# FLIGHT TO Bogotá

# FLIGHT TO Bogotá

England's Football Rebel,

NEIL FRANKLIN

BY JOHN LEONARD

pitch

First published by Pitch Publishing, 2020

Pitch Publishing
A2 Yeoman Gate
Yeoman Way
Worthing
Sussex
BN13 3QZ
www.pitchpublishing.co.uk
info@pitchpublishing.co.uk



A CIP catalogue record is available for this book from the British Library.

ISBN 978 1 78531 654 8

Typesetting and origination by Pitch Publishing

Printed and bound in India by Replika Press Pvt. Ltd.

# Contents

# INTRODUCTION

ON a grey May morning, a couple of families sat quietly and anxiously waiting for their train. They attracted mild curiosity from those others gathered on the platform, both men in the party recognisable to their fellow passengers. The porter was more than delighted to help these celebrities with their luggage. As far as he was concerned, their destination was London.

One of the men boarding the train was Stoke City footballer, George Mountford. The other was an even more feted player, Stoke City and England star, Neil Franklin. As he helped the footballers' families load their bags on to the train, the porter would have naturally assumed they were off for a brief city break in the capital. So did everyone else gathering on the platform. It turned out they were wrong.

The station porters blew their whistles. The steam train burst back into life, next and final stop, London Euston. But, for Neil Franklin, George Mountford and their families there were to be quite a few more stops on their journey. London was by no means their final destination. It was the beginning of a more exotic journey. They were off, in their mind's eye, to El Dorado, destined to board a flight to Bogotá.

It was 1950. No English football lover back then questioned the patriotic statement of the nation being without question the greatest football power on the planet. Logic dictated to every English supporter that the country which gave birth to the beautiful game of association football was without equal.

Yes, there had been the odd glitch, defeats here and there to Scotland, Wales and Ireland. Much to their horror there was a loss at home to Éire, the first 'foreign' team to achieve such a feat. For English fans, it was a mere aberration to be ignored. The English FA now grasped the opportunity to confirm England's formal status as the rulers of the biggest team sport on the planet. Its players were off to Brazil for their first World Cup. But they were in for a shock, several shocks.

Much to the horror of the FA's rulers the first came even before they sent out their players to Brazil. Recognised as the greatest player in the land, destined for legendary status, the very first name to be put on the England team sheet, there was a talisman to help lead his country to World Cup glory. Yet to the dismay, indeed disbelief, of fans he chose to turn his back on his country, informing the Football Association he was unavailable for selection.

In the modern era of football, this seems to be an unthinkable scenario. Yet for England's first ill-fated World Cup finals campaign in 1950, this is exactly what happened. Indeed, he went further than turning his back on his country. As the season closed, he chose to turn his back on his club too, the one he supported from boyhood. Neil Franklin was destined to become the ultimate football rebel.

His decision to desert club and country ahead of the 1950 World Cup naturally shocked the nation. In an era when sports news rarely made the front pages, the antics of England's centre-half did so. A degree of mystery had surrounded his decision to make himself unavailable to the England team for ostensibly 'personal and family reasons'. It turned to bafflement once word got out. He was on his way to Colombia.

Franklin's flight to Bogotá, along, at first, with his Stoke City team-mate George Mountford and their families, both seeking their fortunes as footballing mercenaries, was tracked with stunned amazement. They were audacious footballing rebels, committing, for the English sport purists, an unthinkable act of treachery.

Franklin and Mountford turned up in South America, but not in Brazil to play in the World Cup, their sport's biggest team tournament, but in Colombia to take up contracts with a league outside the jurisdiction of football's world governing body, FIFA. Other top-class British footballers followed them – three other English and Scottish players – Bobby Flavell of Hearts, Billy Higgins of Everton, and Charlie Mitten from Manchester United. Swansea Town's Roy Paul, later to captain Manchester City to FA Cup Final victory, and Everton's Jack Hedley also travelled out to Colombia but, to be polite, demurred from taking up contracts.

Their act of rebellion, the flight of men quickly dubbed the 'Bogotá Bad Boys' by some, 'Bogotá Bandits' by others, arguably gave impetus to the inexorable push for changes to footballers' stifling pay and conditions, the hated maximum wage and the 'retain and transfer' system of contracts. As a result, far from the Football Association's bosses going out to Brazil with an England team to confirm the nation's self-appointed status as the greatest footballing power on the planet, they were worried men in turmoil.

Yet remarkably, as much as the actions of Franklin's 'Bogotá Bad Boys' brought opprobrium from the football establishment, there was a large degree of sympathy from a section of English fans. They acknowledged their heroes' moans and groans about the maximum wage and the despised retain and transfer system of players. It was a time when, as Franklin controversially commented from his bolthole in Bogotá, footballers believed they were being treated as 'slaves' by corrupt managers and owners.

Ultimately, for Franklin in particular, this act of rebellion ended in personal humiliation and failure. Colombia turned out to be no El Dorado for them. There was no crock of gold. Promises of being lavished with riches were broken. One by one they meekly scurried home to Britain, swallowing their pride, pleading for the chance to rebuild their careers. All succeeded apart from one – the rebel Neil Franklin; a man never to be forgiven by the men in blazers at the FA.

Franklin came home to England, back to the Potteries humiliated, facing the wrath of his bosses with club and country. Still in his mid-twenties, his career ended up in tatters. A man who many fans hoped would scale even greater heights than his legendary former Stoke City team-mate Stanley Matthews was temporarily banned from playing the game he loved. Once he was allowed back, it was in Second Division football, with no prospect of a return to the England fold.

Franklin, though a villain to his shocked critics, was arguably a pioneer of the modern game. As a campaigner for justice, he was a man anxious in trying to justify the infamous flight of top-class British players to Bogotá, to concentrate hearts and minds on the fight for footballers' employment rights. On the pitch, as a wonderful footballer, he barely fitted the mould of the chiselled centre-half so common in his era. Franklin was a skilful player, full of artistry. Off the pitch, he was a visionary, an angry young man ready to take on the stern patricians running the English game.

How much the infamous rebel tour of Colombia by top British footballers hampered or helped the campaign for reform in the sport is open to question. The Players' Union, the forerunner to the modern-day Professional Footballers' Association, conducted a fierce battle, constantly threatening strike action throughout the late forties. As I will explain, those threats turned out to be hollow but the behaviour of the Bogotá Bad Boys appeared to reinvigorate their campaign.

It began with Franklin and company, and led to a series of government inquiries held in secret into footballers' pay and conditions, the first held just a year after they returned from Colombia. The inquiries came to nothing. Quite why, we can now deduce from the transcripts of the frosty exchanges I detail, between the unions' lawyers and English football bosses.

Remarkably, Franklin and his fellow rebels never received a mention – early attempts made to wipe them from football history.

This tortured campaign ended at first in the sixties, with the England footballer George Eastham and the Professional Footballers' Association chairman Jimmy Hill successfully going to the English High Court to make their case to scrap the retain and transfer system of contracts, then with a legal battle fought in the European courts by an obscure Belgian journeyman footballer by the name of Jean-Marc Bosman. Far from, as Franklin might term it, professional footballers being 'slaves' or 'serfs', they were the masters.

The Bogotá Bad Boys' role in focusing national and international scrutiny on the treatment of professional footballers prior to the campaigns fought by the likes of Eastham and Hill is often ignored. In a sense this is understandable. Franklin and Mitten appeared to mellow in later life, contradictory figures turning from rebels to pillars of the establishment. In Mitten's case, as manager of Newcastle United, his spat with George Eastham led to the PFA taking out the landmark court case to abolish the antiquated system of players' contracts.

Franklin is so often portrayed as the leader of a misguided band of football rebels. A man rated in the post-war years as the best player in the land seemingly betrayed his country by refusing to go to the World Cup, instead chancing his luck with a bunch of murky South American businessmen. Yet the outcry focused hearts and minds on the medieval treatment of professional footballers in the mid-20th century. Modern footballers, the instant millionaires, arguably owe Franklin and his fellow rebels a debt of gratitude.

Any footballer turning his back on club and country would these days be thrown to mainstream and social media wolves. Yet remarkably in 1950, as detailed in this outline of one of the most infamous episodes in English football history, there was shock expressed by sports writers on the back pages of national newspapers but with a degree of understanding.

The World Cup was not taken as seriously as it is now, remarkably treated by some observers as nothing more than a glorified close-season tour. They were content that in their view British football was vastly superior to any form of the game played elsewhere on the planet. There was no outcry over Franklin's original decision to pull out of the World Cup, citing 'family reasons', instead simple acknowledgement and mere disappointment. For many of them, bringing home the Jules Rimet Trophy was not in doubt. Naturally, they were wrong.

Once Franklin and his mates turned up in Colombia, anger was largely confined to the corridors of power at the FA and the boardrooms of their football clubs, Stoke City's directors expressing the most anger. But for those complacently running the FA, ill-feeling grew, severe punishment needed to be meted out. Their mood was no doubt darkened by the humiliation suffered by the England team, going out of the World Cup after defeat to the part-timers of the United States, the latest shock to those running English football in the summer of 1950. Curiously, Franklin's rebel gang's antics garnered as much publicity as his hapless former international team-mates.

Franklin and his fellow rebels had focused the nation's attention on the treatment of men being worshipped by the paying public in their tens of thousands on a Saturday afternoon. It arguably proved the catalyst for hard-fought reform, turning a future generation of footballers into, in some cases, multi-millionaires. These were riches the Bogotá Bad

Boys failed to even dream of as they set out for their mystical El Dorado in Colombia.

Franklin, for one, found fame but not his fortune as a footballer. He was eventually forced out of the game altogether, left to the stereotypical rôle of a retired footballer by running a pub. He was landlord of the Dog and Doublet in rural Staffordshire where I met him in the seventies. Even as a sports-mad teenager I had barely heard of Neil Franklin – just another name in the annals of Potteries football, nowhere near the level of legends such as Stanley Matthews. Yet he was a legend.

As I walked through the door of the pub with my parents and grandparents, a clue to the greatness of the genial man behind the bar was pinned to the wall: a framed England shirt, the three lions and crown logo, and an international cap. It was the only, but striking, nod to his old career. The convivial landlord had quite a story to tell. This is the story of a fallen idol, his fellow football rebels, of how and why they took their infamous flight to Bogotá.

# BIRTH OF A REBEL LEADER

ANY football team needs its talisman, needs its leader. Decades even before ecstatic England fans celebrated as the consummate, calm, classy, professional leader Bobby Moore lifted the World Cup, they thought such a leader was already born. In the aftermath of war, Stoke City and England fans' appetite for the return of competitive football had been whetted by the emergence of a rising star, a young defender holding his own with the legendary figure of Stanley Matthews. Neil Franklin was identified as England's future talisman, a stylish leader to help guarantee international football glory for years to come.

Instead, Neil Franklin ended up as the de facto leader of a bunch of British football rebels prepared to turn their backs on club and country, angry young men apparently going to desperate lengths to secure their financial future. Of these, Franklin, the most high-profile star to rebel, also turned out to be the most vocal and the angriest.

From an amateur hopeful in the mid-thirties, Franklin had broken into the professional ranks at Stoke City during the wartime years, then eventually came to the attention of England selectors when playing in wartime internationals. He looked forward to competitive action with relish. In the opinion of many, Neil Franklin could look forward to a long and fruitful career with club and country. To their horror, he turned out to be the leader of a gang of mercenary football rebels, unlawfully plying their trade in Colombia.

So just who was this emerging superstar, a young man destined to become one of English football's most infamous rebels? Cornelius Franklin was born in Stoke-on-Trent on 24 January 1922, one of eight children growing up in the Shelton district of the city. His father worked in the local gasworks, his mother staying at home to look after her large family. Neither parent was particularly interested in sport, doing little to encourage their children as they enjoyed kickabouts with their friends using tin cans, rag balls and just from time to time a proper football. He described his young self in his autobiography, *Soccer at Home and Abroad*, as a 'healthy kid, who liked to play'. But he didn't think he was anything special.

All that changed, as with so many sports stars, with the intervention of his games master at school. Neil Franklin went to the Cannon Street School in the largest of the Potteries' six towns, Hanley. He left, aged 14, with few qualifications but, thanks to the guidance of his teacher, Arthur Tams, with a reputation as one of the most promising young footballers in Staffordshire. He had played for both Hanley schools and Stoke-on-Trent schools, but curiously neither of the local professional clubs, Stoke City or Port Vale, came calling at the Franklin household in Shelton.

As far as his mentor Arthur Tams was concerned this was a clear oversight. He encouraged his protégé to approach Stoke City directly, asking for a place on the club's ground staff. Stoke's manager, Bob McGrory, turned him down, the first blow in what would eventually develop into a fractious relationship between the two men. McGrory explained he had enough young players on his ground staff. Neil Franklin, a future England international, was deemed surplus to requirements.

Reflecting on his initial rejection, Franklin had no complaints. 'There can be no criticism of Stoke's decision not to engage me on their ground staff, and my future rise to fame does not affect the case,' he wrote. 'It was impossible to take any more lads on the payroll, so the club had to turn me down.'

Thanks to the persistence of Tams, McGrory did partially relent by offering an amateur contract. Franklin accepted. It meant he still had to find a job. Once again, his old teacher proved to be his guardian angel.

Tams went behind the back of McGrory to approach one of the Stoke City directors, David Duddell, the owner of a brickworks in the Potteries. Duddell, whose son would later become the Stoke chairman, offered the aspiring footballer an office job, little knowing at the time it was to prove to be the best but most troubled signing either ever made.

Franklin commented, 'This was a wonderful arrangement for me because Mr Duddell was a great Stoke fanatic. In fact, the entire Duddell family was, so I was able to work hard in a footballing atmosphere and carry on my soccer playing as a Stoke City amateur.'

Initially, he was confined to playing with the third team, and did so with a string of promising other players from the Stoke schools programme run by Arthur Tams. Many would become first-team regulars in the post-war years, players capable of challenging for the league title. As Franklin put it, in tribute to the club's recruitment of teenage players, 'a player who signed for a transfer fee was a rarity at Stoke'.

Meantime they all buckled down hoping for a breakthrough, Franklin praying the club's manager Bob McGrory would relent and offer him a professional contract. As he had impressed his coaches, Harry Cooper and Stan Clough, a member of Stoke City's staff killed during the Second World War, the offer of a professional contract was eventually forthcoming. On his 17th birthday in January 1939 he was summoned to McGrory's office and offered a professional contract.

Bizarrely, Franklin wanted to accept a part-time contract. He was intent on keeping his job with the Duddell family, a fall-back position just in case a career in professional football failed to work out for him. McGrory turned him down flat. 'Neil, we want you to become a professional player, and as far as we are concerned it is full time or nothing,' McGrory told him. On this occasion Franklin did not argue. The disputes would come later.

He looked forward to a professional football career. Along with the rest of the nation, he knew war was looming. 'I realised that I was on the threshold of a career that would crash any day,' he mournfully reflected. He also realised he was lucky. He was young enough to enjoy a fruitful career once the war was over. On being called up to join the services, in his case the Royal Air Force, he did not see combat, and was still encouraged to play football. It was the policy of the War Office to encourage professional footballers to carry on playing, to do what they did best, thereby providing entertainment for the mass ranks of troops and the civilian population.

Though remaining on the books of Stoke City, Franklin found himself in Blackpool, stationed with the RAF. Among his fellow recruits there was Stanley Matthews. As a consequence, they were seconded to playing for the seaside town's club, Matthews a guaranteed box office draw even in wartime. Franklin, a raw and inexperienced player, struggled to get a game for them.

Once again he was grateful to a mentor. On leaving school, it was his PE teacher. This time he was grateful to an RAF Physical Training Instructor for taking him under his metaphorical wing. Willie MacFadyen, a centre-forward with Motherwell and Huddersfield, told him to go back to the Potteries to fetch his boots. He was to play in a Blackpool 'services' team, ostensibly the professional club's reserve side, alongside him and Stanley Mortensen, another future England star.

Against the backdrop of war, Franklin's career rapidly progressed. A switch from the RAF base outside Blackpool to a military garrison in Hereford gave him the opportunity to go back to Stoke for weekend games. Bob McGrory finally gave him his first-team chance, albeit in a side naturally shorn of its star players.

He also came to the attention of the RAF selectors. To supplement the wartime friendly leagues, there was a series of matches between representative sides: the army, the navy and the RAF. Young Franklin began to impress. Sports writers began to speculate that he might become the future England centre-half, something the player himself dismissed given that the international captain, Stan Cullis of Wolverhampton Wanderers, was firmly ensconced in the position.

His big break, in his words his 'lucky break', came courtesy of a Potteries derby between Stoke City and Port Vale on 18 November 1944. He lined up in a Stoke team, almost at full strength, to take on their local rivals. Matthews and the England centre-forward, Freddie Steele, both laced up their boots to make a rare wartime appearance together in the red and white stripes of Stoke City. An England selector turned up to watch them. Franklin, though, caught his eye in a 2-0 victory for the Potters. From the now defunct *News Chronicle*, correspondent Arthur Shrive wrote, 'Franklin is undoubtedly the finest young centre-half-back in the country, and it cannot be long before the FA selectors recognise his merit.'

Recognition came in the form of a telegram to Stoke's opponents Coventry City for a league game at Highfield Road on 2 December 1944. It read, 'McGrory, Stoke manager, c/o Coventry City Football Club. Franklin selected play at Bradford next Saturday, kindly telephone me Sunday morning – Rous, Football Association.'

He was selected to play for an FA XI against an army team, packed full of internationals. To his surprise, with the first-choice England centre-half, Stan Cullis, unavailable because he had been posted abroad, he was not picked as centre-half. Instead, he played in midfield, a late call-up to cover for his Stoke City team-mate, Frank Soo, who had been given compassionate leave. Soo's brother Ronald, who served in a Lancaster bomber squadron, had recently been killed in a bombing mission over Germany.

The circumstances of Franklin's first call-up for representative honours were tragic. Franklin merely states he was a 'last minute substitute' for Soo. When it came to a replacement for Stoke's mercurial midfielder, the first non-white player to pull on an England football jersey, Franklin dryly noted, 'Happily enough they [the selectors] looked in my direction.'

Franklin, who as a schoolboy played in attack, was not bothered by being played out of position. He was just delighted to receive his first honour as a senior footballer. By calling up someone making his name as a defender and putting him in midfield it was also recognition by Sir Stanley Rous and his panel of international selectors of this promising young player's all-round skills and cultured style of football.

Franklin described the game itself on Saturday, 9 December 1944 at Bradford Park Avenue's ground as 'disappointing', a 1-1 draw contested on an icy pitch, which these days would be deemed unplayable. He acquitted himself reasonably well, viewed by some sports writers present as a star of the future. Another call-up for an FA XI came in the following January, this time in a 6-4 defeat to his companions from the RAF, Franklin among those on the scoresheet. Surely a full international call-up would be forthcoming? It came for a wartime international against Scotland at Villa Park on 5 February 1945.

No caps were awarded for this wartime international, but for Franklin it remained a great honour, not just for him but his hometown club, Stoke City. His famous team-mate Stanley Matthews and Frank Soo, Stoke's pre-war captain, also earned call-ups. Soo became the first non-white footballer to represent England. Franklin described Matthews and Soo taking charge of him and helping to calm his nerves. Matthews, the superstar footballer of the day, even took him to the Scottish team hotel on the eve of the game for a soiree with their opponents.

More than 66,000 spectators crammed into Birmingham's Villa Park, a thousand of them wounded soldiers allocated seats for free. They witnessed a 3-2 England victory; Franklin fearing he had not done himself justice. 'As I walked off the field, I began to wonder whether this would be my first and last appearance for England,' he later commented. He had no need to worry. Football correspondents in the national press wrote approving reviews; the FA selectors agreed with them.

Only the *Daily Mirror* offered any criticism, blaming him for Scotland's second goal, a back header allowing the Scottish centre-forward Jack Dodds through on goal to equalise. But overall, it concluded the debutant English centre-half had done well. The *Daily Mail* commented he did 'a difficult job with success'. The *News Chronicle*'s Arthur Shriver believed he did 'nothing spectacular but was steady and reliable'.

Making the short trip to Birmingham, the Coventry *Evening Telegraph*'s man felt Franklin's inclusion was 'justified', noting he rarely lost Scotland's 'bustling' Dodds. For the *Daily Telegraph*, 'Franklin, Brown and [Stan] Mortensen, England's newcomers played themselves into the national side for Hampden', the reverse fixture being played in Glasgow a few months later.

Franklin was duly called up, his place in England's line-up assured. Pundits of the day deemed him a worthy successor to Stan Cullis, who was on his way into management with his club, Wolverhampton Wanderers. Prior to the fixture at Hampden Park, Franklin went on a brief tour of Belgium with a combined services team, one led by another player about to go into management, Matt Busby.

The irascible Scotsman took a shine to the young lad from the Potteries, offering him advice he would never forget. 'Just remember Neil,' he told him, 'keep playing football at all times and you'll never go far wrong.' In other words, stick to your cultured style of playing the beautiful game, rather than resorting to thuggery as was so common in the day.

Franklin later commented, in admiration of the man who became a managerial legend, 'Those words should be the motto of all young players and were so typical of a great player, great sportsman and great personality like Matt Busby.'

The trip also included a match for a Football Association XI against the Belgium national side, not an international, but Franklin's inclusion in the team gave him a strong hint that the selectors viewed him as their new England centre-half. For the record, the FA's centre-forward for the match, Tommy Lawton of Everton, helped himself to a hat-trick in a 3-2 victory.

Prior to the game Franklin was able to put his new-found fame to good use, cheekily writing to the commanding officer of his brother Harry's army unit, urging him to give his sibling a leave pass. They had not seen each other since the start of the war and wanted to meet up at the game against Belgium. To his delight and surprise, the commanding officer agreed, a gesture the Franklin brothers acknowledged as remarkably generous.

A fortnight after the Belgian excursion Franklin lined up for his very first ever international appearance for England against Scotland at Hampden Park, a severe test of temperament for any young player. A buoyant crowd of 133,000, baying metaphorically for English blood, fell silent before the game in memory of the American President, Franklin D Roosevelt, who'd recently died. Once the whistle went for the kick-off, wartime alliances were put to one side. On the football pitch usual hostilities were reconvened between the two 'auld' enemies.

Scottish debutant Tommy Bogan was carried off with only a minute played after colliding with the England goalkeeper Frank Swift. It incensed the crowd, their mood darkening further as the ten remaining men of Scotland capitulated in a 6-1 defeat. Franklin commented that the Hampden crowd had to be 'seen and most certainly heard' to be believed.

On the eve of England's final home international of the season against Wales, Franklin firmly ensconced in the side, VE Day came, victory in Europe declared. 'Naturally, we had a tremendous celebration,' Franklin remembered. It included stripping out their hotel's blackout blinds, and ensuring its floodlights were switched on for the celebrating crowds on the street outside.

For the English players the celebrations continued with a fortuitous 3-2 victory over Wales at Ninian Park in Cardiff. Much to the embarrassment of Franklin and his fellow defenders the man of the match happened to be their goalkeeper, Bill Williams. His antics between the sticks gained as much attention as Raich Carter scoring a hat-trick up front. Yet despite defensive frailties in the English defence, Franklin's place in the side was safe.

He could not believe his luck. On being selected to play for the first time for England at Wembley he commented, 'In those hectic days there was hardly any close season. I could hardly believe that I had played my first international on February 3rd and within three and a half months here I was turning out for the fifth time.' The game against France ended in a 2-2 draw.

Even missing a penalty for a combined services team against the Irish League did little to dent Franklin's rising fortunes. 'I had always believed that a player should never miss from the spot and I had often voiced my belief,' Franklin embarrassingly explained. 'So, I had to hang my head in shame when their Irish goalkeeper saved my kick and we went on to lose 1-0.'

As the England players gathered at Croydon Airport to fly out to Switzerland, the young Stoke City player considered himself as something of a veteran. He was also about to taste defeat for the first time at international level.

Much to the players' relief they were instructed to leave their service uniforms at home. The Swiss FA had reminded the FA's boss Sir Stanley Rous that Switzerland was a neutral country and Britain was still at war with Japan in the Far East. Army, air force or naval uniforms were not to be worn. 'How happy we were to forget our uniforms for a time,' Franklin reflected.

Thousands of Swiss fans turned out to greet the England team on arrival at Zurich Airport. Their enthusiasm left the man from the Potteries stunned. He commented, 'I got my first insight into how seriously the continentals take their sport.' For their first game in Berne Franklin wished he had never played. It was stifling hot and England lost.

He pointed to three factors contributing to the 3-1 defeat: firstly the heat, secondly Switzerland, at the time, being England's bogey team and thirdly his opponents' flexible tactics, especially his opposite number being given the freedom to roam the field.

English football operated a rigid tactical system at the time, stubbornly and arrogantly holding on to it until the mid-fifties. Players held fixed positions, a pair of full-backs, a centre-half, a pair of midfielders known as out-halves, a pair of wingers, a pair of inside-forwards and a centre-forward. There was no flexibility.

Only when, first, a team of American amateurs knocked England out of the World Cup in 1950, and then, three years later, the fabled Hungarian team, the Mighty Magyars, humiliated them at Wembley in a 6-3 victory did any delusional notions of automatic English superiority come to an end. For both those games Franklin's name was absent from the team sheet, his international career infamously by then at an end.

In the summer of 1945, Franklin appeared to have a bright future ahead of him. He was an established England international playing in all the remaining 'Victory Internationals'. These included defeat to Scotland, 1-0 at Hampden Park, and in May 1946 a revenge victory over Switzerland, 4-1 at Stamford Bridge. Then came the first setback of his international career.

For the game against France in Paris, Franklin was dropped. Stan Cullis had been on active duty with the army in Italy. With the war in Europe now over he became available for selection, his plans for retirement from playing the game put on hold. Cullis was handed back the England number 5 shirt for a forthcoming international against France in Paris, Franklin selected for an RAF team to tour Scandinavia.

He had no complaints. For Cullis, he had the utmost respect. However, on reporting for England duty, Cullis was declared unfit. It left the FA haggling with the RAF for the services of young Franklin. It was agreed he could play for England in Paris before meeting up with the RAF team in Scandinavia. Franklin probably wished he had gone straight to Oslo. England lost 2-1.

Immediately after the game, Franklin and Matthews, along with Bert Brown and George Hardwick, donned their RAF uniforms to fly out to Norway. The RAF tour of the summer of 1946 was to be their last as service personnel. With war at an end, players looked forward to returning to their clubs and the resumption of competitive league football.

Yet in Franklin's case there had already been the first signs of unrest, a hint of his rebellious streak. Along with his team-mate Frank Soo, he seemed none too keen to return to Stoke

City, despite it being his boyhood club. As the 1945/46 season began, they had quite remarkably put in a request to play for Stoke's Potteries rivals Port Vale.

Soo's case attracted more headlines than his young England team-mate Franklin. Soo was the bigger star, the club's captain at the outbreak of war. He, like Matthews and Franklin, was a true local hero. All three clashed with Stoke's manager Bob McGrory. Matthews had done so before the war but backed down, withdrawing a transfer request. Now, Soo actively agitated for a move, fans alarmed their rising star Franklin might follow suit.

Not just at the Victoria Ground in Stoke, but at grounds across the country fans were flocking to grounds in tens of thousands, the beautiful game seeming more popular than ever. Even with war over, austerity remained in place. Football proved the perfect escape. As gates bulged so did club finances. But the strict, archaic and time-honoured restrictive method of paying players remained in place. The maximum wage tied players to their clubs, unable to move freely, subject to the whims of chairmen and managers.

Given the popularity of the game and burgeoning finances, player unrest seemed inevitable. It began bizarrely with Frank Soo and his young accomplice cocking a snook at their club Stoke City with the bombshell request to play for Port Vale.

# STOKING UP TROUBLE

AFTER six years of war, any professional footballer's request to play for any club other than his own seemed a mere trivial matter. Contracts had been put on hold, the finest players in the land enlisted in the forces. Crucially their registration had been kept by their respective clubs, terms and conditions of pay kept at pre-war rates for the return of normality and competitive domestic and international football.

In such an environment, what possibly could be the problem with a couple of Stoke City internationals playing for their Potteries rival Port Vale in a one-off match, a friendly game? After all, in the case of Frank Soo, he had already turned out as a guest player for Vale during the war. But with the war over, his request to play for Vale along with Franklin, the rising star of English football, was met with indignant fury by the Stoke manager and the club's board of directors. They, along with their counterparts at other clubs, were determined to reassert their authority over players.

It was bad enough Soo had already put in a transfer request after apparently being approached by Leicester City's manager Tom Mather, the man who signed Soo for Stoke in the early thirties. But for Soo to be seen to be leading Franklin astray infuriated them. They failed to recognise, though they'd learn later, that Franklin had a maverick mind of his own.

Leaving aside his struggle to secure a professional contract with Stoke in the first place, this proved to be Neil Franklin's first run-in with his manager, Bob McGrory, and the club's board. He had yet to kick a ball in anger, play competitive football. Yet the man who five years later would stun the nation by emerging as football's most infamous rebel gave an early sign of his defiant streak.

Franklin wanted to support Soo, who had been so supportive of him along with Stanley Matthews on England duty. Their influence, especially from the great Sir Stanley Matthews, cannot be overstated. Both those men expressed deep unhappiness at the treatment of players, with Stoke City being considered as one of the least generous of any Football League club. Matthews had already put in a transfer request before the war, believing he might be better appreciated elsewhere, already eyeing up Blackpool as his favoured destination. Matthews, the 'wizard of dribble', was about to give young Franklin lessons in how to run rings around club bosses and the English football establishment.

Franklin's early attempt at rebellion failed. His wilier team-mate Frank Soo succeeded. News of Soo and Franklin's no-show for Port Vale in a Monday afternoon friendly against Norwich City was met with a degree of incredulity. 'Some public concern is evinced owing to the fact that Franklin and Soo, Stoke City's international players, did not play for Port Vale last night when opportunity served,' commented the Staffordshire *Evening Sentinel* in the opening paragraph to a front-page article.

It explained further, 'Franklin, who is in the district on RAF leave offered to play for Port Vale, and Port Vale made formal application to the Stoke City club for the necessary permission but this was refused. Soo, who has been in the news lately owing to his application for transfer from Stoke also offered to play for Port Vale but in view of the refusal in the Franklin case, Port Vale did not think it worthwhile to proceed with a formal application to the Stoke club.'

It then ran the contradictory statements of the respective club chairman for the benefit of bemused readers. According to the Vale chairman, Franklin had contacted them offering to play for his own club's fiercest rivals. He was told to put the request in writing, which he duly did. Port Vale's manager, Billy Frith, went to see his counterpart McGrory to ask for permission to play Franklin. Frith claimed McGrory agreed to consider the matter, and asked the Vale boss to phone him later in the week. Those calls from the hapless Vale manager to the Victoria Ground were never answered by McGrory.

Instead, it was left to the two chairmen to settle the matter. As far as Vale was concerned it was done fruitlessly but amicably. In its statement Vale's chairman claimed, 'I spoke to Mr McGrory. Mr McGrory told me to speak to the chairman [Mr H Booth]. I did so and Mr Booth said it was the first he had heard about the matter and he would let me know. About two hours later Mr Booth telephoned me and said: "I am sorry; we have to refuse. I, personally, am much perturbed about this, as I don't want any dissension on my board."

'I pointed out to Mr Booth that an opportunity to the player had been made by Port Vale. Frank Soo rang up yesterday morning and also offered his services for the match. Mr Frith and I discussed the question and we agreed that after the refusal to allow Franklin to play we did not see that anything would be gained by asking for permission to have the services of Soo.'

From Stoke City's chairman came the stern reply, 'The Stoke Board of Directors were very definite in their decision not to grant permission to Franklin to play for Port Vale. They did not consider that it would be a wise procedure on their part, and there are of course two sides to the issue. In the matter of loaning Franklin to a local club as distinct from one farther afield, my Directors thought it was a little too much.'

As it turned out Soo went on loan to Shrewsbury Town, a club not that much further afield from Stoke than Port Vale. Franklin resumed his RAF duties, turning out in Victory Internationals for England and other representative sides – only occasionally turning out in the red and white stripes of Stoke City.

This bizarre episode signalled an end to friendly relations between two local Football League clubs, wartime co-operation making way for the resumption of peacetime enmity. More importantly it also signalled the beginning of agitation, unrest among footballers, their Players' Union, and their patrician employers, Stoke City Football Club, one of the more notoriously hawkish under the leadership of Alderman Booth and manager McGrory.

As the national newspapers charted the departure of Soo from Stoke City to Leicester City, eventually for a fee of £4,000, their correspondents also noted a growing rift between the Players' Union and all Football League clubs. The union was determined to state its case before the resumption of full competitive action for the 1946/47 season.

It kept out of the parochial spat between Stoke City and Port Vale over the services of Franklin and Soo, the focus on a national clash over players' pay and terms of contracts with Football League clubs. Full-time professional football was not yet available to fans wanting to flock to grounds in their droves. It was set to resume in August 1946. But without the whistle being blown for the renewal of Football League action, there was already the spectre of strike action.

In meeting the Players' Union demands, there were surprising signs of potential splits among the clubs. Stoke, as established, were among the more hawkish. Yet the likes of Charlton Athletic came over as a little more conciliatory. Its directors were irked by the amateurism of those running the Football League in failing to establish an immediate return to normality at the end of the Second World War. To Charlton's bosses it also seemed logical to meet at least some of the discontented players' demands.

From the *Daily Herald*, a Labour-supporting newspaper, Clifford Webb wrote, 'Having been shot at, deservedly, by the players, Football League chiefs must now prepare to receive a broadside from club directors. A memorandum which will urge in effect, "stop fumbling and get the game back to some semblance of business-like basis" is soon to be presented by the directors of Charlton Athletic.'

Webb cited the Charlton chairman, Albert Gliksten as being 'deeply disturbed' by what he called the 'footling' manner in which 'big football is being allowed to drift through transition back to normality'. Gliksten accused fellow football club directors of ignoring the parlous state of the nation's economy in the aftermath of war and the rise in the cost of living. In summing up his opinion piece, Webb wrote, 'The worried world of football is one of the few spheres where it is apparently not recognised that the £ sterling has undergone a change in value. At least 30 per cent is Gliksten's estimate of the increase in pay a full-time player would need to enable him to live close to the pre-war level.'

Unfortunately for the unlikely rebellious Stoke trio of Franklin, Matthews and Soo, the view from Charlton's Thames-side location was a minority one. The Stoke board's traditional view of the relationship between club and player was more widely shared. A clash between clubs and players, both individually and collectively, appeared inevitable. Matthews, Soo and Franklin were just the first.

Collectively, the Players' Union withdrew its threat of strike action. They agreed to play 'under protest'. For the more militant members, at a heated meeting held on 20 August 1945, this was a lost opportunity. Not one professional footballer in the country was reliant on the game for his livelihood. They were either in the forces or a 'reserved' occupation. There was unlikely to be a public backlash given there was to be no resumption of a full league season for another year, just a continuation of the wartime leagues with clubs fielding guest players. Yet, at this meeting the players decided to back down. The club bosses won, not for the first and not for the last time.

The *Herald*'s Webb gloomily warned, 'I have heard it said in soccer circles quite recently, "We are in for a boom. The crowds will turn up whatever football they see." Football has a hold on the public but it is no unbreakable iron grip. Entertaining play from contented players should be a number one priority.' Unfortunately, fans and players being taken for granted seemed to be the order of the day, especially to a large degree, as today, the supporters.

There was no darker example of this disdain for fans, the working-class masses flocking to football grounds, than the Burnden Park disaster, some months earlier. In the annals of football history, it seems a long-forgotten tragedy, though not in the minds of Bolton Wanderers and supporters of Stoke City, their opponents for the day. Franklin and Matthews lined up in the FA Cup quarter-final for Stoke, both dreaming of Wembley glory.

Franklin by then had been forgiven by his manager McGrory for his act of rebellion in the late summer of 1945 by volunteering to play for Port Vale. McGrory even appointed him captain, perhaps reasoning it was the easiest way to keep his young recalcitrant player quiet. A fairer assessment is that he actually had a soft spot for Franklin, proud to have helped to develop him into an international player. For the Burnden Park disaster, the Stoke captain of the day devoted an entire chapter to the tragedy in his autobiography, simply calling it 'Black Saturday'.

A post-war generation had experienced enough tragedy, witnessed enough horrors, suffered personal loss, with footballers, the majority called up for the services, no different. As mentioned earlier, Franklin's youth-team coach at Stoke City was among those killed in action. But at Burnden Park, this was no battle. It was peacetime. It was a football match. Naturally the horrific events of the day would have a profound effect on anyone there that day, even for those who did not know any of the victims.

Just as at Bradford, and Hillsborough some four decades later, fans going along happily to an English football ground, men, women and children, ought to have returned home safely. The tragic fact they did not, the scandal of the authorities failing to learn lessons, instead continuing to treat the national sport, a working-class sport, with disdain verging on contempt, is a source to all of immense shame.

The game took place on Saturday, 9 March 1946, the second leg of an FA Cup quarter-final. Stoke City had lost the first leg at the Victoria Ground 2-0 a week earlier. There was no competitive league action in that post-war season, just the FA Cup. As a result, and arguably for financial greed, the FA decreed that cup matches had to be played over two legs, rather than one as is the normal practice. If the tie had been run on traditional lines the game would never have taken place, as Franklin's Stoke City would have been knocked out. Nevertheless, the game did go ahead with tragic consequences.

Despite playing poorly at home and losing, Stoke's players felt confident for the return leg. 'After all, we had a good side,' commented Franklin in his recollections of the match. 'We had the one and only Stanley Matthews so we felt there was still some fight left in us.' Stoke fans agreed with them. They made the short trip north from the Potteries to Bolton in their thousands. Bolton fans, confident of victory, also turned up in their tens of thousands.

Tellingly, Franklin believed there was also a strong contingent of neutrals, not to see him play but Matthews and Bolton's star draw of the day, their inside-forward Ray Westwood. 'The neutrals might have thought a Bolton victory was a foregone conclusion, their money's worth of class football from those two great artists.'

Pointedly he goes on to comment, 'This fact was forcibly made at the inquiry into the disaster and it surely underlines the drawing power of the star. Whenever they appear the gate is increased. People with no real interest in the competing teams want to see the stars in action.'

Even in assessing a human tragedy, Franklin, albeit out of condemnation of the football authorities and club bosses, rails against top footballers being undervalued. It irked. Maybe it did so out of guilt because, though he never admitted as much, he too was one of the stars the crowds were flocking to see. Forget players being undervalued, he would have had more reason to be concerned by spectators being treated like cattle, herded to their deaths.

On arriving at the ground, the Stoke players noted the thousands cramming the streets and packed into the car park outside the main stand of Burnden Park. It was clear they could not all get in. It did not help that one of the stands was closed, commandeered by the government as a storage dump during the war. It had not yet been handed back for the use of its owners, Bolton Wanderers Football Club. Thousands of football fans would miss an eagerly anticipated game. They turned out to be the lucky ones. By the end of the day 33 fans had been killed, hundreds injured.

Estimates put the crowd that day at more than 85,000. But the ground, official capacity was almost 20,000 less. The average crowd for the 1945/46 season had been 43,000. The police and the ground authorities were simply unable to cope. Franklin in his account of the tragedy refused to blame them. He said they had been placed at a 'disadvantage', first by the reduced capacity. Secondly, 'no one could have expected such a large crowd', Franklin reasoned. At 20 minutes to the scheduled three o'clock kick-off the decision was taken to close the only entrance to the ground, located on the Manchester Road. Yet still the fans tried to get in.

Accounts of how fans managed to get into Burnden Park after the gates were closed differ. It is not in dispute that many sneaked in via the railway running past the back of the ground, removing the flimsy fencing as they did so. In an eerie echo of the Hillsborough disaster four decades later it was also alleged others stormed the gates. Yet there's no evidence they did so. Eyewitnesses say a father anxious for the safety of a young child managed to pick one of the locks of a gate at the rear of the ground to escape from the melee inside. Once he had taken his child outside to safety other fans poured into the already overcrowded terraces with crowd-control barriers about to give way.

Matthews' and Franklin's accounts of the unfolding tragedy are unsurprisingly harrowing. At first the players were unaware of any problems, just buoyed up by the exuberance of the crowd. Stanley Matthews in his autobiography, *The Way it Was*, shared similar sentiments. 'As I ran on to the pitch I was amazed by the size of the crowd,' he wrote. 'They were packed like sardines and during the pre-match kick-in I glanced up and saw the heaving masses on the terraces swaying like the great swell of an ocean. Even at this stage young boys were being passed over the heads of the adults towards the relative safety of the cinder track that ran around the pitch.'

Franklin wrote, 'When we took to the field, we were greeted by a tremendous roar that sends the blood tingling in the veins.' He continued, 'It was the familiar cup tie scene. Some of the crowd, especially youngsters, had been allowed to come on to the track and many people were lying on the ground just outside the touchlines.'

Within seconds of the referee George Dutton blowing the whistle for the kick-off two barriers gave way with deathly consequences. Mr Dutton, his linesmen and the two sets of players were unaware. As those barriers gave way the mass ranks on the terraces collapsed in on themselves. Mayhem ensued, fans spilling on to the pitch for safety. The game was stopped but, even then, the ref and the players were still unaware of the gravity of the unfolding tragedy. Franklin commented, 'At that time we thought it was nothing more serious than enthusiasm run riot.'

Matthews, perhaps conscious the swollen crowd, the neutrals, had come along to see him play, confessed to be not so optimistic. He remembered, 'I glanced over my shoulder and saw the crowd and saw the crowd swaying and tumbling towards the front of the terracing behind the goal at the far end of the pitch. People were screaming and clambering over the perimeter wall on to the cinder track and the pitch itself. I had a terrible feeling in the pit of my stomach that this wasn't just overspill from a big crowd.'

The game was temporarily stopped. Play resumed but at 3.12pm, as victims were being stretchered away, the police decided to once again halt the game. Matthews had just received the ball from Franklin. 'I was aware of someone approaching me and turned to shield the ball,' he remembered. 'I saw it was not a Bolton defender but a police sergeant waving his arms frantically trying to get Mr Dutton's attention. It stopped me in my tracks.'

After the briefest of conversations with the police sergeant, the referee called over Franklin, the Stoke captain and Harry Hubbick, the Bolton captain. 'He told us that some people had been injured and suggested we leave the field until some sort of order had been restored,' Franklin stated. The players and officials trooped off the field.

As fans on one side of the ground were losing their lives, those packed on to the surrounding terraces were oblivious of being in the midst of tragedy. They even booed the officials and the players as they headed for the dressing rooms. There was no public address system. They were blissfully unaware the emergency services were treating the scores of injured, removing bodies, counting the mounting death toll.

For 20 minutes the players sat in their respective dressing rooms waiting for instructions from the officials. There had already been word that people had died. Remarkably, the authorities were determined to carry on with the game. After the dead and injured had been moved, it was then left to the mounted police to clear the pitch of spectators. It would have been better for them just to get the referee to call the game off. But he explained to the players that the Bolton Chief Constable had personally ordered the game to continue. Matthews commented, 'We stood up but my legs felt like lead. I didn't want to go back out. None of us did.'

Franklin's recollections were also vivid and stark, but a little matter of fact. 'At long last we got the order to go back on to the field, but as soon as we left the dressing room the full force of what had happened hit us,' he wrote. 'When you leave the visitors' dressing room at Burnden Park you walk along a corridor past the home team's dressing room, and then turn right into the tunnel leading to the pitch. Usually the corridor is clear, but on this occasion, it was full, full of bodies. We saw the victims laid out there and suddenly realised they were dead. How many were dead we didn't know, but we knew that it was a frightening number, and as soon as that realisation hit us, all thoughts of football left us.'

The game ended in a goalless draw, the players just going through the motions. 'No longer was this a cup tie in which Stoke City had to battle against a two-goal deficit,' Franklin explained. 'It was now just a mere formality that we completed 90 minutes and to hell with the result. No one wanted to score, let alone win.' When referee Dutton blew the final whistle, he described it as a 'blessed relief'. Players of both sides walked dejectedly off the pitch. The result didn't matter. Stoke were out of the FA Cup. Bolton lost the subsequent semi-final to Charlton. Again, that result didn't matter either.

As a man who would live on in infamy as a rebel in the minds of the football authorities, Franklin appeared to back them in the handling of the Burnden Park disaster. He did so despite obvious failings on the day, also the lamentable failure to learn any lessons. That failure eventually led to disasters at Ibrox in Glasgow, Bradford, Heysel and finally Hillsborough.

A public inquiry into the Burnden Park disaster was held but it made little difference, aside from a recognition of the immediate need to strengthen crowd barriers. Recommendations to install efficient turnstiles to count crowd numbers, making high-profile domestic league and cup games ticket-only, were wilfully ignored by many clubs, those with scant disregard for players and fans alike.

Indeed, for the tragic events at Bolton's Burnden Park in March 1946, Franklin allegedly held errant fans as mainly responsible for causing death and injury to their fellow supporters. 'The cause of the disaster was simple,' Franklin concluded. 'People locked out of the ground had fought their way on to the railway, broken down the fence and poured into the enclosure. This saw the crowd surging forward in one mad rush, and the victims had been crushed to death by the weight of bodies.'

Warming to his theme, he continued, 'Despite the precautions taken by clubs and the police, the co-operation of the public is necessary if we are going to prevent another Bolton disaster. It only needs a couple of people to lose their heads in a big crowd, and deaths and injuries can follow in a matter of seconds.' That passage was written in the mid-fifties. The leader of the band of football rebels, defying their bosses and flying off in search of riches in Colombia, firmly sided with the establishment. The players had their complaints. They were ignored. Fans, herded like cattle, had their complaints too. They were fatally ignored.

Sadly, as we know, further tragedies did follow. At Heysel in May 1985 there's no question that fan disorder contributed to the disaster, along with decaying stadium infrastructure, woeful facilities at a ground not fit to stage a European Cup Final. But at Hillsborough, fans being wrongly and shamefully blamed. Perhaps, in hindsight, it was all too easy for those involved to blame over-exuberant fans for 'Black Saturday' 9 March 1946.

In contrast to his young protégé, Matthews offered no criticism of the fans' behaviour, quite the opposite. Franklin did so, insisting his comments were heartfelt and well meant. He also backed the controversial decision to carry on with the match, despite body bags being piled up outside the dressing rooms, one taken by the referee on the advice of the police. According to Matthews, Bolton's captain Harry Hubbick, unlike his Stoke counterpart, disagreed with the resumption of play. It was a similar scenario to Heysel when Liverpool and Juventus players were told to walk out to play a European Cup Final, knowing a tragedy was unfolding. Again, that decision was heavily criticised, no lesson learned.

In fairness, Franklin felt the hapless Chief Constable had no choice but to advise the players to go out and play. There was one key difference between the events at Burnden Park and Heysel some four decades later – the absence of mass communication. The police did not possess radio communication. There was no public address system to inform the crowd of the problems unfolding before them, hence the booing mentioned earlier. If the game was abandoned the police feared a riot. The disaster could have been worse.

In summing up his feelings Franklin movingly wrote, 'My career in football has been full of experiences, some of them pleasant, some of them not so pleasant. I have been involved in thrilling cup ties. I have taken part in a club's fight for the championship, and a club's equally grim fight against relegation. I have represented my country at home and abroad. I have struggled against injury. I have been classed as a rebel and an outcast because I left the closed shop and went to find alleged fame and fortune in Bogotá.

'So, I have plenty of memories and although some of them might not have been pleasant, I would not have missed it for world. It has been fun. It has been thrilling. But although I have probably made my full quota of mistakes – who doesn't? – I don't regret a minute of it all. Except one thing. I shall always regret Black Saturday, that unforgettable disaster at Burnden Park, Bolton.'

As Matthews put it, football was about to enter a golden era. All the Burnden Park tragedy did for those running the so-called 'beautiful game' was to remind them of the voracious appetite for football of the sporting public. Forget the tragic consequences of cramming fans into decaying, badly maintained stadiums, just think of the money to be made, not human welfare.

Much to the football bosses' dismay, they discovered the players also wanted a share of any fortunes to be made, not least the greatest star of the day in the guise of Stanley Matthews, and the rising star, his Stoke City captain, Neil Franklin. Curiously Franklin appeared to take the events in Bolton a little more stoically than his more illustrious team-mate. Those events tragically and darkly illustrated the failings of those running football in the forties, both at club and national level.

Both Matthews and Franklin, along with others, were determined to take on the authorities in their battle for fair terms of employment. Meantime, a new season beckoned for 1946/47, at last a return to normality, a full programme of competitive league and cup football. Franklin rather than Matthews would arguably turn out to be a greater thorn in the side of his club, Stoke and the Football Association, but not before this particular pair played a heated and controversial part in their hometown club's doomed tilt at a one and only league title.

# POTTERS CRACK

THEORETICALLY of course a resumption of competitive domestic league football after a seven-year break marked a welcome return to normality for football fans and players alike. In reality these were anything but normal times for football or wider society. On the one hand, post-war austerity measures remained in place. Clubs even put out appeals for extra rationing coupons for clothes in order to replace shabby and torn playing kit. On the other hand, the voracious demand for the game from eager spectators meant pound note signs lit up in the eyes of club directors. One snag for players just happened to be their bosses' determination not to share out the spoils, much to the chagrin of the Players' Union.

As players demobbed from the armed forces returned full time to their clubs, the threat of strike action loomed. 'The players wanted to share in the post-war boom for football,' Franklin bluntly explained. The union demanded an increase in the maximum wage available to players to £12 a week, up from £9 a week, with a minimum payment of £3 a week.

Football League bosses, backed by the clubs, turned them down flat. They complained they were only able to meet the Players' Union's demands with financial help from the government, namely a cut in entertainment tax. Once, no doubt much to their surprise, the newly elected Labour government of the day agreed to do so, this quite remarkably brought the football bosses into conflict with fans as well as players.

On announcing this concession to Football League clubs, both in England and Scotland, in his budget, the Chancellor of the Exchequer, Hugh Dalton, expressed his hope of this being passed on to the fans. He wanted the minimum entrance fee to be reduced from 1s 6d (the princely sum of 7.5 pence in decimal currency) to 1s 3d (6 pence). Initially the clubs agreed. But once the fans flocked to the grounds for the beginning of a new season they were in for a shock. They were allowed in for 1s 3d each. But once inside they were then charged again to access terracing with a view of the pitch. The *Daily Herald* newspaper accused the clubs of reaping the rewards of the cut in entertainment tax while avoiding their 'moral obligations'.

As this row with disgruntled fans rumbled on, the Players' Union also turned to the government for help in its dispute over pay and conditions. It was a pattern later to be repeated after the infamous flight of disgruntled British players to Bogotá in the summer of 1950.

In calling for government intervention in the summer of 1946, union General Secretary, James Fay, commented, 'I hope the Ministry of Labour will be able to persuade the League to meet the Union as the situation is serious.' Initially, while Fay claimed the support of a substantial minority of clubs, the Football League turned down the demand for talks. 'There had been talk of strike action before, and no one had taken it very seriously. But this time it was serious,' observed Franklin. Players and fans alike were at loggerheads with those running their beautiful game.

At Stoke's Victoria Ground, another dispute loomed as the season kicked off, a simple clash of personality between manager and players, most notably involving its greatest player, Stanley Matthews. Yet again, he wanted out. Franklin, as the club's newly appointed captain, naturally ended up embroiled in the maelstrom of what was turning out to be a deeply personal conflict between Matthews and his manager, Bob McGrory. It gave the future Bogotá rebel leader an early indication of life in the eye of the national media, even then quite intense in its scrutiny of football and national icons such as Stanley Matthews.

Eight years on from his first dispute with Stoke over pay and conditions, Matthews put in his latest transfer request with the 1946/47 season barely days old. To compound matters for Franklin, as he tried to keep the peace in the Stoke dressing room, his understudy at centre-half, Billy Mould, also put in a transfer request. Just for good measure, Matthews' understudy as right-winger, George Mountford, the man with whom Franklin was to later make his infamous flight to Bogotá, also put in a transfer request.

In such a scenario it seemed difficult to envisage Stoke City challenging for the 1946/47 league title. A dreadful start to the season on the pitch, allied to the troubles off the pitch, hardly helped. Stoke picked up a solitary point from the first four games, including losing home and away to Bolton Wanderers. Much to Franklin's embarrassment Stoke's defence took the flak from disgruntled fans, especially after a remarkable 5-4 defeat to Middlesbrough at Ayresome Park. 'We couldn't grumble at the forwards,' Franklin wryly commented. 'They were averaging two goals a game and we were still without a win!'

But then came a total reversal in form. It also came largely in the absence of the injured Matthews. Stoke won six games in a row, including a 3-2 victory over the league leaders Manchester United in front of 40,000 fans at the Victoria Ground. It culminated in a 5-2 victory over Chelsea at Stamford Bridge.

This game was played with both sets of players believing it was a strong possibility they were about to go out on strike in the dispute between the Players' Union and the Football League. 'When we trotted on to the field at Stamford Bridge on that October Saturday afternoon, we were all wondering whether this would be our last game for some time,' reflected Franklin. 'In case it was to be like that, we decided to celebrate, and we entertained the crowd to a scorching match which ended with our winning 5-2.'

As the players returned to Stoke, the threatened strike was averted. Talks between the union and the Football League under the guidance of officials from the Ministry of Labour had been tentatively agreed; the dispute had been called off at least for the time being. Jimmy Guthrie, chairman of the Players' Union announced, 'There will be no strike while negotiations are in progress. We have not whittled down our demands one fraction, and we feel we are advanced in getting the Football League to discuss all matters at issue.'

It meant a brief lull in hostilities between players and their employers. In contrast, at individual club level, hostilities in the dressing room and on the training pitch at Stoke lingered despite their tremendous run of form. Specifically, the club's legendary talisman Stanley Matthews and his manager Bob McGrory renewed their long-running public feud. Matthews backed down in their first altercation just before the war, withdrawing a shock transfer request at the behest of his fans. This time he was in less of a mood to back down, much to his new international team-mate Neil Franklin's frustrations and embarrassment.

After thrashing Chelsea, the Potters were due back in London to face Arsenal. For this game Matthews had been declared fit. Matthews sought out his manager, presumably thinking he'd be delighted by the news. McGrory's response left him stunned. Instead of turning out for the first team against Arsenal, the manager suggested his star player might be better off with a run out in the reserves against Aston Villa.

Stoke City had been on a winning streak. Matthews' replacement, George Mountford, demonstrated the fine form that would later bring him to the attention of Colombian money men. For McGrory, in fairness to him, it was hard to change a winning side, even if it meant leaving out an absolute footballing legend at the peak of his powers. Franklin in his autobiography understood his decision but still thought it was wrong.

'The dispute or misunderstanding, call it what you like, came when Stan recovered from a pulled muscle, the bane of the professional footballer's life,' he wrote. He continued, 'George Mountford was his deputy in the Stoke team, and although we lacked our great star, we had one of those good runs which every club has now and then. Once the run starts you get tremendous confidence and can do no wrong.' Franklin also pointed out that Stoke's star performer in the 5-2 thrashing of Chelsea was Mountford.

As for the straightforward choice between Matthews and Mountford, he commented, 'There was much speculation as to whether he [Matthews] would be chosen, and if he was, where would Mountford play. Obviously, Mountford couldn't be dropped. But just as obviously Matthews if fit couldn't be left out. Some people might say here that you should never change a winning team but that is absolute nonsense. You won't change a team because it is winning or losing. You change the team to give you the best team available from your resources. It would be madness to keep a good player out of the side just because you had won without him.'

Franklin and his team-mates clearly had expected Matthews to return to the side. Somebody other than Mountford would have to make way for him, both to play against Arsenal. They were unaware of McGrory's private chat with Matthews, consigning his star player to the reserves. His omission from the side surprised Franklin and the Stoke players. For Matthews, it left him more bruised than from any Neanderthal full-back's brutal tackle. His pride above all was hurt. Someone would need to smooth his furrowed brow; the task would fall to Franklin.

An exasperated Matthews, who was living in Blackpool and training with the seaside town's football club, told the Lancashire *Evening Post*, 'I quite understand Stoke City being reluctant to change the team after winning six games in succession. I would have had no objection if they reached that decision and told me I could take an extra week's rest. It is true I have been on the injured list, but it was only a simple pulled muscle at the back of the thigh, which has healed completely. I am completely fit again. I do not require any tests in a reserve team.'

While readily acknowledged that Mountford had been playing well in his absence, he strongly felt that he ought to be restored to the starting line-up. 'I honestly couldn't take seriously McGrory's suggestion that I was not worth my place in the first team when fit,' he later told his biographer, the journalist David Miller. 'He [McGrory] and I had words and I told him to leave me out of the reserve side.' Rather than simply 'having words', judging by subsequent events with Matthews' departure from the club in the very same season, it seems they had a full-blown row.

As far as Matthews was concerned, worse was to follow. As soon as it became known he had been left out of the Stoke side, despite being fit, newspapers speculated that not only had he refused to play in the reserves but put in yet another transfer request. Stoke City's directors insisted he would not be sold. Matthews dismissed talk of him being transferred as 'rather premature'.

To make matters worse, there was also talk of a split in the dressing room of a club fielding the form team of the English First Division. Rumours spread of the players approaching the manager, asking for Matthews to be left out. Tales abounded of them being jealous of him and his superstar status, one incidentally bringing him relatively little financial reward. 'That was hurtful,' Matthews later reflected. 'For the next few days life was a turmoil.'

It was time, as club captain, for Franklin to intervene in the dispute and act as peacemaker. He set out, first, to quash what he saw as mischievous rumours, not least those circulating among Stoke fans. Unlike a modern-day Premier League star, he lived and worked in the community. He had heard the gossip first hand. First of all, he needed to call a meeting of the players – discover, though he knew it was highly unlikely, whether any of them were harbouring any grievances with Matthews.

'We players could do nothing. The affair was purely one between Matthews and the club, but the rumour-mongers wouldn't leave it at that,' he recalled in his autobiography. 'They immediately said that we players had approached the management and demanded – I like that one! – Matthews earn his way back into the first team. Others said we had told the management we didn't want Stan in the side. As soon as these rumours reached me, I realised that as captain of the team I could no longer stand aside.'

In describing the meeting, he wrote, 'I pleaded with the players to own up and tell the truth, pointing out it would be best for everyone and that, after all, we were all entitled to our opinion. Everyone present assured me that he had nothing against Stan and that he had never even thought of approaching the management.'

Satisfied he had the support of his players, Franklin addressed the national press. He commented, 'We are all the best of friends with Stan and think very highly of him.' He then decided to write to Matthews, who had returned to the guest house he ran in Blackpool to lick his mental wounds.

It arrived through his letterbox on the Monday morning after the Arsenal game. Stoke had lost 1-0, their winning streak at an end. The controversy over Matthews could hardly have helped.

In his autobiography, *The Way it Was*, published in 2000, Matthews insisted he took 'no satisfaction' from the result. He wrote that he was 'still totally committed to the Stoke cause, whether playing or not'. The commitment would not last but for the time being he took comfort from Franklin's overtures towards him. 'I received a letter from the Stoke captain and my good pal Neil Franklin that gave me a tremendous lift.' He added, 'Knowing that I had the support of my team-mates, including George Mountford who had replaced me, made me feel a whole lot better about the whole sorry affair.'

Franklin's intervention in Matthews' dispute with the Stoke board drew praise from their fellow England international Tom Finney, a friend of Franklin and fierce rival of Matthews for a place in the England team. Finney commented, 'That was Neil Franklin, a man with principles who liked to see right triumph.'

This 'sorry' affair left Franklin baffled and perhaps a little contemptuous of those commenting on the game – closer to home, those running his football club. 'It is rubbish to say that Stan was not popular,' he commented. 'He was a man admired by us all. Every footballer recognised his genius, and no player would be silly enough to be jealous of a genius in his side.'

Commenting on the temperament of one of England's greatest ever footballers, Franklin added, 'Matthews, of course, is the reserved reticent type, but that does not mean he is unpopular. Everyone at Stoke knew Matthews. They knew how reserved he was. How shy he was in fact. They knew too that he was a fanatic about football. And, we all admired him for it.' Matthews did not need such a fond endorsement but he remained grateful for the rest of his life.

He counted Franklin as a 'pal', so much so he would end up being one of Franklin's sternest critics once he and George Mountford had their own infamous brush with club and country less than four years later. For now though, Matthews resolved his differences with Stoke's manager and the club's board of directors. His earlier suggestion of his absence being explained away as him 'taking a rest' was taken up. Stoke's hapless chairman Harold Booth commented that he had been given an extra week's holiday, 'owing to the controversy during the last few days and will continue to train at Blackpool'.

At the time it was seen curiously as an early victory for player power, one only the greatest footballer in the land was capable of achieving. 'This ends a soccer chapter without precedent in this country,' commented Clifford Webb of the *Daily Herald*. He went on, 'Phrase it how you will, it is impossible to gloss over the fact that the player wins. There was no mention of a transfer, or of transfer offers, or of any desire of Matthews to leave Stoke. In my opinion, Matthews has won a victory, which puts him in almost a fantastic position as a football player.'

His team-mates, Franklin and George Mountford, could be forgiven for treating the bold, disruptive antics with envy. Indeed, players up and down the land probably felt the same. There were lessons to be learned for a later date, the key one being just don't walk out on your club. It was one the Bogotá rebels would spectacularly ignore.

In Matthews' case, it was argued that he would never leave Stoke City mainly because he was too expensive to buy. Unless, as Webb of the *Daily Herald* put it, 'an earthquake occurs to alter the trend of thought'. When it came to dealings in the forties transfer market top players would have the upper hand in any dispute with their clubs, he wrongly argued. Such an earthquake, of course, was decades off. In the meantime, there was an unlikely challenge for the league title for Matthews, Franklin and George Mountford to focus on.

All this furore, what Franklin termed 'the Matthews sensation' overshadowed the Stoke captain's own personal triumph, finally winning a 'full' England cap. With the full return of domestic competitive football, the various national associations restored full international status for games between countries for the first time since the outbreak of war in the autumn of 1939. England resumed awarding 'full caps' for two games in two days in Ireland, beginning in Belfast and then in Dublin. Even then the occasion of him receiving this great honour threw up controversy in what was turning out to be a madcap season of football.

Franklin and Matthews were selected in both games, a return to international duty for Franklin after being left out of the final Victory International against Scotland. Matthews, thanks to injury, dropped out. It allowed Preston's Tom Finney to take his place, indeed, much to the Stoke winger's consternation, threatening to do so for the long term. To his dismay, he was battling for his place at both club and international level.

A fractious build-up to Franklin making his 'full international' debut in Windsor Park, Belfast ensured a bumper crowd. More than 60,000 turned up fuelled by anger over the behaviour of England's Football Association. It had been at loggerheads with the Irish Football Association, a bizarre dispute throwing the fixture into doubt.

At the time, the Irish Football Association (IFA) and the Football Association of Ireland (FAI) both claimed jurisdiction over the running of the sport on the island of Ireland. For international purposes the IFA, based in Belfast, ran the Ireland team and the FAI, based in Dublin, ran their team using the Gaelic word for Ireland, Éire. Much to the chagrin of the FA in London, neither Irish association was too fussy at the time about where on the island of Ireland they selected their players from.

Sir Stanley Rous, the FA boss, wanted the British associations to re-join the international governing body FIFA, noting the success before the war of the fledgling World Cup and fearing the home of association football was losing international influence. It was vital, in his view, to send an England team to the forthcoming World Cup in Brazil to establish his country as the greatest football power on the planet.

To assist his campaign, Rous wanted to appease FIFA, which frowned on member associations selecting players born outside their territories. As a result, Rous demanded the IFA only selected players from Northern Ireland. He sent a similar missive to the FAI, insisting it only fielded players born in the Republic of Ireland.

For Rous, later to become the FIFA president, it turned out to be an early diplomatic failure. The competing Irish associations had their differences, to put it mildly. The hapless English FA boss managed to unite them. He united them in anger at his impudence. Clifford Webb of the *Daily Herald* noted their anger at the behaviour of 'the dictatorial English'.

Rous made a demand for the IFA to leave out players born outside Northern Ireland. The IFA refused point blank. Its selectors picked four players from the Republic of Ireland: Johnny Carey of Manchester United, Bill Gorman of Brentford, Davy Walsh of West Bromwich Albion and Tom Aherne from Belfast Celtic. In contrast the FAI did comply with the English request, leaving out any players born in Northern Ireland. It did so while selecting all of the above players for the Éire squad with Carey as captain. Effectively they were playing for two different countries against England in the space of two days.

This quasi-comical row guaranteed interest from those not normally interested in football. As an estimated 60,000 spectators filed through the gate, the Windsor Park authorities struggled to cope. As Franklin lined up with his England team-mates, memories of the horrors of Burnden Park must have flashed by as fans spilled on to the pitch. Kick-off was delayed by a quarter of an hour for some order to be restored.

The *Belfast Newsletter* reported that the warm weather and the 'crush' had made some people faint. Fortunately, there were no major injuries. Appeals on the tannoy were heeded, The *Newsletter*'s correspondent describing the heaving crowd as 'good-humoured'. After the game had been threatened by political controversy and the spectre of crowd disorder, it could finally go ahead. Neil Franklin was finally able to make his full international debut.

Franklin described it as his 'first real international honour'. After the mayhem prior to the game, it could not have gone more smoothly for Franklin and England. It turned out to be a comfortable 7-2 victory. As one correspondent put it, the Irish were 'overwhelmed'. Franklin assumed the game against Éire would be even easier. He was wrong.

England fielded the same 11 players as those who took to the field in Belfast 48 hours earlier. Éire picked two of the men the English faced at Windsor Park, Johnny Carey and Bill Gorman. The Irish centre-forward Davy Walsh, who had originally been picked to play in both games in a green shirt, missed out on them because of injury. Both centre-forwards picked to replace him posed Franklin problems.

'We got a tremendous shock,' commented Franklin. 'Never have I met such enthusiasm, no not even at Hampden Park in Glasgow, and it wasn't until five minutes from the end that Tom Finney scored the goal that gave us a 1-0 victory.' He was relieved, not least because he had been given the run-around by the Irish centre-forward Michael O'Flanagan of Bohemians.

'I was certainly glad to see the back of him,' Franklin ruefully reflected.

Having begun his full international career, he returned to the Potteries harbouring dreams of domestic honours as captain of his hometown club. It first meant helping to sort out the domestic spat between the man absent from the England squad, his old friend Stanley Matthews and his manager Bob McGrory. Once they temporarily settled their differences there was a realistic chance of Franklin captaining Stoke City to the league championship. Frustratingly for him, they failed.

How could a club the size of Stoke City leave out one of England's finest players? It was the question on the lips of Arsenal fans as they queued for a sell-out match between Arsenal and the form team of the division, Stoke City. As it turned out, the Potters, minus Matthews and with his replacement George Mountford coming under inevitable intense public scrutiny, cracked. They would do so again at the end of a tumultuous season as Matthews finally bid farewell to Franklin, Mountford and the rest of their team-mates.

On international duty, burly part-time professional centre-forward Michael O'Flanagan had tormented Franklin during England's fortunate 1-0 victory. His brother Kevin O'Flanagan, a young doctor based in north London, was also on the field that day, his hobby being playing football for Éire and Arsenal. As Franklin looked across the Highbury pitch before the match, the sight of O'Flanagan warming up, he could have been forgiven for thinking a recurring nightmare would be about to unfold. It duly did. Stoke's right-winger, Mountford, struggled, unable to reproduce the fine form he showed during Stoke's recent impressive winning run. Arsenal's right-winger, the flying doctor O'Flanagan, enjoyed the game of his life, scoring the winning goal.

The subsequent press coverage made for difficult reading for Franklin, his team-mates, and their manager after his heavily publicised spat with the most famous footballer in the land. It was generally agreed among the watching press that Stoke were unlucky to lose. But the overriding conclusion was summed up in one headline, 'Serves Them Right'.

The *Daily Herald*'s George Chisholm wrote, 'More than 70,000 went to see the team that could leave out Stanley Matthews and the 62,000 who got inside quickly decided that it was all wrong.' In commenting on George Mountford's contribution, he concluded, 'Trouble was that in a few days George Mountford, deputy for Matthews, had grown in public imagination from a very good player to a super player. Which is exactly what no one ever claimed for him.'

As for Franklin and the Stoke defence, they were considered shaky. In contrast, Franklin's opposite number, the England cricketer Denis Compton, was considered man of the match. Franklin merely dismissed the defeat at Highbury as 'a bit of a setback'. He was confident his side, still minus Matthews, would get back on track by beating the then league leaders Wolverhampton Wanderers at the Victoria Ground. Once again, he ended up disappointed. 'Defeat it was to be by three goals to nil,' he dryly noted.

One disgruntled fan blamed Blackie, Stoke's club cat, for the defeat rather than the players. 'On Saturday my wife saw a woman in a fur coat, who had come in a car with some Wolverhampton supporters, stroking Blackie at the club entrance,' he sternly informed the *Sentinel* newspaper. 'It is my belief that luck went to Wolverhampton like the points.'

Early on in the game Franklin's mate, George Mountford, missed a sitter, the Wolves goalie Bert Williams saving from him at point-blank range. He then picked up an injury, pulling a leg muscle. He was unavailable for the next run of fixtures, which Franklin considered as 'not particularly difficult'. Cue manager McGrory to phone a guest house in Blackpool. Matthews was back in the Stoke side for the next match away to Sunderland.

Incredibly, news of his recall was deemed worthy of mention on the front pages of the national tabloid press. Much to his annoyance, some claimed he was refusing to play against Sunderland. Dismissing the story as an 'invention', Matthews told the Lancashire *Evening Post* that he was 'flabbergasted'. He commented, 'I knew nothing about it until I opened a daily newspaper this morning and saw a long story on the front page stating I would not play for Stoke. I had no such thought in my mind and where the idea came from I do not know.' His mood darkened with the announcement of the England team for the upcoming international against Wales. Matthews, once the first name to go on to the team sheet, was omitted. His Stoke team-mate Franklin was, of course, included.

On reading the coverage, a bunch of Sunderland students came up with what they considered to be a bright fundraising idea for rag week. It was quite simple. They plotted to kidnap Stanley Matthews on arrival at the Stoke team hotel in Sunderland and hold him to ransom. There was just one snag. For some unfathomable reason, they did not know what the most famous footballer in Britain looked like.

To solve the problem some of them posed in the hotel lobby as autograph hunters. Another passed herself off as a member of hotel staff. What could possibly go wrong? Well, asking one of the mischievous young Stoke players to point out Stanley Matthews for them is the answer. Instead of pointing to Matthews, he guided them in the direction of Neil Franklin.

As he waited to check in, a phone began to ring in a phone booth near him. He was advised by the rogue member of staff it was a call for him. He walked towards the ringing telephone only for the students to pounce on him and drag him out on to the street and into a passing tram. Stoke's England international centre-half had been kidnapped. The students had taken the wrong player captive. But it didn't really matter to them. Franklin was a decent prize hostage.

'I pleaded with my "captors" telling them that the Stoke team would soon be leaving for Roker Park,' recalled Franklin of this bizarre episode. 'But it was no good.' In fairness Franklin saw the funny side. His manager failed to do so. McGrory was also summoned to the phone with Franklin telling him the students were demanding a £5 ransom for his release.

A furious McGrory pointed out that he had already phoned the police. Meantime, Franklin, assured by the students they would let him go in time to play the game at Roker Park, happily allowed them to parade him through the streets as they set about collecting their fundraising target of £400. They managed £450 to be donated to the local hospital.

Franklin was duly 'freed', and driven back to the hotel by one of the college lecturers with the police waiting to talk to his students. He dryly noted, 'They had been told very firmly by the police that I had to be returned or else!' On his return to the hotel, he discovered the Stoke entourage had already left. McGrory decided to take advantage of the unseasonally temperate weather by holding a light training session on the beach.

Franklin made his own way to Roker Park to be eventually reunited with the Stoke team. The unusual build-up worked in their favour. They won 1-0, the club's first-ever away victory at Sunderland, Franklin insisting that throughout his capture by students celebrating their rag week he had kept his 'mind on the afternoon's game'.

As for the man of the match on this occasion, it inevitably went to Stanley Matthews. One observer implausibly commented the Sunderland crowd were 'roaring with laughter at the ease with which Stan beat his man', the Wearsiders' left-back Jack Jones. More importantly, there were smiles back on the Stoke players' faces. Their league title challenge was back on track.

They were disappointingly led to a goalless draw with Aston Villa at home. But as Franklin put it, the Stoke team were doing 'exceptionally well on tour'. The away victory over Sunderland at Roker Park was followed up by a 3-1 win over Portsmouth at Fratton Park. Matthews was described as being in 'scintillating' form, Franklin noted for 'controlling the centre of the field'.

In confident mood, Stoke saw off Everton 2-1 in controversial circumstances. A late winner from Antonio sealed the victory in the gathering gloom on a bleak November Saturday afternoon. Floodlights had yet to be installed at Stoke's Victoria Ground. Everton players furiously protested to the referee but the goal stood. Antonio later admitted he had handled the ball into the net.

By now Stoke fans as well as players were dreaming of title-winning glory. 'There's no doubt that a terrific roar won us the match,' commented McGrory. 'Wouldn't it be a strange thing if that late goal won us the championship?' The following week came a match which Franklin firmly believed cost Stoke the title: defeat to Huddersfield Town.

'As always the trouble came from the lowly club, Huddersfield Town,' mused Franklin. 'When we visited Leeds Road they were at the bottom of the league, but they beat us 1-0. At the end of the season, this was one of the games we looked back on and said about it, if only we had won?' To make matters worse, Franklin was blamed for the winning Huddersfield goal. Their winger Metcalfe dispossessed him before lashing home the goal.

Undeterreded, Franklin put this latest 'setback' behind him, putting in a man of the match performance the following weekend against the club haunting his manager McGrory: Blackpool. Ironically, Matthews, the star player who spent the week training with the Seasiders, scored the fourth Stoke goal. Franklin made sure their England team-mate, Stanley Mortensen, would have no such joy for the visitors.

Quite bizarrely Franklin led the applause of both sets of players in tribute to Matthews as he left the pitch. He had played with one set, trained with the other. In praising his performance, the Stoke *Sentinel* correspondent commented, 'Matthews' goal will be talked about for years and those who saw it will describe how he progressed by acute zigzags over half the length of the field, with four or five Blackpool players trotting at his heel like a pack of dogs, and finally he even made the goalkeeper go the wrong way and tapped the ball into the net.'

It was a comprehensive victory for the Stoke fans, one of many to savour during a memorable season. In the aftermath, Franklin sportingly had some warm sympathy for his Blackpool opponents, given they were caught up in an accident while embarking on a morning tour of the Potteries' factory shops. 'Perhaps there was some excuse because on the way to the ground a taxi, in which six of the Blackpool players were travelling, was involved in a collision with a lorry,' he explained. 'None of the players were injured, but they must have been shaken up and their form was quite probably affected.'

There were no travails for Stoke as they enjoyed another 4-1 victory, this time away to Brentford before playing out a goalless draw at home with Blackburn Rovers on an icebound pitch. Franklin claimed that game put them 'in fighting trim' for the Christmas holiday games. They did beat Liverpool, the eventual title winners, 2-1 on Christmas Day. But 24 hours later on Boxing Day, they lost 2-0 to the same opponents at Anfield.

Defeat away to Charlton Athletic by a goal to nil a couple of days later ensured Franklin's team would go into the new year eight points behind the leaders Wolverhampton Wanderers in an era of two points for a win. Indeed, Wolves were five points clear of their nearest challengers Manchester United and Blackpool. Franklin commented the odds on Stan Cullis, the man he took over from as England centre-half, winning the title had 'shortened alarmingly'.

'We, of course, slipped up where so many other clubs slip up – in holiday games,' he groaned. 'These annual feasts of league games at Christmas and Easter can make or break a club. Three games in four days is a great strain on any team fighting for honours.' No doubt Franklin, if alive today, would have little sympathy for Premier League players and managers complaining about playing three games in the space of a week.

Stoke, including the goalless draw with Blackburn just a couple of days before Christmas, had played four games in the space of a week but just garnered three points. Dreams of winning an elusive league title were fading away. More alarmingly, the winter weather was closing in. One of the harshest British winters on record would have a significant impact on the outcome of the Football League season.

'Ice was commonplace. Snow, too, was becoming frighteningly commonplace,' complained Franklin in his autobiography. 'Playing football, in fact living at all, was far from comfortable.' A combination of the poor weather and a bruising FA Cup run, which ended with a disappointing 1-0 fifth-round defeat to Sheffield United at the Victoria Ground, limited Stoke's league outings, much to Franklin's frustration. Despite the odd, at times bizarre, setback he confidently believed he would be lifting the league trophy at the end of the season. Fixture congestion would, in his optimistic view, be the only problem.

'Out of the cup, but still in the league fight, and now in the middle of some of the worst weather ever known in Britain,' recalled Franklin. 'Snow hurled its fury down on every part of our island. Roads were blocked, villages were cut off, transport was reduced to chaos, and the whole nation began to grind through to an agonising crawl, to an even more agonising stop.'

As the list of postponed fixtures throughout the league mounted up week by week, the natural thing to do would be to reschedule fixtures in midweek. But this was banned by the government. Given the country was still trying to rebuild in the aftermath of war, it was decreed that nothing should interfere with the task of keeping industry going in the middle of the harshest winter in living memory. Sport was seen as a potential distraction. Events could only be staged on Saturday afternoons.

Remarkably, for all of the Stoke players' moans and groans, their club was not as badly affected by postponements as others. Somehow, the Victoria Ground staff managed to keep it open, admittedly with a pitch which these days would be deemed unplayable. There was no under-soil heating of course. Instead braziers were strategically placed all over the pitch, Stanley Matthews famously being captured on camera warming his hands by one of them.

After helping to secure a 1-1 draw with Manchester United for their side at Old Trafford, Franklin and Matthews warmed to welcoming Chelsea, the team Stoke thrashed 5-2 in the winger's absence. Matthews was once again missing, suffering a boil on his leg. George Mountford returned to the side. The outcome was no different than back in the autumn. 'We hit the Londoners with an outsize blizzard,' crowed Franklin. 'By half-time we led 6-1; there was no scoring in the second half, but I bet news of that half-time score got them talking on most grounds.'

A week later the defeat to Arsenal, which Matthews had controversially missed, was avenged. Franklin dryly remarked, 'We wallowed through the snow well enough to pick up another two points to a 3-1 victory.' It put Stoke just three points behind the leaders Wolves with two games in hand on their Staffordshire rivals. Next up, they were optimistically making the short trip to Molineux.

Wolves' form had frozen. It thawed with the visit of Stoke City. Losing the game 3-0 was a bitter blow to Franklin's players. March 1947 turned out to be an unhappy month for them as they tried to secure an historic league title. After Stoke's home fixture with Sunderland became yet another casualty of the snow, the Football League reluctantly tore up the fixture list, sanctioning an extension to the end of the season. It meant Stoke would now play their final game on 14 June 1947.

Their game at Aston Villa was abandoned in the snow with an hour played and the score at 2-2. Neil Franklin played after turning out for the English Football League against the Scottish League at Hampden Park in midweek. Matthews, who played alongside him in that game, failed to turn out, a precursor for yet more off-the-field drama to come.

Back on the pitch a 1-1 draw at home to Portsmouth and a 2-2 draw away to Everton proved to be another of Franklin's disappointing setbacks. Franklin went as far as describing the result of the game at Goodison Park as 'tragic'. His team had thrown away a 2-0 lead at half-time. Stoke's title challenge was faltering. But so too were the campaigns of their rivals.

Another series of 'make or break' holiday fixtures loomed. Easter was on its way. A thaw in the bitter winter weather was also on its way. Unfortunately for Franklin and Stoke's league title-winning ambitions there was no complete thaw in relations between manager, Bob McGrory and talisman, Stanley Matthews. This time, a breakdown in relations proved terminal.

Their spectacular personal spat overshadowed the wider national dispute between the Players' Union and their clubs over pay and conditions. It staggered on with once again the players threatening strike action on the eve of Easter. The clubs had offered a maximum wage of £11 a week during the season, and £9 in the summer. The union rejected the offer, demanding the matter be taken to compulsory arbitration.

Its secretary, James Fay, explained, 'I shall proceed with my instructions from the players to ask the Ministry of Labour for compulsory arbitration. Some of them have blamed the union committee for not taking strike action earlier. If the league challenges our right to go to arbitration there would be no illegality in our striking to bring the matter to the test.'

Once again talk of a strike turned out to be an idle threat. The only walkouts were from the pitch and on to the pitch, not out the main doors to form a picket line. The dispute dragged on. Franklin, Matthews and the legendary winger's unlikely rival for Stoke City's number 7 shirt all took their own unilateral action to resolve their concerns over pay and conditions. Matthews' action in comparison with the two Bogotá rebels appears in hindsight a little more subtle. His long-running feud with his bosses was coming to a disastrous conclusion for Stoke City in the spring of 1947.

Back then clubs played three games in four days over the Easter weekend – Good Friday, the following day and then on Easter Monday – with no complaints from any of the protagonists. There had been plenty of complaints from Bob McGrory over Matthews' failure to turn up for the abandoned league game against Aston Villa at Villa Park. Franklin and Matthews battled back from international duty in Glasgow through blizzards with their English colleagues for the journey south to re-join their clubs.

Franklin made it back to Stoke so he could report for duty to go to Birmingham to play Villa. Matthews went home to his wife at their hotel in Blackpool. Worse still, another Stoke player, Jack McCue, had played for a British army team against a French army team in Paris. He managed to make it back from the French capital through storms and blizzards, turning up in North Staffordshire in the early hours of the morning of the Villa game. Given the abandonment of the match, perhaps Matthews had a better weather forecast or just saw little chance of the appalling weather abating, making him not a bad judge. But his no-show for the game set the tone, ahead of rows over selection for those vital Easter holiday games.

Matthews claimed he was happy to be left out of the side to travel to Grimsby Town for the Good Friday fixture because he wanted some rest ahead of England's international against Scotland a week later. He was also absent from the team for the home games against Huddersfield and the return fixture against Grimsby on Easter Monday. Stoke won all three games comfortably.

Matthews had called McGrory on Maundy Thursday asking to be excused the trip to Grimsby. McGrory agreed but initially picked Matthews for the Saturday game against Huddersfield before changing his mind. The legendary number 7 was furious. He wrote in his autobiography, 'There are times in the career of any footballer when he doesn't agree with certain decisions a manager makes, but out of respect accepts them. Bob McGrory's behaviour not only galled me, it started to eat away at what remaining respect I had for him as a manager.'

Still, there was no transfer request. This came a fortnight later after a game against Brentford. For this, Stoke's programme publisher can apparently be blamed as much as anyone. Once again, there was a genuine selection dilemma. George Mountford had played well in a run of four successive victories, the latest a 2-0 win away to title rivals Blackpool, naturally the club keenest to sign Matthews. Franklin breezily commented, 'We helped Blackpool on their way out of the honours race.'

On face value, McGrory decided to accommodate both players for the Brentford game, moving George Mountford to the inside right position, something he had been reluctant to do earlier in the season. Matthews and Mountford both scored in a 3-1 victory and Matthews was pleased with a job well done until he sat down and picked up the matchday programme.

In those days, players were named from one to 11, the team line-up reflecting the manager's selection barring any last-minute injuries. It was only when Matthews glanced at the programme it dawned on him; he had been duped by the manager. Mitchell's name was on the team sheet. He was not dropped. He was injured. Cue a showdown between the board of directors and their star player. A transfer request was duly slapped in – the final transfer request. Matthews was on his way.

This time there was to be no intervention from Franklin. He had his own difficulties with McGrory despite being appointed captain. He made only passing mention of Matthews' departure in his autobiography, merely noting, when mentioning Matthews' goals in the wins over Brentford and Blackburn Rovers, that their star player was 'within weeks of leaving us'.

A deal between Stoke and Blackpool was struck in Glasgow where the great and the good of British football had gathered for a charity game at Hampden Park. It was billed 'The match of the century', Great Britain versus the rest of Europe, Matthews making what turned out to be his final international representative appearance as a Stoke player. Franklin missed out on selection, Ireland's Jack Vernon preferred at centre-half instead. For the record, the British team won the game 6-1. The beneficiary of the match was the world-governing body FIFA to the tune of £30,000, money donated despite the English, Welsh and Scottish FAs not being members at the time.

As it turned out in hindsight, the other beneficiaries were Blackpool and also Liverpool, the eventual league champions thanks to the agreement reached in Glasgow by the Stoke chairman Harold Booth and his directors to sell Matthews. The loser was Stoke City. For all of Matthews' tantrums, he was still their star, their talisman, his name on the team sheet putting fear into the opposition. For the final three games Matthews' name was absent from the team sheet – a fatal blow to Stoke City's league title ambitions.

Further hampering Stoke's bid for title glory just happened to be the intermittent absence of the club's skipper, Neil Franklin, thanks ironically to his brilliance. In those days, international matches, including the Home Nations Championship, coincided with a full programme of league matches. To compound matters, the FA had arranged an England tour to Switzerland and Portugal. It went ahead despite the Football League extending the domestic season. Other clubs could just about afford to lose their better players. Stoke heavily relied on Franklin, especially with Matthews going out the door. Pleas to the FA to leave him at home were ignored.

'The dates for our matches in Switzerland and Portugal had been arranged beforehand and the Football Association is not the sort of organisation to break a contract,' commented Franklin. 'So away we went on the usual tour with the Football League championship still undecided, and Stoke City still being in with a great chance.' For Franklin, a game listed as a B international against Switzerland in Zurich proved memorable, sadly for the wrong reasons.

While he confidently boasted his England side had 'outclassed' their Swiss opponents, they struggled to score. They were also frustrated by lenient refereeing, the Swiss constantly being given the benefit of the doubt for some horrendous tackling. 'To me football is a game to be played with the head and the feet, and when I say the head, I also include the grey matter which we are all supposed to have inside our heads,' Franklin stated in summing up his football philosophy. He went on, 'If you have nothing more than physical strength then you can never hope to be a success at soccer. Any lout can knock a man off the ball, but it takes a footballer to take a ball off an opponent and then beat others, either by dribbling or by passing the ball correctly.' The Swiss failed to live up to his version of the beautiful game.

Towards the end of the game with the score still 0-0, the Swiss winger Hans Siegenthaler raced clear. Franklin moved across to tackle, timing it, in his view, 'perfectly'. His opponent, the referee and more ominously the crowd disagreed. 'As I went up to the player and was helping him to his feet, I suddenly saw that the crowd was in a whale of a temper,' revealed Franklin. 'Some of them were advancing on to the field, and two empty beer bottles and an umbrella were winging towards me.'

Franklin admitted that he was 'scared'. The police intervened but his saviour turned out to be the England goalkeeper Frank Swift. 'As soon as he saw the trouble developing, Swifty moved out of his goal and approached the crowd, who were thirsting for blood,' he recalled. 'He picked up the offending umbrella, waved it at the crowd, and with that unfailing charm and humour of his did what the scores of policemen could never have done. He led the spectators back to their seats and the "riot" was over.'

Franklin was forever grateful to Swift, a man sadly to lose his life as one of the victims of the Munich air disaster. 'Big Frank was the hero of Switzerland,' commented the England centre-half. 'He also earned my undying thanks. Looking back on the incident, I can laugh, but I assure you it was far from pleasant. My knees felt like unset jellies, and I cannot imagine what I would have done if the crowd had got hold of me.'

Back home, the Players' Union leader, James Guthrie, was less than amused with Franklin and Swift, but not because of their clash with the Swiss crowd. Guthrie's revelation that they were behind with their subscriptions made front-page news rather than the crowd trouble in Zurich. He suggested other professional footballers ought to refuse to play with them.

Given Stoke City's players were hoping to lift the championship trophy, they were unlikely to agree to Mr Guthrie's demands. An angry Franklin responded, 'I am still a member and support the union policy. I shall send on my subscriptions, paid up to the end of the season at once.' Meantime his manager agitated to get him back from international duty to play with his team-mates.

'Club's "Fly Home" cable to Star' ran one headline. 'Stoke City believe their hopes largely depend on whether Neil Franklin can get back from the continent in time for their Whit Monday game with Aston Villa.' Franklin was due to play for England in Lisbon against Portugal the day before his club were due to play Villa. His manager, McGrory, asked him to catch a flight home straight after the game rather than fly back with the rest of the England squad on the Monday morning. Franklin was unable to do so.

As he eventually flew home with the England squad, Stoke travelled to Villa Park, Frank Mountford deputising for the absent club captain at centre-half. Stoke won 1-0, George Mountford scoring the winning goal. It set up the final game of the season. All their title rivals had already played all their 42 games. Stoke had just one left, away to Sheffield United, a fixture to be played on 12 June.

Given Stoke's superior goal difference a win would mean the league championship would be coming to the Potteries for the first time in history. A draw or a defeat would hand the title to Liverpool. In theory, Sheffield United had nothing to play for apart from pride, and unfounded rumours of an illicit bonus from the Merseyside club.

Sadly, Stoke blew their opportunity in the Sheffield rain. 'Sheets of it came down, and the Bramall Lane turf looked like something the cat had brought home,' remembered Franklin. 'Fancy fighting your way through a ten-month season, and then having to play the vital game in summer, and in mud!'

Sheffield United took the lead in just the third minute of the game. But within a couple of minutes Alec Ormston had equalised. Yet, perhaps remembering Sheffield United were the team who had knocked Stoke out of the FA Cup earlier in the season, Franklin's men struggled. He was grateful to goalkeeper Dennis Herod.

'Dennis was great that day,' wrote Franklin in his autobiography. 'He saved them from every angle, and every time he saved a shot or a header, he seemed to look imploringly at the rest of us, asking us to score the goal that would put us into the lead. For a draw was no good to us. We had to win.'

They failed to do so. Just as they started the first half slowly, the same occurred in the second half. Walter Rickett put Sheffield United back into the lead. Liverpool had won the Football League title, champions of England once again. Franklin and his devastated team-mates went back across the Pennines to the Potteries dreaming of what might have been. They also posed a simple question. Did the transfer of Stanley Matthews cost Stoke City the league title?

Quite a few of them, including Franklin, thought so. They blamed the club, and in doing so the manager, for missing out on winning a league winners' medal. Franklin in an interview to the Stoke *Sentinel* some years later commented, 'Stan was the best player I ever played with. If he had not been sold to Blackpool in 1947, I am sure Stoke would have won the First Division championship.'

Goalkeeper Dennis Herod, recognised by his skipper as the man of the match, described the funereal mood among his colleagues. He told Stoke City historian Simon Lowe, 'The atmosphere was dreadful. I can't tell you how depressing it was. Actually, it took me six months to get over it.'

As for the sale of Matthews, Herod goes on: 'Bob McGrory's jealousy of Stan's fame cost Stoke the First Division title. Before our last game at Sheffield United, he sold a world-class player and we lost that game without him. I am not taking away anything from McGrory who did a great deal for Stoke City. But he wanted the limelight himself and was jealous of players like Stan and Neil Franklin. It was folly to leave Stan out and the decision to sell the best forward in the world to Blackpool was sheer stupidity.'

Sir Stanley Matthews did offer his own take on the impact of his sale to Blackpool on Stoke's title chances. He wrote in his autobiography, 'Whether or not my presence in the team would have aided Stoke in their quest for the Championship is a matter of conjecture. Suffice to say that Stoke not winning it that season was, for me, a sad end to what had been 17 wonderful years with my home town club.'

Franklin offered other theories too. He felt Stoke City should have won the league title that madcap season even with Matthews absent for the final games. He put it down to a simple lack of experience. 'We had no special training for this grandstand finish,' he observed.

In commenting on the fortnight's gap between playing the penultimate game against Villa and the final match in Sheffield, he further offered, 'In fact it was difficult not to over-train, during this great waiting period. The worst trouble was, of course, nerves. After all, we played only three games in six weeks, and had to wait 14 days before our vital game at Sheffield. It just got us down and I think this waiting period was our undoing.'

Philosophically, he looked back with pride on a 'great fight' and a 'great, if tough season'. With Matthews gone, he alone was the star man. But as Dennis Herod alluded to, it also meant Neil Franklin, the club captain, would be next in line to clash yet again with his taciturn manager, Bob McGrory. George Mountford, Matthews' understudy, was set to do the same. It was to end with one of the most spectacular fallings-outs in football history.

# A ONE-MAN STRIKE

QUITE how and why Neil Franklin, along with his Stoke City team-mates, eventually became easy prey for Colombian moneymen setting up a pirate league became evident in the aftermath of their crushing disappointment in failing to win the English Football League. Already an odd, if not to frustrated Stoke fans a dysfunctional, dressing room, one enduring an appalling relationship with the club's bosses, matters deteriorated sharply. The national scene, the fractious relationship between Football League club and the Players' Union, appeared little better.

There was little time for Franklin and his Stoke team-mates to recover before they were due to return to pre-season training in preparation for the next campaign. Any psychological scars would linger – the post-mortem into how the title was lost in the previous season hardly over before the new one kicked off.

For Franklin there was a personal fillip. Generally, the football sages hailed Franklin as one of England's finest players, his position as the international team's centre-half unassailable. In an era before football writers began formally voting for their player of the year, some informally gave the honour to Franklin. His prospective Colombian suitors duly noted from afar.

Clifford Webb of the *Daily Herald* revealed he wanted Stoke City to win the 1947 league title. 'It would have been so fitting a finale for the player of the season – Neil Franklin, the City's and England's centre-half,' Webb declared. 'Neil was man of the match at waterlogged Bramall Lane where Stoke failed to get from Sheffield United the points which would have won the title. He carried a shaky defence on his strong young shoulders. His tackling, strong and scrupulously clean, was instructional. His distribution was invariably correct and direct.'

It was high praise, but he did conclude Stoke were 'well and truly walloped'. In his assessment of Franklin, the *Herald*'s correspondent took a swipe at critics, not least sceptical England fans. Webb insisted his player of the season had been 'England's pivot' in all international matches at home and abroad. He also boldly suggested Franklin might go on to be Stoke's greatest player ever.

Yet for all the praise coming his way Franklin felt unhappy. In the inquest into Stoke's failure to clinch the league title, McGrory and Matthews took a lot of flak for falling out not just once, but twice in the season, the second embarrassingly during the final run-in. Surprisingly, the Stoke captain also came under scrutiny from a minority of Stoke fans. For the time being Franklin ignored any criticism from those fans and more pertinently his manager.

Stoke's talented team of players returned for the 1947/48 season in optimistic mood, despite losing their talisman Matthews. Club-record signings helped to boost morale, forwards Jimmy McAlinden and Tommy Kiernan coming in from Portsmouth and Celtic respectively. It proved impossible to repeat the feats of the previous campaign, not least because of a catalogue of injuries. Franklin was among those spending time on the injured list.

At one point, there was a danger of Stoke being relegated less than 12 months after being involved in a title challenge. Defeat to the champions Liverpool in their third game of the season began a run of seven successive defeats – but, with injured players returning the Potters recovered, eventually settling for mid-table mediocrity. As for the personal state of their captain, Franklin, he became more and more unsettled.

'For a long time I had felt that Stoke City did not like my style of play,' groaned Franklin. 'There had been a lot of criticism of it, but it was the only style I knew and I had no intention of changing it. I thought that the only solution was for me to move to another club.'

Above all he took umbrage at the coverage of him in the local press, especially one stinging comment with analysis of the club's defensive record with him in or out of the team during the troubled 1947/48 season. The correspondent pointed out that in games Franklin was missing Stoke had won three and drawn three. Of the remaining games with the club's captain at the heart of the defence, they'd lost half their games.

His critic concluded in citing a game with Franklin missing from the line-up, 'Stoke, who with that hang back defence, rarely avail themselves of the protection of the offside law, were winning more free kicks for offside on Saturday than in half a dozen home games previously. We cannot blame this season's troubles entirely on injuries, and it seems we shall have no guarantee against a repetition next season unless a better understanding in defence checks this goal against toll.'

Perhaps it was better for Franklin to ignore this critique of the Stoke defence, one seemingly based on their ability to play the offside trap. Instead, he bit. It was further proof of how he was not wanted, even by people with whom, as a kid, he had shared the Victoria Ground terraces.

It seemed to him he was appreciated nationally, especially with his performances for England, but not locally, at least not by, albeit a minority but vocal, Stoke fans. For any high profile it is always thus, not least at Stoke City! To sum up his style of football, the type unappreciated by his critics at home in the Potteries, he cited the admiration of former Scottish international Andy Cunningham.

Cunningham told the Scottish *Sunday Express*, after England had beaten Scotland in a game at Hampden Park, 'Franklin's play all through had an international stamp. Never flustered, scrupulously fair, he was the complete centre-half. Franklin does not believe in giving the ball the boot. He uses it intelligently, and with a gliding header or a slick ground pass to his wing-halves initiates as many attacks for his side as any of the old-time classical pivots did when the position was less onerous.'

He concluded, 'He does not look exceptionally tall for a centre-half, but his timing and accuracy in the air or on the ground stamp him as outstanding among the dominating players of recent years.' It was high praise but it wasn't just disgruntled Stoke fans but also manager Bob McGrory who felt their England centre-half ought to have concentrated more on his defensive duties.

The constant sniping provoked him into first of all resigning from the captaincy of the club, then putting in a transfer request ahead of the 1948/49 season. 'I believe a change of club would be to my benefit,' commented Franklin to the consternation of fans, let alone the club itself. His shocked manager Bob McGrory retorted, 'I am both surprised and sorry that Franklin has asked to leave.' In contrast the Stoke chairman, Harold Booth, indicated the club might agree to the transfer, but only on the basis of a player exchange. His fellow directors disagreed. At a board meeting they refused to grant Franklin's request to be put on the transfer list, despite firm offers for his services from Arsenal and Manchester United.

Franklin reluctantly agreed to stay. He had no choice. Back then, only a player of Matthews' legendary stature could hold his club to ransom. But as Franklin admitted years later his transfer request in the summer of 1948 was the 'beginning of the end' of his career at Stoke City. It also put him on the path to catching his fateful flight to Bogotá.

To soothe his furrowed brow, a welcome honour came from Stoke-on-Trent City Council, if not Stoke City Football Club. Forget the poisoned pen letters to the local paper. The people of the Potteries, not just football fans, appreciated his efforts, especially in the national shirt of England.

On 30 September 1948 the council invited Franklin, his wife Vera and son Gary, to one of its meetings. Before it began, the Lord Mayor presented him with an illuminated address. It read, 'We the Lord Mayor, Aldermen and Citizens of the City of Stoke-on-Trent desire to express our great appreciation of the distinction and honour you have brought to the city by playing for England in 26 successive international matches. By your activities you have rendered magnificent service to your city, not only nationally but internationally, and we hope and trust that you have many more years to play in the sport of football. We are gratified that you were born in this city and that the whole of your career has been spent so successfully with the Stoke City Football Club.'

Those councillors politely ignored his request to be transferred from 'the Stoke City Football Club'. For his part Franklin described the presentation as a 'great moment', noting that by then the only footballer to be given a similar honour was Stanley Matthews. Nobody thought at the time it would be less than two years before the end of Franklin's Stoke City and England international career.

In trying to secure his future, Franklin was about to take matters into his own hands. Meantime, the Players' Union was stubbornly campaigning to improve the lot of all players but with little success. 'Above all it is security which the players want and to which we think he is entitled,' the Union Secretary, James Fay, commented as yet more talks were arranged in October 1948, those players yet to, either individually or collectively, take strike action, and defy their clubs.

Fay acted amid a rebellious atmosphere among his members. Franklin was not alone in following Matthews' example and asking for a transfer away from his hometown club, the one that helped to nurture his talent as a kid. Newcastle United's then England centre-forward and now a revered Geordie legend stunned his fans by putting in a similar request.

Jackie Milburn even went to the extent of echoing Franklin's personal concerns, the health of their families. 'My reason is that the North East is not suiting my wife's health,' Milburn explained. 'We have given it a good trial since our marriage last February but she still suffers from headaches and sleeplessness. She has lost weight.' Given the impending birth of their first child, Milburn wanted a move nearer to his wife's hometown of Willesden in north London.

Newcastle United turned him down flat. Like Franklin, he reluctantly agreed to stay at his hometown club. For Milburn, his career was to turn out a lot more happily than the one of his England team-mates from Stoke-on-Trent. At first, Franklin put his transfer travails behind him, happily settling back into life as a high-profile footballer in Staffordshire, enthusiastically supporting a scheme from the county's FA to help teenage footballers.

Along with another Stoke international, Freddie Steele, and the Wolves and England captain, Billy Wright, he gave up his Sundays to coach the youngsters. All seemed peace and light but it was not to last. The hullabaloo over the return of Stanley Matthews to the Victoria Ground with Blackpool for a fourth-round FA Cup tie served as a reminder of how certain players were somehow able to beat the restrictive system, even if most individuals and their union were unable to do so.

Blackpool's manager, Joe Smith, who spent years trying to lure Matthews to his club allegedly with financial incentives unavailable to any other footballer, taunted the Stoke fans in the pages of the national press. 'At Stoke, his old friends may see a different Stanley, playing better than ever before,' crowed Smith. He added, 'I believe Matthews can be more dangerous if he is a bit selfish. Instead of making chances for others all the time, I want him to have a crack at going through on his own.'

Franklin singled the game out as one of the most 'memorable' he'd played in, though more for the performance of the referee than the original target of Stoke fans' ire – Stanley Matthews. Arthur Ellis, later to find fame beyond the footballing world as a co-presenter of the BBC TV series *It's a Knockout*, took charge of the match. Much to Franklin's frustration even Ellis admitted he had a stinker. Five times Stoke put the ball in the back of the net. Five times, to the horror of players and fans alike, Ellis ruled 'no goal'.

In his autobiography, *Refereeing Round the World*, Ellis recalled his nightmare, being caught up in the frenzy surrounding hero turned villain Matthews returning to the Victoria Ground. 'No matter how hard I tried, things happened which I didn't see,' Ellis wrote. 'It was not rough play, but things like offside, and before long the crowd was cat calling and shouting, "Get back to Halifax!" [his home town].'

The most-anticipated game in decades ended disappointingly in a goalless draw. Afterwards, Ellis apparently asked a Stoke fan what he thought of the game. 'We drew but we had the world's worst referee,' came back the curt reply. Franklin simply concluded, 'He had given us a raw deal.'

Stoke won the replay at Blackpool's Bloomfield Road ground 1-0, Franklin's mate George Mountford scoring the winning goal. Even then there was controversy. Franklin went up to Ellis with yet more complaints. 'Most of our players were sporting scratches on their legs,' the Stoke captain recalled.

'He [Ellis] inspected the Blackpool players' studs and found six of them had worn their studs so low that the nails were protruding. He also found the same fault with the studs of two of our players!'

Franklin accepted there was nothing malicious going on, just par for the course for forties football with studs often being worn down on rock-hard, ice-bound pitches. He was less sanguine about the behaviour of his bosses at Stoke City. Once the club had been knocked out of the FA Cup in a shock defeat to Third Division North club, Hull City, an ambitious outfit making no secret of its admiration of Franklin, rumours circulated of his impending departure from the Potteries.

Humberside was a possible destination. Prior to the fifth-round cup tie in February 1949, the *Hull Daily Mail*'s football correspondent wrote gushingly of Franklin. 'They [Stoke City] possess the finest centre half in the land,' he told his readers. 'Hull City's best chance would seem to be in keeping the ball clear of centre half Neil Franklin as much as possible, and being on the lookout for any quick Stoke change from defence to attack.'

If that was the tactic, it worked spectacularly well. Hull City won 2-0. The *Hull Daily Mail* called it a thrashing. 'Neil Franklin, the Stoke captain, had to be on his best England form on such a day, but masterly though he played, doing two and three men's work at times, he could not stem the tide. If one had taken Franklin out of the Stoke side there would be little of their work to appraise, apart from brilliant goalkeeping by Dennis Herod.'

Once again Franklin and his Stoke pals ended a season with nothing to play for. Yet again his club was also in turmoil. A group of supporters had turned against one team-mate in particular. Sid Peppitt, an inside-forward, became the favourite target for the boo boys at the time on the terraces of Stoke's Victoria Ground.

One anonymous group even sent him a telegram threatening demonstrations if he was ever picked to play for the first team. 'He [Peppitt] was very upset and said that if I thought it best for the club he would willingly be transferred,' commented his manager, Bob McGrory to Potteries journalists. 'Last season they made his life a misery and I had to drop him for his own sake. He was to the point where he was almost ready to leave the game.'

Even Neil Franklin, despite being feted on the national stage, felt prone to criticism from a volatile and fickle group of his club's supporters. He noted that after agreeing to remain at Stoke after putting in his transfer request in the summer of 1948, the criticism of his style of play from the naysayers in the Victoria Ground crowd was never, in his words, 'erased'. The barbed comments from some of his own townsfolk left him puzzled, frustrated and just plain annoyed.

Once again, he felt his future in football lay elsewhere. Humberside served as an option with Hull City winning promotion and keeping a weather eye on the travails of the Stoke captain. In July 1949, he put in a transfer request. Hull City put in a bid, thought by the national press to be in the region of £23,000, then a British record. Among the First Division clubs, Chelsea emerged as favourites to sign him. A bidding war began with the fee rumoured to be spiralling up to £30,000.

Franklin held talks with his club's board and the manager, Bob McGrory. They refused to allow him to leave the club, despite him being out of contract. In turn, Franklin refused to sign a new one. Twice McGrory asked him on 29 July 1949 to put pen to paper. Both times he declined to do so. Once again, he cited his wife's ill health as his main reason for wanting to leave the smoke-filled air of the Potteries. It was agreed in a joint statement from player and manager to put the terms of his contract in 'abeyance'.

Effectively, Franklin went on strike, forced to train alone at the City of Stoke-on-Trent Police Sports Ground, rather than with his mates at Stoke City's Victoria Ground. For all the efforts of the Football Players' Union, their members remained tied to their clubs even while out of contract. On the eve of the season McGrory made a last-minute plea to Franklin to re-sign. He refused point blank. McGrory was forced to leave out his best player for the opening game of the 1949/50 season against Bolton Wanderers. 'There appears to be nothing more we can do in the matter,' the Stoke manager commented.

Stoke were duly thrashed 4-0. The man rated as Stoke's worst player on the day? He was the club's hapless reserve centre-half, Roy Jones. He was dropped for the following game just two days later against Liverpool at home; Frank Mountford moved to play at centre-half instead. As for Franklin, he had spent his Saturday afternoon meeting and greeting fans, signing autographs at the Lewis's department store in Hanley. *The Sentinel* correspondent dryly noted, 'There was a long queue of boys and girls, men and women at Lewis's store eager to secure Neil's "£30,000 signature" as it has become known since Hull City offered that amount for his transfer.'

National newspaper writers were an enthusiastic audience for Franklin and his views, eagerly following the impasse between club and player. Franklin told the press on the eve of the Bolton game, 'I am still prepared to hold out. I have not changed my mind about wanting to leave Stoke.' From the *Daily Herald*'s Clifford Webb came a sympathetic hearing for Franklin. Webb used the dispute to lambast the treatment of players by clubs. 'The Stoke City Football Club locked all doors except their own against international centre-half, Neil Franklin, when the directors after a special meeting, again refused his application for a transfer,' commented Webb in the opening line to his piece published on 17 August 1949, just three days before the start of a new season.

Webb further noted, 'Before the war, when clubs were allegedly on the poverty line, players never knew from one season to another where and how they were going to be pushed around. It was a habit to sell a couple of men in order to pay summer wages. Now there is so much money in the till that a £30,000 offer [the rumoured record bid from Hull City to Stoke City for Franklin] can be turned down, even at the expense of keeping the player out of the game.' It appeared hubristic nonsense, in Webb's view, for Stoke to sideline their best player. As far as the club's directors were concerned, Franklin had effectively staged a one-man strike. They had the whip hand. They were not going to give in to his demands.

Summing up the dispute, Webb commented, 'It is difficult for the soccer follower to understand why a player, having signed a contract for one year and having completed that contract satisfactorily should still be so completely tied to the same club.' Now, players and their agents wield the power in professional football. Back then, especially in English and Scottish professional league football, the clubs had all the power. They wielded it jealously, even to the extent of Stoke City casting aside the club's captain and best player, a regular England international.

As the *Daily Herald*, a Labour Party-supporting newspaper, concluded in headline form, 'Great Footballer is Handcuffed – Something Wrong'. In the body of the piece the strident Clifford Webb opined, 'There must be something wrong with the Soccer system when a great player in Franklin's unique position is apparently prepared to deliberately sabotage his career if not permitted to move.'

Eager managers at other clubs kept an eye on developments, not least the ambitious owners of Hull City. They had increased their record offer from £23,000 to £30,000, astonishingly in the context of the modern game a mere £1.1 million in today's money. Yet Franklin had an alternative, coming from suitors from a rather more distant option than Humberside or the capital.

This opportunity became available to him thanks to a mystery correspondent to Stoke City Football Club, one Franklin's unsuspecting manager thought was just doing nothing more than sending innocent fan mail. Instead, preparations were being made for a bombshell to be dropped, one designed to shake the English football world to its core. El Dorado beckoned; Neil Franklin a prime and easy target for Colombian prospectors.

# EL DORADO

JUST what was this footballing El Dorado? Disgruntled, disillusioned British footballers of the post-war years considered going there in search of a golden ticket: financial security for life, an impossibility back then in English and Scottish football. Latin American players, mostly Argentinian, had already beaten a path there, destination Colombia, home to the legend of El Dorado, a city of immeasurable riches.

As European explorers or conquerors began to arrive in South America in the early 16th century, they plundered vast amounts of gold from the native tribes on the continent's northern coast. From those natives they began to hear tales of a tribe high up in the Andes with a chieftain anxious to appease the gods. He did so, according to the mythical tale, with a ceremony at Lake Guatavita in what is now Colombia, covering himself in gold dust, his flunkies flinging copious amounts of jewels and gold into the waters to be gathered by an underwater god.

Spanish settlers dubbed this tribal chief El Dorado or the 'Golden One' and began to set out in search of his gold. Even the English explorer Sir Walter Raleigh joined in, battling with the Spanish in search of a mythical golden hoard. They did find some gold on the shores of Lake Guatavita but not the vast riches they hoped for. El Dorado remained out of reach but the myth became steeped in American and European folklore.

By the mid-20th century, football curiously offered up its own version of El Dorado. Young ambitious men embarked on their own search for a golden future. For an equivalent of an ancient tribal chief of the Andes, laden with gold, Colombian football offered its own gang of unlikely candidates. These men, seemingly dripping in wealth, ran the country's emerging professional clubs.

Up until the forties the growth of the popularity of football in Colombia, unlike most Latin American countries, was stubbornly slow. As was the case elsewhere, the sport was brought to the country in the early 1900s by British businessmen. They operated out of the Caribbean port of Barranquilla and for the early decades football, under the stewardship of a federation recognised by FIFA, Adefutbol, remained largely confined to the region.

Inevitably with Colombia becoming more and more industrialised, the capital Bogotá growing in commercial strength, the 'working man's ballet' of football grew in popularity throughout the country, the prospect of professionalism beckoning for its leading clubs. The catalyst happened to be a tour to Colombia by Argentinian club, San Lorenzo. It was a massive commercial success.

As a result, the owners of Bogotá's biggest clubs, Alfonso Senior Quevedo of Millonarios and Luis Robledo, a London-based Colombian diplomat, of Independiente Santa Fe, moved to set up a professional league, DiMayor. It began inauspiciously, Quevedo immediately falling out with the domestic governing body, Adefutbol; then caught up in Colombia's political turmoil, violence and tragedy.

Firstly, Adefutbol asked FIFA to outlaw the new professional league, DiMayor. It duly obliged. For Quevedo, this was hardly a setback. It was an opportunity. His nascent league was not encumbered by international regulations concerning the transfer of players. Millonarios and Independiente Santa Fe began a recruitment drive, their main targets being players in the Argentinian league. Attracting them to Colombia proved impossible at first. The opening games of DiMayor were put on hold as Colombia veered into a state of near civil war. Even for Argentinians, quite used to political turmoil and violence, Colombia hardly served as an enticing destination.

In the spring of 1948, it seemed certain the Mayor of Bogotá and leader of the Colombian Liberal Party, Jorge Eliecer Gaitan, would win the next race for the country's presidency. A charismatic figure, offering a mantra familiar to modern-day British political followers of 'for the many, not the few', Gaitan proved deeply popular among the working classes.

His political career recovered from a disastrous decision to run against the official Colombian Liberal candidate, Gabriel Turbay, and the Conservatives' Mariano Ospina Pérez. Gaitan felt by attracting Communist supporters he might win. All he succeeded in doing was split the vote. Pérez was elected President but opted to form a fragile 'unity' government with Turbay.

Gaitan and his supporters regrouped. The CIA station in Bogotá noted in declassified cables back to the USA that the unity government was 'never entirely satisfactory to the Liberals'. Gaitan recovered from his political miscalculation to be selected as the Liberals' sole Presidential candidate. American spies expressed alarm at 'armed clashes in various parts of the country between Conservatives and Liberals'. On 9 April 1948, Gaitan became the latest victim of the growing conflict. He was assassinated, shot dead on a city centre street in Bogotá.

Gaitan's murder provoked an orgy of violence. Crowds gathered outside the National Palace, where the Colombian Conservative Party leader, Laureano Gómez, was hosting the Inter-American Conference of American States, along with the US Secretary of State, George Marshall. They stormed the building but were repulsed by troops firing into the crowd. Scores were killed.

Pérez, along with his friends among South American leaders, blamed Communist agitators acting on the instructions of their Soviet backers for the murder of Gaitan. For CIA operatives in Bogotá, it was an embarrassment – allowing their Secretary of State to be placed in serious danger 'an intelligence failure'. They also noted a growing narrative that supporters of Gómez were to blame for Gaitan's assassination. It was a 'popular insurrection' against Colombia's Conservative government and its pro-American policies.

Gómez, unpopular, among other things, for openly supporting Hitler and Spain's General Franco, temporarily fled the country. He left it to a man more or less up until then his puppet, President Mariano Ospina Pérez. By the time the violence ended weeks later, it's estimated more than 20,000 had died. Against this dark backdrop, Colombian football chiefs were selling their football version of El Dorado to international players, hoping no doubt they never read the papers. Either that or in the case of South American players they were unfazed, given the volatile nature of their own home nations.

The new Colombian league, DiMayor, was due to stage its opening games in May 1948. Thanks to the uprising, it did not begin until August of that year. By then relative order had been restored in Colombia, seen until the outbreak of violence in the aftermath of Gaitan's murder as one of the least volatile Latin American nations. It was no longer the case.

DiMayor kicked off during a lull in the 'Bogotuzo', as Colombians termed the uprising; a de facto civil war between forces loyal to President Pérez and guerrilla units backed by Liberal politicians, who in the chaos had given up on the democratic process. Most of the fighting was confined to rural areas. Cities were made relatively safe thanks to intensive policing with curfews imposed at night.

In 1950, the year a group of rebellious British footballers made their infamous flight to Bogotá, and Laureano Gómez was elected President after returning from exile, it's estimated that more than 50,000 Colombians died in civil conflict. Against this background, football with DiMayor proved for Pérez, Gómez and their thugs a useful distraction for the masses.

Millonarios boss Alfonso Senior Quevedo later recalled, 'People were desperate because of the political situation. So, the government, President Pérez, supported our bringing in foreign players and gave us the dollars.' Quevedo added Pérez knew 'we would fill stadiums'.

For all Colombia's political and civil unrest, the recruitment drive of footballers from across Latin America intensified; Colombian club owners, boosted by government cash, boasted of meeting their promise of a footballing El Dorado as their rogue league began in earnest.

Quevedo despatched his club's Argentinian manager, Carlos Aldabe, in the spring of 1949 to Buenos Aires. A week or so later with no need for a transfer fee and the offer of generous wages he pulled off a shock signing: Argentina's legendary player of the day, Adolfo Pedenera, talisman for La Maquina or 'the machine' as River Plate fans described their club. Pedenera, a star of the thirties with River Plate, was past his best but crucially he had a bright, young, emerging prospect under his wing, Alfredo Di Stefano.

At the time Di Stefano was on loan from River Plate to Huracan, being mentored by Pedenera. Once news emerged of La Maquina's defection to Colombia, alarmed River Plate bosses recalled Di Stefano to Buenos Aires. They were unable to keep him out of the clutches of the moneymen from the Argentinian capital for long.

Padernera arrived in Bogotá to a triumphant welcome, paraded before a packed house of Millonarios fans, its owners pocketing $18,000, five times the average for a match, without even a ball being kicked. Pointedly, he told the Colombian daily newspaper, *El Tiempo*, 'I want to express a perfectly logical human aspiration to enjoy the same freedom as all men. You understand that it is perfectly impossible that the fact of exercising a profession, that of football, should put us in an exceptional situation in relation to the other professions, in that we are obliged to give up the freedom of Labour.'

Argentinian players proved easy pickings. Unlike the British players taking up contracts in the DiMayor league, there was curiously no serious way of them being sanctioned by either FIFA or their domestic governing body, the Argentine Football Association (AFA). They were constantly in open rebellion with their bosses, mostly over the familiar gripe of a post-war footballer's pay and conditions. In stark contrast to their British counterparts the Argentinians were not afraid to go out on strike.

Their other beef, so to speak, was over the AFA's curious decision to pull out of international competition, including the FIFA World Cup, at the behest of the country's charismatic but controversial President and de facto dictator, Juan Domingo Perón. In a football-mad country, Perón's swift rise to power inevitably had a significant impact on the sport. For his legion of critics, a detrimental impact.

Argentina's civilian government declared neutrality at the outbreak of the Second World War, but it was openly sympathetic to the Axis powers of Hitler and Mussolini. On 4 June 1943 the country's military staged a successful coup, deposing the President, Ramon Castillo, accusing his regime of being run by 'sinister persona, motivated by the vilest passions'. The new Argentinian military junta of army generals and junior officers were hardly themselves scions of liberal virtue, not least in the persona of Juan Perón.

Appointed as Minister of Labour, the young army colonel built up growing influence beyond his rank. To consolidate power, Perón grew in popularity among Argentina's working classes largely thanks to his whirlwind reforms of the labour market. His own generals feared him, and rightly so. Indeed, foreign diplomats quickly identified him as the de facto leader of the military junta. Successive presidents, General Pedro Ramirez and General Edelmiro Farrell, were deemed to be his puppets.

An attempt by rival army officers in the autumn of 1945 to clip his wings failed. They put him in jail following mass protests by groups opposed to dictatorship. He did not stay there long. Hundreds of thousands of protestors, corralled by his supporters in the trade union movement, took to the streets of Buenos Aires. They gathered in the Plaza de Mayo, in front of the Presidential Palace, demanding the release of their hero, Juan Perón. His alarmed captors released him.

Triumphant, he addressed the crowds from the balcony of the Presidential Palace, promising to be the people's champion in the planned forthcoming Presidential election. A few days later he married an actress, Eva Duarte, or Evita as she was hailed by their supporters. Together, they plotted to gain power in a democratic vote with promises of widespread social, political and economic reform. They succeeded but only after a campaign marred by police intimidation of their opponents – their supporters accused of orchestrating an orgy of anti-Semitic violence.

Naturally, as populist leaders in a football-crazy nation, the people's sport was not immune to the Peróns' dubious charms. Once confirmed in power, their focus was on developing solely the domestic game, the AFA happily going along with this policy by refusing to send the Argentina national side to the forthcoming competitions, the 1949 Copa America and most strikingly the 1950 World Cup in neighbouring Brazil. Inadvertently, this made it harder for Argentinian clubs to retain its players, to prevent them falling under the spell of the millionaire owners of Mexican and, pertinently in the case of El Dorado, Colombian clubs and their ambitious DiMayor league.

It is no surprise the AFA complied with the Perónist demands. Successive presidents of the governing body of Argentinian football, Oscar Nicolini and Valentin Suarez, were direct Perón appointments. Every club acquired a *padrino* (godfather), who linked them to the tightly wired new circuits of power in Perón's government. But the grip on power of these patrician powerbrokers in Argentinian football was, ironically enough, vulnerable to a key aspect of Perón's popularity among the working classes: reform of the Labour movement.

The first Argentinian Players' Union was formed in 1944 and named the Futbolistas Argentinos Agremiados. It sought recognition in 1948, demanding the implementation of a minimum wage, notably no maximum wage, and freedom of contract. The clubs and the Argentinian football authorities ignored the players' demands so a strike was set for April 1948. It led to recognition of the union and the strike being called off, but the AFA and the clubs still refused to give in to the players' wage and contract demands.

So, in effect, the strike was merely postponed until July. With the authorities refusing to relent, the Argentinian players, unlike their English counterparts, who threatened but then bottled such a drastic step, went on strike. Argentina's best players refused to turn up for work – the febrile packed stadiums of Buenos Aires, Boca Juniors' famed La Bombonera silenced.

With restless fans starved of football, Perón's government intervened by appointing a tribunal to look into the players' demands. They agreed to return to work but once the tribunal published its findings the Argentinian players deemed them insufficient. The strike was back on, clubs being forced to field amateur players just to finish the 1948 season off; cue a flight abroad of the professional Argentinian players, most notably to the new pirate league in Colombia.

Only one club was immune: Racing. Its 'godfather' on the board happened to be Perón's Finance Minister, Ramón Carejo, managing even to hand over three million pesos to the club in the form of a loan to be paid off over 65 years. The loan went to the funding of a new stadium. President Perón, despite earlier in his political career expressing his devotion for Boca Juniors, duly attended the opening ceremony.

Racing dominated Argentinian football. Given the loss of players to Colombia and Mexico, the more traditional powerhouses of Boca Juniors, River Plate, Independiente and San Lorenzo were simply unable to compete. Their loss was to the gain of Colombian club owners with their fledgling DiMayor league, the infamous footballing El Dorado. One of the greatest young players of the era, Alfredo Di Stefano, pursued his career in Bogotá rather than his home city of Buenos Aires.

Indeed, the cream of Di Stefano and Pedenera's old club River Plate steadily took up Quevedo's lucrative offers to ply their trade with Millonarios, among them Argentina's creative midfielder, Néstor 'Pipo' Rossi and the Argentinian national team goalkeeper, Julio Cozzi. Not to be outdone by their Bogotá rivals, Robledo's Santa Fe club picked up one or two promising Argentinian players of its own for the 1949 season. They included striker Héctor Rial, who would later play with Di Stefano at Real Madrid, winning five European Cups in a row.

As they headed north to football's El Dorado, the Argentinians cared little of their international playing prospects, with FIFA sanctioning them for taking up contracts in a pirate league. Di Stefano and company knew they were not going to grace the 1950 World Cup in the light blue and white stripes of Argentina. Victory in the 1947 Copa America proved to be Argentina's last international triumph for a while. Perón's insular, ultra-nationalist policies meant a curious boycott of the world showpiece of the 'working man's ballet' by the AFA. Instead, Di Stefano happily played in the blue kit of Millonarios, a Bogotá-based club nicknamed by its fans 'Ballet Azul' – the blue ballet.

There were no complaints. Di Stefano revelled in the financial opulence and reflected on what he described as the ability to play football as art. He commented, 'The Millonarios players really were living the life of, well, millionaires. Every day they went training at the end of the morning, then everyone was invited for lunch at the club headquarters. The Colombian cuisine, based on rice, manioc and pork meat, and fried banana was a discovery for us. They drank a special kind of beer, the Bavaria, which was fantastic. And after that we had a Colombian coffee, rightly considered the best in the world. Later a siesta and sometimes the cinema and a quick visit to the dancing. When you come from the country of the tango, you aren't ashamed to show that you possess the art of dancing.'

As the 1950 World Cup kicked off in Brazil, there were 109 foreign footballers playing for Colombian clubs, 57 of them Argentinian. Millonarios and Santa Fe both had their strong contingent of players from Argentina's top clubs. Deportivo Cali followed suit. In contrast, Deportivo Pereira signed Paraguayans. Cucuta Deportivo recruited Uruguayans, eventually signing eight of the 1950 World Cup-winning team. Independiente Medellin opted to raid the Peruvian league.

There were just five British players lured to football's El Dorado. Quevedo of Millonarios and Robledo of Santa Fe craved for British players to boost their mercenary league. Recruiting top Argentinian players proved particularly easy, thanks in part to the inadvertent greed and negligence of their country's ruler Perón. Instead of sending the cream of Argentinian football to a World Cup in neighbouring Brazil, his wife organised the inaugural Evita Football Championships instead.

Despite the riches on offer, Colombian club owners found it infinitely more difficult to prise top British players away from their clubs. As mentioned earlier, their main target happened to be England's top player of the day, Neil Franklin. Robledo, the boss of Santa Fe, recognised the former Stoke City captain might be more vulnerable to an approach, more than any of his English peers. Nevertheless, luring him to Robledo's version of El Dorado required intrigue, subtlety and secrecy. He began by popping what appeared to be an innocent piece of fan mail into the post. As it rested in the mailroom at Stoke City's Victoria Ground, the letter served as a ticking time bomb for English football.

# A MYSTERY CORRESPONDENT

DURING the protracted and fractious talks with his club throughout the summer of 1949, Franklin dropped a hint at where his ill-fated future might lie. To the puzzlement of English fans, he revealed that a South American club had been in touch to offer him a contract, one far more lucrative than Stoke City might offer. It was put at £2,500 per year, then considered a small fortune. He did not reveal who had approached him, not the club, nor the country; the identity of the South American correspondent making overtures towards him, Franklin kept a mystery.

Few took his comments seriously, certainly not his club or the FA. Even the legions of sports writers following his heated travails with club and manager dismissed the notion of him sailing off to play South American football. He was 'handcuffed' to his club. There was no way of unlocking its grip on him. Franklin mulled over how to escape. He was thinking the unthinkable, spurred on by his mystery correspondent from Latin America. El Dorado beckoned.

First Franklin needed to return to playing football. The spur for him was an imminent meeting of the England selectors to choose the team to play Éire at Goodison Park in a friendly international pencilled in for 21 September 1949. For a brief period, he went off to Desborough in Northamptonshire with his wife and young son to relax, away from the pollution of the

Potteries. The break was ostensibly for the benefit of his wife's health. But it conveniently put Franklin for the time being out of sight from agitated Stoke City supporters, annoyed by his absence from the side.

Franklin returned to Stoke-on-Trent, first to watch the club he supported from the stands in a welcome victory over Birmingham City, then to put pen to paper on a new contract. In what were described in the press as 'swift and secret moves' he re-signed on Wednesday, 31 August 1949, in time for the forthcoming game with Derby County. 'I am glad to be back and in a couple of days I shall be ready to play against Derby County,' Franklin told Stoke's *Evening Sentinel*. It splashed the story on its front page complete with a photograph of player and manager, smiling as they shook hands. 'I am very pleased it's all over,' commented McGrory. 'It is for the good of the game and everyone else.'

Relieved England international selectors no doubt agreed with McGrory. The end of the five-week deadlock between club and player meant they were able, once again, to pencil in Neil Franklin's name as their first on the team sheet. He had made more than 30 consecutive appearances for England. Thanks to having little choice but to cave in to his club's demands, this proud sequence of international appearances was not about to be broken.

Nevertheless, just by putting pen to paper failed to put an end to his travails. Football League bosses, deeply suspicious of Franklin's sudden about-turn, ordered an inquiry into his new deal at Stoke City. They also questioned just how a newly promoted Second Division club, in the guise of Hull City, could afford to put in a record transfer bid, throwing the promise of a house into the deal as an added incentive for the player. Nothing came of these inquiries but for Franklin it served as proof his quibbles were not just with those running Stoke City Football Club but with the bosses of British football in general.

Just to add some mischief, his old friend Stanley Matthews saw fit to comment on Franklin's new deal, seizing the opportunity to take another swipe at Stoke's directors. Writing in a ghosted article for the *Sunday Express*, he questioned whether Franklin's motive for wanting to leave the Potteries was the good of his wife's health. 'I am certain there is more to it than that,' Matthews wrote. 'Neil's case is similar to mine at Stoke. He is being taken for granted and does not get on too well with certain officials.'

It was not the most helpful of interventions. But Stoke fans, many still angered by Matthews' departure a couple of years earlier, were relieved by Franklin's decision to stay. 'All Stoke breathed a sigh of relief when Neil ended his five-week deadlock with the club by re-signing on Wednesday,' commented the Derby *Evening Telegraph* in its preview of Franklin's return to action at the city's Baseball Ground. It turned out to be a winning return to duty.

Not surprisingly, Franklin was considered a little off the pace as Stoke struggled in the early stages of the game, an uncharacteristic error from him allowing Derby to open the scoring. It possibly didn't help from Franklin's point of view that inevitable comparisons were on offer between him and his biggest rival for the England number 5 shirt, Derby County's Leon Leuty. England selectors turned up at the Baseball Ground to check on the form of both players amid speculation Franklin's international place was in jeopardy. Franklin began the game poorly but as he slowly grew into the game Stoke turned around a 2-1 deficit to emerge 3-2 victors.

After yet again being called up for England, his form was being questioned in a game at Old Trafford against Manchester United. Stoke drew 2-2. James Stagg of the *Daily Mirror* commented, 'If Stoke had armed themselves with sawn-off shot guns and rifled the League points box, it would have been no greater robbery.' He singled out Franklin for polite criticism, remarking, 'the England centre half did not quite hold his own'.

Franklin, despite struggling to recapture his usual form after his early season absence, did though remind everyone, for all his off-field woes, that he remained one of the finest players in England, if not, for some, the best. Franklin was nicely set for his brush with history and infamy. Unwittingly, his first taste of making history came sooner than he anticipated. He made it, as far as English football fans were concerned, for the wrong reasons. It came courtesy of the Irish players, who had tormented him and his England team-mates in Dublin a year or two earlier.

England took on Éire at Goodison Park in Liverpool, boasting a proud record at home. An English international football team had never lost on home soil to a 'foreign' side, just the home nations. Éire, despite fielding players regularly turning out for the Irish Football Association's 'Ireland' team at Windsor Park in Belfast, counted as 'foreign' opposition, even if some of the more jingoistic English fans and sports writers thought otherwise. They were intent on upsetting England's proud home record.

England fans and players were confident of victory; nothing more than a comfortable win against the Irish would do for them. Franklin, along with his half-back partner Billy Wright, were considered key. According to the *Liverpool Echo*, 'The strength of the England side lies in its brilliant half back line, which will bear comparison, no matter what the veterans may say, with the best of previous decades.' Its correspondent predicted England would 'romp home'. Franklin and company didn't. Much to the shock of English football fans they lost.

'England's Display Without a Saving Grace', intoned the *Daily Herald* in its headline. 'Football history – bleak, black history – was made on the Goodison Turf', its correspondent mournfully noted. He continued, 'For let it be known that this was the first time that any country outside the [Home] International Championship has won here [on English soil]. Éire, small and weak, by Soccer standards, triumphed where the great European teams in their pre-war heydays always failed.' He suggested the lucky England players were those, such as Stanley Matthews, left out of the side. He called for wholesale changes, including in the fabled half-back line.

'ÉIRE LOWER ENGLAND'S SOCCER FLAG, PROUD RECORD IS ENDED', ran the *Daily Telegraph* headline. Its correspondent Frank Coles predicted an 'easy win' for England on the morning of the game. In his post-match comments, he wrote, 'International football history was made at Goodison Park this afternoon. Éire, on their first appearance in his country, gained a startling 2-0 triumph and won fame as the first foreign team ever to make a successful invasion of England.' Of Franklin's performance Coles noted, 'David Walsh [Éire and West Bromwich Albion's centre-forward] had never led an Irish attack with such dash and skill. He had Franklin genuinely worried.'

The *Daily Mirror*, looking ahead to the following summer, splashed its back page with 'Oh England! What a World Cup warning by Éire'. It commented, 'England Soccer pride was tumbled at Goodison Park, Everton, when the unfancied Éire team won 2-0 – football's biggest surprise for years.' It concluded, 'England's display in the first match of the World Cup season was disappointing. The inside forwards were below form and the defence too shaky.' It called for the selectors to make changes. But despite being given the run-around by the Irish forwards, Franklin and Wright at the heart of England's 'shaky defence' were spared the axe, both destined to make English football history, but for very different reasons.

For the time being Franklin enjoyed a revival in playing fortunes to the extent of him being touted as a rival to Billy Wright for the England captaincy. On Monday, 7 November

1949 the England selectors met at FA headquarters at Lancaster Gate in West London amid speculation they would choose Stoke City's centre-half to lead England out at Old Trafford for a Home International against Ireland rather than the Wolves half-back.

The *Daily Express* would turn out to be something of a mouthpiece for Franklin on his eventual escapade in Colombia. It supported his credentials as a possible England international in late autumn 1949 but only with some barbed comments. Desmond Hackett wrote on the morning of the selectors' meeting, 'Last month this same flawless Franklin was a club problem child, a player with such a load on his mind that the locals who saw their team going nowhere fast, demanded that he should be given his transfer request.'

Warming to his theme, Hackett suggested, to use a modern cliched term, his head had been turned by what he dismissed as 'soccer spivs', men more interested in fame and money than football. It shows such concerns were not just the preserve of the Premier League era. This was the 1940s with Franklin, Wright and company kept by their clubs, the FA and the Football League under a metaphorical lock and key.

He did not name names, South American or otherwise, instead quoting the concerns of Stoke City director, Len Duddell. He moaned, 'These men are known. They are just too clever to be caught and there is nothing that can be done about them.' In support of Duddell, Hackett wrote, 'Franklin has had a showdown with his club, and Stoke City, that good old family football business that turns local boys from fumbling footballers to highly skilled players, listened in silence.'

He added with an oblique reference to the departure of Stanley Matthews from the Potteries club, 'They had heard this story before. Quietly and firmly they satisfied the worries of the restless Franklin.' Furthermore, the correspondent noted Franklin had been restored to the Stoke captaincy, leading his club to victory against Billy Wright's Wolves, knocking them off the top of the league table.

How any of this supported Franklin's claims to the England captaincy was not made clear by his lukewarm supporters. While hailing Wright as a 'half-back genius' they simply questioned his suitability for the captaincy, a bizarre assessment given the hindsight of history. Wright kept the captaincy. England, with Franklin enjoying one of his easiest international games at centre-half, duly beat the Irish 9-2.

At the time both Franklin and Wright seemed destined to go together to Brazil, leading England's campaign to lift the World Cup. English fans were confident the earlier defeat to Éire was a blip, not a portent of what was to come in South America. None realised Franklin was already considering a trip to South America in the following summer, but not to the World Cup in Brazil. He may have suffered the odd brickbats in the English national press, but one foreign admirer was leaving him an offer he was unable to refuse in the fan mail arriving at Stoke City's Victoria Ground.

'I make no secret of the fact that I was unhappy at Stoke,' commented Franklin in his autobiography. He went on, 'True, I got on well with the crowd and with the other players but my style of play was not popular with Bob McGrory, who was then manager of the club. As readers of this story know, I had previously asked for a transfer, which the club had refused to grant, and yet the continual niggling about my style of play did not cease. Even my delayed re-signing at the end of the 1948/49 season did no good.' He further commented his England call-ups were of little consolation to him as a professional footballer, given his unhappiness at Stoke.

'After all any workman would feel unhappy and unsettled if his boss continually criticised his work, while at the same time the heads of the industry praised it,' Franklin explained to his readers. 'Surely, any normal workman would feel that he would be better off with another firm. That is exactly how I felt at Stoke, but footballers cannot change their employers as easily as other people.'

By November 1949, he was still contemplating how to leave Stoke City. It was then the surprise offer was made, a more substantial proposition to him from the owners of a South American football club than the one put to him some months earlier. It came from a man more noted in the gossip columns of British newspapers than the sports pages.

He recalled, 'I had turned over in my mind frequent transfer requests, but had dismissed such a course of action because I did not want to become known as a malcontent, as a trouble-maker. I also thought of refusing to re-sign at the end of the 1949/50 season and staging a [second] one-man strike. It may well have come to that although I don't think I would have been able to afford the financial complications.

'But right out of the blue came a letter from the officials of the Santa Fe Club in Bogotá,' he revealed. 'It was signed by a Mr Luis Robledo.' He also wryly noted, 'The original letter was addressed c/o Stoke City Football Club. So, although they did not know it at the time, officials of Stoke City had handled the letter which was the cause of me leaving them before I had done. It simply asked me if I would consider signing for the club. In it, Mr Robledo told me that the financial rewards would be much greater than I could ever hope to gain by continuing to play in Britain.'

For Franklin it was an attractive offer, not least for a top-class footballer seemingly in mental turmoil. He reasoned, 'Even if I continued as England's centre-half, received my benefits and bonuses, and even if Stoke City were so often in the honours list as to give me special bonuses, my gross income would still be much lower in England than it would be in Bogotá.'

Robledo certainly appeared busy at the time. Not content with running Santa Fe in Colombia's DiMayor league, he kept up his business and diplomatic duties in Europe. For much of the late forties, he split his time between Bogotá, London and cities in West Germany, there to set up trade deals between Colombian and German businesses. Up until making his overtures to England's regular centre-half, he had been more noted in England for his romantic endeavours with aristocratic young British women.

In October 1948, he married debutante, Lady Bridget Poulett, considered one of the great Society Beauties of the day. Their marriage was kept secret because Colombian diplomats were banned from marrying citizens of the country in which they were stationed. News of the wedding was splashed on the front pages of British tabloid newspapers some 13 months later once gossip columnists got word of the nuptials, just the time Robledo was sending his 'love letters' to Franklin.

The *Daily Express* gushed, 'Lady Bridget Poulett, famous as a debutante and most photographed 'society girl' of the 30s revealed today that she married a Colombian diplomat 14 months ago. She is 37. Her husband is handsome Senor Luis Robledo.' It went on, 'Often Lady Bridget was a wedding guest. Often her photography got more prominence than the bride's. And often it was asked: When and to whom she'd be the bride. Now the answers are known.'

Senor Robledo captured an aristocratic bride, a woman 13 years his senior. Now in further promoting his business interests at home in Colombia, namely Santa Fe FC, he set about wooing not just Franklin, but some of the prize assets of English and Scottish football. They were far more difficult to capture than the hordes of Argentinian players, eagerly making their way to Bogotá.

His new bride, an aristocratic woman more familiar with Henley, Royal Ascot and the Monaco Grand Prix, was about to become key in achieving his aims. She gave someone knowledgeable followers of English football would treat with deep suspicion, with his ties to Colombia's pirate DiMayor league, an air of respectability.

Señora Robledo, aristocratic daughter of the Earl of Poulett, was a woman, much no doubt to her own surprise as anyone else's, destined to whisk away a working-class couple from Stoke-on-Trent in secrecy to her new husband's Colombian homeland. She was to act as a minder and confidante to Mr and Mrs Neil Franklin. As the initial approach was made by Robledo, Franklin was unaware the same applied to his Stoke team-mate, George Mountford, and his wife. The Colombian diplomat and businessman wanted to whisk them away too.

In contrast, the tactics adopted by Robledo's rival at Millonarios, Alfonso Quevedo, appeared a little less subtle, certainly not romantic. As with Robledo's recruitment drive, any negotiations were carried out in secret. A much more grounded character, Quevedo used his Anglo-Colombian business contacts including, in the case of the Everton player Billy Higgins, a Merseyside-born businessman based in Bogotá. Higgins declined to name the man, only revealing he had been approached by this individual while he was home for the Christmas holidays of 1949.

Additionally, the Millonarios owner hired a grizzled old professional from the English and Scottish game, the former Blackpool player Jack Dodds. From his office in the seaside town Dodds worked to lure players away to a footballers' El Dorado. He was assisted by another former Blackpool player, George Eastham senior, father of the English footballer of the same name who would later play a pivotal role in reforming English professional football.

Both the owners of Millonarios and Santa Fe targeted players they deemed to be vulnerable to an approach to play in what was an internationally outlawed league. Quite simply, they went for footballers at odds with their clubs. Both Higgins and Swansea's unsettled and ambitious young player, Roy Paul, for example, fitted the bill. The most rebellious player in English football, of course, just happened to be the nation's best defender, Stoke City's Neil Franklin.

In summing up Robledo's initial proposal to go to Bogotá, Franklin commented, 'It all seemed most attractive, so attractive, in fact, that only a fool would have turned it down without going into the matters more fully. There was of course the question of climate, and living conditions, but Mr Robledo assured me in his first letter that Colombia would boast spring-like weather all the year round. That really was an attraction! So, the whole proposition looked most attractive, especially to a man who was discontented and unsettled.'

He was aware, even at that stage, there were severe risks, the chance of bringing an illustrious career to a premature and humiliating end. He recognised there was, classic understatement, 'a snag'. If the Colombian Football Association, under whose jurisdiction the Santa Fe club fell, was affiliated to FIFA, then he would not be able to, in his words, 'accept or even consider the offer unless Stoke City agreed'. There was absolutely no chance of the Potters doing so.

Yet he persevered. In the late forties FIFA was only just beginning to exert total control of English football. His own FA had only just agreed to re-join, its patrician boss Sir Stanley Rous persuading the Irish, Scottish and Welsh Associations to do the same. There were still disputes with other national associations and their respective leagues and clubs, among them Colombia. Franklin wrote back to Robledo seeking clarification of Santa Fe FC's relationship with Colombia's FA and the world governing body FIFA. As he explained, 'I told him that although I was interested in his proposition, the whole thing was impossible because of FIFA control.'

Much to Franklin's surprise, Robledo replied almost immediately, anxious to offer reassurance. This time he wrote to Franklin's home address, now it was in his possession rather than adding to the fan mail in the post room at Stoke City's Victoria Ground. As there was no sign of FIFA lifting the suspension of DiMayor at the request of the Colombian FA, Adefutbol, Robledo at best twisted the truth, at worst simply lied to Franklin.

'In his second letter, Mr Robledo assured me that the Colombian Football Association was not a member of FIFA so there were no obstacles of that sort in my way,' Franklin explained in his autobiography. 'Obvious then, the route to Bogotá was clear. It only needed the details sorting out, because I admit that I was very interested. Whenever I thought of the way my style of play was criticised at Stoke, I became even more interested.'

Franklin insisted he carefully assessed the implications of the venture on which he was about to embark, giving it the most 'careful consideration'. It's doubtful he was able to assess the scale of the fury he was about to unleash, at club, national and international level. Neil Franklin's name was going to go down in footballing infamy. Perhaps, naively, it was one consideration the automatic choice for England centre-half at the time, just ahead of a first World Cup, was able to factor into his calculations.

He simply explained, 'I realised that if I decided to accept the offer, I would cut myself off from English football for ever. I realised too that I had to weigh the pros and cons of that along with the offer of increased pay, living conditions and the hundred and one other considerations which obviously arose. So, my correspondence with the Santa Fe officials was long and involved and, let this be said for both sides, confidential.'

Technically, there was one breach of this mutual confidentiality between Robledo and Franklin – the Colombian's decision to put another player and his family on the flight ticket to Bogotá. Among the other British players Robledo was approaching just happened to be one of Franklin's team-mates, George Mountford. A fine player, equally disgruntled with his plight as an English professional footballer, he and his family were destined to become Franklin's travelling companions.

First, both men needed to work out the vexed details with their Colombian suitor. Quite rightly, at this stage, they appeared suspicious of promises of a footballing El Dorado. The negotiations became protracted and painful but then for Franklin came, what he euphemistically termed, 'a snag'. His wife, Vera, informed him she may prefer to stay in Stoke-on-Trent for one simple reason. She was pregnant.

Franklin had not immediately accepted Robledo's offer, one his club, the FA and FIFA would later denounce as illegal, despite the Santa Fe boss's false assertions to his British players. Nevertheless, Franklin described himself at that early stage of negotiations as 'favourable towards it'. His wife's pregnancy then cast, for the first time, doubts in his mind.

It forced him to assess what he termed as 'serious complications'. First, the couple were anxious about the nationality of their new arrival. They wanted the baby to be a British rather than a Colombian national. They also wanted guarantees about the state of Bogotá's hospitals and the general levels of healthcare in the Colombian capital.

Robledo gave the necessary assurances, insisting the medical and hospital services were 'first class'. The Colombian diplomat also confidently asserted the new baby, even if born in Colombia under the UK nationality laws of the day, would be British, not Colombian. It gave Franklin and his pregnant wife peace of mind.

But here the story becomes a bit murkier. Franklin claimed in his autobiography that he not only informed Robledo and the Santa Fe club of his dilemma; he also told the FA. 'I would not, under any circumstances, agree to leave my wife and fly to Bogotá on my own. No matter what happened I insisted on being with my wife when the baby was born,' he wrote.

One thing is certain. Franklin did not inform the FA that he planned, all being well, to go to Colombia to play club football rather than represent his country at the World Cup in Brazil. Perhaps as a criticism it's unfair but Franklin used the impending arrival of his second child to excuse himself from England's World Cup squad. Barring injury, his place was guaranteed. Franklin had no intention of going to the Brazil World Cup 1950, regardless of whether or not his wife was expecting a baby.

'I made it quite clear to them [the FA] that honoured as I would be to be chosen to represent my country in the forthcoming World Cup series in South America [the first World Cup series which included England] I would prefer not to be considered because of this domestic complication,' Franklin insisted.

He continued, 'Some people may think I was silly to do that but I don't think I was. I would not have gone to Rio and given of my best for England, when I knew that my wife was having a baby thousands of miles away at home. It would not have been fair to my wife. It would not have been fair to myself, and probably most important of all, it would not have been fair to England.'

Given the FA, his club Stoke City, and fans across England were unaware of his planned 'flight to Bogotá' with George Mountford, such an explanation was taken on face value. There was undoubted disappointment and, contrary to Franklin's own claims, FA officials hoped for a change of mind. The England selectors wanted Franklin to travel with them to Rio. He wasn't going to do so.

Indeed, contrary to the claims in his autobiography, Franklin does not appear to inform the FA of his decision until the very last minute, once he had played what turned out to be his last game for England, a Home International against Scotland at Hampden Park, a game also serving as a World Cup qualifier.

On 28 April 1950, the *Daily Telegraph* ran the story headlined, 'FRANKLIN TO MISS RIO'. The article stated, 'Neil Franklin, Stoke City 27-year-old centre half, who has played in every England full international since the war, will not be available for the World Cup competition in Rio. His decision was contained in a letter to the Football Association, when he also stated that he did not wish to be considered for the Continent tours [games away to Portugal and Belgium] next month.' His reasons were simply given as 'domestic'. That much was true. There was another over-arching reason – the planned unauthorised move to Colombia.

Back then the World Cup was not taken as seriously as it is now, at least not in the UK. After all, England along with the other Home Nations had only just deigned to agree to compete. Scotland, in a fit of pique, refused to go to the World Cup because their 1-0 defeat to England meant they qualified as runners-up in the British Championship with the English going as champions. But they were going without one of their automatic choices, much to the frustration and disappointment of fans.

Franklin had taken his place in the heart of the England defence for the game against Scotland at Hampden Park in Glasgow on 15 April, already aware it was more than likely his last game in a 'Three Lions' shirt. Tom Finney described Franklin as his 'best mate' in the England set-up but claimed to be oblivious of the defender's plans to go to Colombia.

In his autobiography, Finney describes Franklin's agitated state in the build-up to the Hampden Park clash. 'As we were lining up before the game, we had to wait until the marching bands cleared the pitch,' recalled Finney. 'Neil was standing alongside me, somewhat pre-occupied. "See that lot Tom," he said, indicating the band. "They're probably on more money than us." I looked at him and laughed but he wasn't laughing.'

Finney noted, 'We were all concerned with turning over the old enemy and putting ourselves in line for World Cup selection. Neil gave his usual faultless performance and nobody would have guessed he had other matters on his mind. But he clearly had.'

Franklin in his own autobiography made just a short, and in tone almost lamentful, reference to the match, one attracting a crowd of 135,000. 'My international career ended in April 1950 when Roy Bentley scored the goal by which England beat Scotland at Hampden Park, thereby sending England to the World Cup and leaving Scotland to stay at home because they had previously said they would not go unless they were the home champions,' commented Franklin.

Just for the record he added proudly, 'To settle any arguments I have been capped 27 times for England since peacetime football was resumed, and never once was I dropped from the international side.' It was his decision to walk out of the England side. He was never to be allowed back.

For English fans, indeed for his fellow England players as Finney commented, there was little hint that the international career of a player at the peak of his powers was at an end. There was just puzzlement but polite acceptance of Franklin's decision not to go to the World Cup for 'domestic reasons', something the player himself acknowledged. But at the risk of being harsh, England's first-choice centre-half had effectively duped FA officials, and also the fans at club and international level.

Franklin's correspondence with Robledo and officials at Santa Fe in Colombia was of much more interest to him than arrangements to go to South America for the Brazil World Cup. It was possibly what Finney described as pre-occupying his mind in the moments before kick-off against Scotland. Franklin harboured doubts, needed reassurance.

His primary concern was for the welfare of his wife and family, including the citizenship of their unborn child. He wrote to his Colombian suitors seeking guarantees for the welfare of his wife and family. 'Santa Fe officials replied [by letter] that I had nothing to worry about concerning the new arrival [of his wife's baby]. That as good as clinched it. I would go to Bogotá.'

Along with George Mountford, he had for months embarked on a cloak and dagger operation, liaising with an agent for Santa Fe, based, apparently, in Switzerland. His identity, the players were informed, needed to be kept a secret. As the 1949/50 season drew to a close, Franklin also took time out to travel to London to finalise arrangements at a London hotel, with one of Robledo's team, a certain aristocratic beauty by the name of Lady Bridget Poulett, the new Mrs Luis Robledo.

In later interviews with the press, she claimed not to know the identity of the Santa Fe agent in Switzerland, a man dubbed Senor X. That's frankly difficult to believe but nobody, at the time, was going to question the word of a 1940s aristocratic beauty. It's safe to assume, given her husband's meanderings in West Germany and Switzerland promoting trade with Colombia, she did know the identity of Senor X.

His name was later revealed by Robledo's colleagues at the Colombian Embassy in London. 'The Santa Fe representative who negotiated the Franklin arrangements is George Mendes, an official of the Santa Fe club. His headquarters are in Switzerland,' commented Ernesto Anzola-Cupides, the Colombian Commercial Attaché in London. 'He has made several flying visits to Britain to watch star players in action and send back reports to Santa Fe.' Scouting reports on

Franklin were immaterial. All along he was Santa Fe's chief target, a prize asset to be poached.

As Franklin admitted, his 'days in England were numbered'. He, his wife, Vera, and son, Gary, along with his Stoke City mate George Mountford, his wife, Phyliss, and their daughters, Jill and Kay, were off to Colombia, were about to take their long, arduous and tortuous flight to Bogotá.

# THE BOMBSHELL

ONCE the local evening newspaper dropped through letterboxes in the Potteries on Monday, 8 May 1950, it landed on doormats with a bombshell for eager readers. 'FRANKLIN'S SECRET FLIGHT SENSATION' blazed out of the front page of the Stoke *Sentinel.* It revealed that Franklin and George Mountford had arrived in New York with their families, intent on going on to Bogotá in Colombia, supposedly to take up coaching contracts with Santa Fe Football Club.

Crucially, the paper described the Colombian outfit as 'the wealthy, black-listed' Santa Fe Football Club. Understandably, it also focused most attention on Franklin, the England international who turned down the chance to go to the World Cup in Rio for 'domestic reasons'. For all English football fans, not just Stoke City fans, he was about to become a sporting pariah. A city, a nation was in shock.

Franklin, the key player, who just on the eve of England going off to South America for their first World Cup excused himself from international duty for 'personal reasons', had indeed turned up on a continent of football fanatics. He just happened to be on his way to the wrong country: Colombia, not Brazil. He had done so as a 'mercenary'.

George Mountford's role in the drama was crucial, aiding and abetting his mate Franklin. But along with all the other prominent English and Scottish players about to follow them to Colombia he was also in reality something of a bit-part player in this drama. The national focus was on England international defender Neil Franklin.

The *Daily Mirror* ran with, 'FRANKLIN FLIES OUT, SHOCK FOR CLUB, FA' on its back page. As for the *Daily Telegraph*, it was worthy of front-page news with 'FRANKLIN HAS GONE TO SOUTH AMERICA, SURPRISE TRIP AS COACH'. From the *Daily Herald* came the simple headline, 'SHOCK FOR ENGLAND SELECTORS'.

It, along with other newspapers, indeed Franklin's club Stoke City, harboured the belief he might be persuaded to change his mind and play for England at the 1950 Brazil World Cup. Such speculation was sparked by an injury crisis in the national side's defensive ranks, especially the lack of a top-class centre-half.

'Is it possible that Stoke City centre-half Neil Franklin will reconsider his decision not to play for England against Portugal and Belgium?' wondered the *Daily Mail*'s Roy Peskett. He added, 'Though I completely understand Franklin's personal problem and deeply sympathise with him, I am hoping that he will be able to change his mind.'

The FA intimated the selectors wanted him to at least play in the warm-up games against Portugal and Belgium. There was no point wondering whether Franklin would be available to go to Lisbon. He was already in the air, flying west to the Americas, not east to mainland Europe. England selectors, the press pack, were to be left, not just disappointed, but shocked and angry, any sympathy for Franklin's 'plight' completely evaporated.

To compound matters, Franklin and George Mountford acted as if they didn't know what the fuss was all about. They both knew full well what it was about. They had turned their backs on club and country. Franklin's previous protests of wanting to be left out of the England team to go to the World

Cup sounded hollow. Not just for the directors of Stoke City and committee men of the Football Association, for English fans Franklin became overnight public enemy number one.

Yes, there was sympathy for professional players of the day, their terms and conditions a universe apart from those of footballers of the modern day. But to skulk out of the country with a degree of subterfuge and seeming dishonesty provoked mild intrigue and curiosity from some and outright condemnation from most.

Franklin, Mountford and their families began their arduous flight to Bogotá under the cloak of secrecy. All along, once word got out, their journey ended up being tracked by not just the British but the international press. Their trip began by rail from Stoke-on-Trent station, just families on a day trip to London. Curious bystanders no doubt simply wished them luck, the more curious wanting to mull over with Franklin and Mountford Stoke's previous day's 5-2 defeat at home to Arsenal.

Fans had no clue that within the following 48 hours they may be contemplating a more important talking point than a post-mortem on another disappointing season for their club. Franklin recalled in his autobiography, 'I can say, though, that there were one or two people in Stoke, who knew that George and I were going with our families and that we were not coming back. Not for a year, anyway. Those few people kept our secret wonderfully well.'

Instead of taking in the usual tourist sights, the Franklins and the Mountfords headed for Mayfair, specifically an address they had been given, the home of the aristocratic wife of Santa Fe director Luis Robledo, Lady Bridget Poulett. It was there they would briefly rest before heading off to the airport.

Quite bizarrely, they claimed to have been supplied with her address solely by the mystery agent based in Switzerland, Senor X, rather than her husband Senor Robledo. She told a bemused *Daily Mail* reporter, 'All that happened was I received a telephone call from Senor X early in May informing me that Mr and Mrs Franklin and Mr and Mrs Mountford and their children were going to Bogotá.

'He went on to say that Mrs Franklin was very shortly going to have a baby and that the party included three small children. I thought that the least I could do was to invite them to rest at the flat and have a wash and brush-up on their way through instead of having to sit in the airport.' On the matter of the identity of Senor X, she was taken at her word. She maintained she did not know he was one of her husband's business friends, George Mendes.

Indeed, both Mrs Robledo and quite bizarrely the Colombian Embassy in London were anxious to distance themselves from the cloak and dagger operation to spirit the Franklin and Mountford families out of the country. 'They asked me many questions about Bogotá,' she told the Stoke *Sentinel*. 'I told them, and that was my sole contribution.'

Meanwhile, the Colombian Embassy Commercial Attaché, Ernesto Anzola-Cupides, maintained that neither the embassy nor any individual member of staff had anything to do with Franklin and Mountford's flight to Bogotá. Asked how they managed to obtain visas to travel to Colombia without the embassy being involved, Anzola-Cupides replied, 'I have since discovered that they were obtained in the normal way from the Consulate. [Separately based away from the Colombian Embassy near Regent's Park.] Anyone can get them if they have a reason for going.'

Helpfully, he further explained, 'Franklin says his reason was to visit the country for a short while for pleasure. It was not until he arrived there that he had made arrangements to sign a contract which I understand is for one year, with an option of two. He has been in touch with us from time to time on routine matters and, except for this, it is the only contact we have had with him.'

Having enjoyed Mrs Robledo's hospitality, they headed off to Heathrow for their first stages of their flight to Bogotá with stopovers at Shannon Airport and Goose Bay before landing at LaGuardia Airport in New York to be met, to their own shock, by a throng of reporters. Interest in soccer in the United States in the forties was next to zero. Yet these English footballers had caused something of a stir.

Neither Franklin nor Mountford would comment on whether they planned to stay in Colombia or return to England for the start of the new season. Franklin sniffily retorted to his questioners, 'You can't stop a man from taking his family on a trip.' Mountford merely stated, 'I don't understand what all the excitement is about. I am not worried. For my part it was a chance to earn more money and give the family a holiday.'

Franklin then breezily commented, 'If I like it [Bogotá], I might stay down there. I decided to leave England about a fortnight ago.' As Franklin well knew, the latter point was a blatant lie. Also, rather disingenuously, Franklin insisted there was no subterfuge involved in planning his trip. 'There is nothing secret in the football world,' he commented.

Those answers didn't satisfy their inquisitors at LaGuardia. They persisted, forcing Franklin to offer an answer further enraging club and country. 'We had permission from Mr Robert McGrory, Stoke City, manager,' Franklin claimed. 'What arrangement the club made with the FA is none of our business. We plan to return to Stoke City by August. The Club Independiente Santa Fe at Bogotá have offered us an agreement to coach and perhaps play a bit until then.' The latter point hinted at a formal contract to play competitive games but at this point they denied such a possibility.

Commenting on his motives Franklin said, 'The money they are paying is considerably more than what we earned in England. The only trouble is I only recently learned the club isn't in the world federation [FIFA]. We did not leave England secretly, nor did we wish to hide anything from the football authorities.'

Yet later, Franklin would look back with pride on how he and Mountford kept the arrangements secret. He also admitted he had not been granted permission by Stoke City or the FA for the trip to Colombia. Naturally in response to the players' comments in New York, Stoke City denied it knew anything of their plans. The FA, still smarting from Franklin's refusal to go to the World Cup and his false claims for doing so, began to consider disciplinary measures.

Stoke City's frazzled manager, Bob McGrory, told the Stoke *Sentinel*, 'The news has come as a complete shock to me. I had no idea that either of the players was going by air. The club will have to take the advice of the Football Association.' The club's president, Sir Francis Joseph, commented, 'I spoke to both men in the dressing room on Saturday. Neither gave any indication that they planned to leave the country over the weekend. The matter is really for the FA, more than the club.'

True, both men had made it known to Stoke City prior to their flight out of the country they wanted to take up coaching appointments during the summer of 1950. They just didn't say where. Stoke had given Mountford permission. But the club refused to do so for their England international Franklin. He would have to clear the matter with the FA.

As Franklin explained, given his plans, that would be a pointless exercise. 'I never, of course, requested the permission of the Football Association, for if I had done it would have been refused,' Franklin later admitted. 'Obviously, they would have told me that if I was available to leave Britain during the summer of 1950, I would have to go with the England World Cup party.' Instead he was off to Colombia.

After their impromptu press conference at LaGuardia, they went to another prearranged venue, this time an apartment in Manhattan. Franklin reflected after receiving his grilling from journalists, 'Although our departure caused a sensation in Stoke – and in fact, throughout Britain – and came as a shock to most people, it was well planned.'

Unfortunately, once they arrived in New York those plans began to unravel. Once they got to the address they had been given to rest before embarking on the final few legs to Colombia, they discovered nobody was at home. The door, firmly locked. It was a sign of things to come.

'At the time both George and I were annoyed at the breakdown in the arrangements, but we thought it was just one of those things,' noted Franklin. 'Little did we know that it was only the first of the many examples we were to get of the complete lack of organisation in Bogotá.'

Fortunately, a student living in a neighbouring flat came out and took pity on them, offering a place to rest for a short few hours. 'But for this extremely thoughtful student we should have been in a real fix, because I had very little American currency,' remembered Franklin. 'Fortunately, I did have a cheque, which the Santa Fe officials had given me, so I was able to cash it to avoid being absolutely broke.'

Once refreshed they headed for Idlewild Airport by taxi for the next leg of their journey – a flight to Miami and an overnight stay in an airport hotel. For their brief stopover in New York, the travellers from the English Midlands found it difficult enough to cope with the searing heat. In Miami it was far worse.

'It was almost unbelievably hot in Miami,' recalled Franklin. He also shared an anecdote in his autobiography, at the expense of his Stoke team-mate. He wrote, 'George Mountford raised a laugh when he asked the hotel porter where the boiler room was. He wanted to dry some nappies that Mrs Mountford had washed. Quite rightly, the porter told him to hang them out of the window and they would be dry in a matter of minutes.'

The journey was beyond a joke for the Franklin and Mountford families, especially the pregnant Mrs Franklin. They were up at the crack of dawn to catch a seven o'clock flight from Miami to Havana in Cuba, then on to Kingston, Jamaica.

'Jamaica. Here, the heat was even worse and Vera was beginning to feel the effects of it all,' groaned Franklin. 'She was terribly exhausted and most unhappy, but we had only two more stages of the journey before we arrived in spring-like Bogotá.'

The first stage of the journey took them, at last, into Colombia, the flight landing in the Caribbean port city of Barranquilla. There they were met by a doctor, sent by the Santa Fe club to assist Vera Franklin. He sat alongside them on the flight for the final leg to Bogotá.

'We were glad to have him too, because the last stage of our journey was the roughest flight I have ever experienced,' recalled Franklin. 'I don't think the aircraft flew on a level keel for more than a minute at a time and we were all tossed about like so many corks in a rough sea. This sort of thing, of course, upset my wife more than ever, although I am thankful to say she never needed the attention of the doctor.'

As Franklin and Mountford flew into Bogotá, the Football Association, back home in England, furiously began to draw up its full list of threats and sanctions against the men. Their mood was further darkened by the news of other players making plans to fly to Colombia. Everton's Billy Higgins and Charlie Mitten of Manchester United were both drawing up their travel plans. Higgins, though Franklin and Mountford did not know this, was originally due to fly out with them to Bogotá.

What initially stopped Higgins was the advice coming from the sports editor of the *Liverpool Echo*, in whom Higgins had confided. 'Eventually, I accepted the Millonarios club's offer and should have travelled on the same plane as Franklin and Mountford, though at the time I had no idea they were going out,' revealed Higgins. 'The reason I delayed my departure for four days was that "Ranger" [*The Echo*'s sport's editor] persuaded me not to leave until I had got a cabled guarantee that my passage would be paid back to home whenever I wanted it. I cabled asking for it, but got no reply. Despite this I decided to take a chance and began packing. If I'd only known what I was heading for I should have at once unpacked quicker than I packed.'

The Scottish Football Association were also about to join their English counterparts in erupting with fury once it emerged Scotland international Bobby Flavell of Hearts was also on his way to an airport bound for Colombia. Two other players, Welsh international Roy Paul of Swansea Town and another Evertonian, Jack Hedley, were also contemplating offers.

At first, the FA offered Franklin and Mountford an olive branch. If they didn't play or coach in Colombia and simply returned home to England there would be no disciplinary sanctions. The FA secretary, Sir Stanley Rous, sent 'warning telegrams' to them both, lodging the missives with his counterparts from the Colombian Football Association.

His final telegram, a plaintive plea, simply singled out Franklin, the errant England international. It read, 'Neil Franklin, English international, flew to Bogotá yesterday. He is under contract to play only for Stoke City. Must not play for any other club until clearance certificate obtained. Please inform him and Santa Fe club.'

In response, Santa Fe put out a statement initially denying Stoke's footballers were in Bogotá to play for the Colombian outfit. Pleading innocence, an official told the Colombian press, 'We do not think the FA quite appreciate the point that they [Franklin and Mountford] had been engaged as trainers not players.'

Those telegrams from the FA at Lancaster Gate in London simply warned the players against associating themselves with a club, which at the time was not affiliated to the world governing body of world football, FIFA. It meant any 'football engagement', coaching as well as playing. There was no mention, yet, of any sanctions if they chose to ignore the warning.

In his 1978 autobiography, *Football Worlds: A Lifetime in Sport*, Sir Stanley Rous revealed he made far greater efforts than just sending off a missive by telegram. 'I contacted the Bogotá officials to see if conflict could be avoided, explaining to them the long-term damage to Franklin's prospects,' Rous recalled.

Most of the FA's ire was directed at Franklin. Mountford, at least, had asked for permission from his club to be excused for the summer to take up a 'coaching' contract abroad, albeit in an unspecified country. Franklin, the England centre-half turning his back on his country on the eve of a World Cup, had done no such thing.

Just to press home the FA's initial warning via telegram, officials from the Colombian FA agreed to meet the players once they landed in Bogotá to give them the warning from their English bosses. They would be in breach of the rules of international football, set by FIFA, if they accepted what was termed a 'football engagement'. That meant coaching, not just playing.

For the benefit of football fans, following the unfolding scandal, newspaper articles cited Rule 23 of the Football Association, the measure of which Franklin and Mountford were allegedly in breach. It read, 'Clubs and players under the jurisdiction of this Association, or an affiliated Association, shall not play with or against any Club, which is not a member of this Association, or some other recognised Association. Associations, Leagues or Clubs of another nationality, must apply for the consent of the Football Association.' In the case of Franklin, Mountford and the other rebel players about to join them there was no consent.

Not surprisingly the Stoke City manager and his board of directors rapidly distanced themselves from the actions of their recalcitrant players, once again insisting no permission had been given to them to fly out to Colombia.

Bob McGrory told the Stoke *Sentinel*, 'The Stoke directors did not give permission to Franklin to go on a coaching trip. When Franklin and Mountford made their requests, the latter was told that he could go, although there was no mention of the club concerned, but Franklin was told that permission would only be granted if the FA gave their consent in view of the fact that he would probably be wanted for Rio [the 1950 World Cup finals].'

As pointed out earlier Franklin did not seek permission, simply citing 'personal reasons' for not wanting to be considered for the World Cup. McGrory also revealed the England manager had telephoned Franklin, hoping to persuade him to change his mind. According to McGrory, 'The player [Franklin] re-iterated his reasons [to Winterbottom] for not wanting to be included on the tour and again never mentioned anything about a coaching appointment.'

Of course, Franklin and Mountford were not just in Colombia to take up coaching duties. They were there to play, something they made clear on arrival at Bogotá Airport to what Franklin described as 'a reception worthy of visiting monarchy'.

There to greet them was a phalanx of Colombian FA and Santa Fe club officials, including the man who had recruited the Stoke players, Luis Robledo. It was the first time they had met in person. Robledo had his own warning to the players. 'Watch your pockets,' he told the bemused Englishmen. They soon discovered the meaning. Franklin claimed Colombia's capital was full of 'the world's most expert pickpockets'.

Meantime, there was another encounter with the gentlemen of the press, the eager Colombian media, international correspondents, and the few British journalists able to catch up with them, sports writers diverted by their news desks from their original journey to Rio to preview the World Cup. Instead, they were sent to Bogotá to quiz the England centre-half on his real reasons for not wanting to play for his country.

Standing on Colombian soil, Franklin was more open about his plans. 'Neither George Mountford nor I were willing to admit that we were going to stay in Bogotá,' Franklin later explained. 'We thought it was much wiser not to admit that until we were safely in the country.'

In answer to questions, yes, he would play for the Santa Fe club, initially for three months, before returning to England. He refused to answer any questions about Santa Fe's status as a club with no affiliation to FIFA via its domestic governing body. He simply responded, 'I am tired. I am going to bed.'

It was then off on what Franklin described as a 'triumphant drive' from the airport to their city centre hotel. He recalled, 'We travelled by car and were accompanied by a whole procession of vehicles, all sounding their sirens and blowing their horns. We had been led to expect a bright modern city on the lines of say, Rio de Janeiro. We found that Bogotá was nothing like that at all. But we were there, while back home the controversy raged.'

The last comment was an understatement. Their story was being carried on the front pages as well as the back pages in an era where sport rarely caught the attention of national newspaper leader writers. The entire English football establishment was against them, only limited and measured support coming from the Association Football Players' Union, forerunner to the PFA.

Jimmy Guthrie, chairman of the union, acknowledged the threats being issued by the FA's Sir Stanley Rous to Neil

Franklin and George Mountford. If the threat to suspend them was carried out then the union would, of course, fight their case. His members would not have taken such a dramatic and drastic measure if the terms and conditions of employment with Stoke City, as determined by Football League rules, were, to put it politely, a lot more reasonable.

'I don't suppose they are coming back at all. What's the point of them wasting their talents here when they can earn higher wages elsewhere?' commented Guthrie to the press. Alluding to Franklin's initial insistence he was only off to Bogotá to coach, Guthrie asserted, 'Franklin is quite right. I am in entire agreement with him. The official season operates from 1 August to 31 July. During the close season, players get a reduction in wages. Franklin is under contract at the moment with a reduction in wages.

'There is nothing to say that he cannot accept an appointment in South America. The close season is set aside to give players a rest. Franklin is quite justified in refusing the Rio trip so far as I am concerned. Overseas trips are all very well, but the players get very little of the profits. Players should get a bigger "cut" out of tours.' Intriguingly, Guthrie, the Players' Union leader, was quite content for one of England's best players to miss a World Cup.

Indeed, he took the opportunity to condemn FIFA, arguably in stronger terms than his modern-day counterparts. 'FIFA have too much control over football. Star foreign players should be able to come here, and ours should be allowed to go wherever they like. There is no democracy here, only monopoly.'

He even raised the possibility of forming a rival world governing body of football, given the anger ignited by the shock flight of Franklin and Mountford to Bogotá. 'When our own troubles are smoothed out, the Players' Union is going ahead, in co-operation with unions of other countries to form a World Charter. The object of this will be to break down the monopoly of FIFA.'

Summing up, Guthrie declared Franklin had, on behalf of all British footballers, struck 'a blow for freedom'. He asked, 'Why should they be restricted? It is a disgrace that players should be lured away by other countries because of the poor summer wages paid by English clubs.'

In the meantime, as the furore erupted in Britain, the Stoke footballers settled with their families into a new life thousands of miles away from home, beginning in the luxury of Bogotá's finest hotel. Early on they must have wondered what exactly they had just done and not only because of the opprobrium heaped on them from Stoke and London – that much they predicted, but not the chaotic organisation in Bogotá.

Their doubts may have set in during their travails en route to Colombia with their brief stopover in New York serving as a warning. Life in Bogotá, both off and on the pitch, was not quite what the smooth-talking Colombian diplomat Senor Robledo had cracked it up to be. Threats of dire sanctions from the Football Association were, for the time being, the least of their concerns. First off, the Stoke City players needed to prepare for their eagerly anticipated debuts in the red and white colours of Independiente Santa Fe.

# SANTA FE DEBUTS

AFTER a journey lasting more than 48 hours involving seven different flights and only a couple of the briefest of stopovers, an athlete in any normal scenario might be expected to rest and acclimatise. But this was far from any normal scenario.

Having secured his prize assets and secreted them out of England, Luis Robledo wanted an immediate return on his investment. The owner of Independiente Santa Fe wanted the now former England centre-half, Neil Franklin, out on the pitch alongside his mate George Mountford for their new club's very next game.

It did not matter that Santa Fe's doctor advised against the idea. Given Bogotá is a city in the northern Andes, some 9,000 feet above sea level, he urged patience so they could adjust to the altitude. Even an attaché from the British Embassy turned up at the hotel to check on the players and their families and offer the exact same advice. The British diplomats pointed out it was vital the players spent a few days getting acclimatised before contemplating going out on to the pitch to play a game of football.

Robledo ignored his own club doctor, and the overtures from his diplomatic counterparts at the British Embassy. As far as he was concerned, Franklin and Mountford were in the Santa Fe team for their forthcoming home fixture against Medellin. Even his club manager had no say in the matter.

Robledo ended the pretence of the players simply being in Bogotá to coach, something the Santa Fe club kept up until the players were ensconced in their hotel. Instead, he happily promoted the match on the radio, guaranteeing an instant sell-out given the hysteria over the arrival of the English football stars.

'Both George Mountford and I were willing to take the advice of the British Embassy about the height, but the Santa Fe Club were terribly anxious that we should play on the Sunday, although we had only arrived the previous Tuesday,' Franklin recalled in his autobiography. 'The officials wanted to show us off to the public, and one can hardly blame them for that because they had gone to a lot of trouble to sign us, and our arrival had received tremendous publicity.'

Rather than arguing whether or not to play, for Neil Franklin his first priority was his pregnant wife, Vera. Naturally, she was struggling after the gruelling journey from England and with acclimatising to altitude. To compound matters, their son Gary went down with dysentery or, as his dad called it, 'the Bogotá tummy'. The doctor ordered both to bed, giving Franklin junior the appropriate medicine. It was an inauspicious start to their visit to Colombia.

Vera and her son Gary may well have struggled to rest given the commotion outside their hotel. As her husband recalled, 'The whole town was alight with the news. Crowds gathered outside our hotel, and we were rocketed into the same sort of position television stars find themselves in after a few successful appearances, but we had not yet appeared. So, it would have been a terrible let-down if it had been announced that we were not in the side for that game on the Sunday. Knowing that, both George and I decided to turn out.'

On the morning of the game, the now defunct British newspaper, the *Sunday Empire News*, ran a front page with Neil Franklin's byline, headlined, 'Franklin: I did it for my wife'. It was ghostwritten by the paper's chief football correspondent, W. Capel Kirby, who had been diverted on his journey to the World Cup in Rio to intercept the rebel English footballers in Bogotá. Kirby, no doubt for more than the odd US dollar, set up a rapport with Franklin, acting not so much as a reporter but the England international footballer's public relations agent.

Once again, Franklin insisted there was nothing secretive about his flight to Bogotá, a difficult argument to keep maintaining. 'They say I slipped off to Bogotá, Colombia and ratted on England and Stoke City FC without saying a word to anybody. It is not true,' Franklin protested. 'Because I am a footballer who happens to be more in the public eye than most, it still doesn't follow that I should put country and self before the happiness and well-being of my wife and family.'

Basically, he argued he was putting his international career in jeopardy for the sake of the health of his wife. 'One of the conditions of my engagement here [in Colombia] is that she will be given the best medical attention for nervous trouble arising from her condition, which believe me was the one and only reason I wrote reluctantly to the Football Association begging them to release me from the World Cup trip to Rio. Nobody in their right mind would think that I would jeopardise an international career of 38 consecutive appearances for England without a very good reason.'

Yet he had done so. In an opinion piece termed by his new-found journalistic friend, Capel Kirby, as a 'Capelgram', warning was offered to anyone wanting to join Franklin and Mountford. It was high risk, almost certainly more than the errant Stoke City players realised. Kirby commented, 'Neil Franklin and George Mountford have gone over to a pirate organisation, a body of wealthy Colombian goal prospectors not recognised by FIFA or any other sports federation. As a freelance concern they can poach world stars without honouring transfer obligations but what of the players tempted to this soccer El Dorado? They have put themselves beyond official world football legislation.'

As a consequence, Kirby suggested the players were no better off with Santa Fe than at Stoke City, aside from the obvious benefit of vastly inflated wages. 'Suppose for instance, Neil, George or both sustain a serious injury this weekend [during their debuts], and believe me the possibility is greater out here than at home, they would be at the mercy of their unrecognised employers. The chances are that they would get the brush-off and neither FIFA, the FA, the Football League, Stoke City, nor the Players' Union could do anything on their behalf.'

As far as the writer was concerned it was a high-stakes gamble. If so, there was only limited sympathy for Franklin back home in England. His international career was not just in jeopardy but, while nobody contemplated such a scenario at the time, it was over. Nevertheless, Franklin remained unrepentant, citing the welfare of his family rather than any personal concerns. His priority happened to be his pregnant wife, who like so many in the Potteries suffered from the intense pollution in the district at the time. Taking her thousands of miles away to a different continent did, for many of even his supporters, appear a bit drastic.

'There are thousands of wives, who at a time like this, cannot bear the thought of their husbands being separated from them for a day or two, let alone going nearly 7,000 miles away for several weeks. And that is what it would have meant if I had allowed my name to go forward for the World Cup team,' he plaintively elaborated.

Once letters began to arrive from their families in the Potteries, informing them of the negative and stunned reaction to their behaviour from football fans and the public at large, Franklin and Mountford began to soften their stance. Overtures were even about to be made by the Santa Fe club to the English FA, offering Franklin's services to England for the World Cup.

In the meantime, they prepared to play in a competitive club game deemed by the World Cup organisers FIFA as illegal. Santa Fe registered them with the rogue Colombian League on the Friday before the game. Both passed their medicals, deemed to be in perfect condition. Fans began to queue outside the stadium on the night before they were due to trot out to make their Santa Fe debuts.

Just a week earlier they had been playing at the Victoria Ground, Stoke-on-Trent, in a fairly meaningless end of season game, losing to Arsenal in front of a largely unenthusiastic crowd. This time they turned out in front of tens of thousands of fanatics with players they had barely met, unable to communicate with them because of the language barrier, and against unfamiliar opposition.

'I couldn't help thinking during the game how strange it was that we should play at the Victoria Ground, Stoke, one Saturday and lose 5-3 to Arsenal and eight days later we should be playing in Bogotá, a city no one had ever heard of and in a country few people knew existed!' mused Franklin. His memory deserted him. Stoke actually lost 5-2. To make matters more surreal for Franklin and Mountford, Santa Fe turned out in Arsenal colours of red shirts with white sleeves and white shorts. Their new boss Robledo chose the kit because he became an Arsenal fan while being posted on diplomatic duty in London.

It turned out to be a successful debut for them. Santa Fe beat Medellin 3-2 in a match witnessed by English journalists, most of them at a game of South American football for the very first time in their careers. 'Neil Franklin, England's centre-half, and his Stoke City club-mate, George Mountford, made an impressive debut for Santa Fe in the Colombian Premier Division,' ran the copy from *Reuters*' correspondent at the game.

He went on, 'Santa Fe beat Medellin 3-2, Mountford making the openings for his side's first two goals and scoring the winning goal himself. Franklin was brilliant in defence and continually broke up dangerous Medellin attacks. Both Franklin and Mountford expressed satisfaction with their first match, but said they had felt a little tired towards the end due to the heavy ground and high altitude.'

It was a debut to live long in the memory for Franklin, not just the football, or the unusual circumstances, but the febrile atmosphere. He thought Stoke fans could be passionate. The Colombian supporters were of a different order. 'A Colombian crowd in action has to be seen to be believed,' he wrote. 'Everyone is so excitable and biased. We all know that in Britain you stick up for your favourite team and get into tremendously heated arguments about the merits or otherwise of a player or team, but in Britain it is all done in a friendly spirit. In Colombia there is nothing friendly about it.'

Arriving in Bogotá just in time to witness Franklin and George Mountford's debut for Santa Fe, Everton's Billy Higgins gave an account of the match to the *Liverpool Echo*. He wrote, 'The players at last came on to the field. You never saw such a fuss in all your life. They dashed about from one touchline to the other, waving to the crowd and shouting remarks which obviously I couldn't understand. With the crowd also cheering frantically the scene was indescribable. During all this Franklin and Mountford, who certainly had a rousing reception stood bewitched and bewildered, looked as though they didn't know whether they were on their heads or their heels. No wonder!'

Contrary to the views of the match expressed by their *Reuters* correspondent, Higgins noted the crowd were unhappy with Franklin's performance. 'Apparently, Franklin was not coming up to expectations,' wrote Higgins. 'I was hardly surprised at that, for the defensive formation out there is vastly different to what it is in England and obviously Franklin was finding this a problem, apart altogether from the fact that he was getting no cover from the men alongside him. He did as well as anybody could under the circumstances, but spectators continued murmuring "malo" [Spanish for bad] several times.'

During those early days in Bogotá, Franklin anxiously tried to put forward a positive view of life as a footballer in Colombia. But clearly, just as there were problems during the flight to Bogotá, doubts as to the wisdom of his actions must have already set in during the course of Franklin and Mountford's Santa Fe debut. After witnessing them take to the field Billy Higgins left the ground feeling horrified. Already, Higgins thought he had made a mistake in taking up the offer to play for Millonarios. He suspected the Stoke players felt the same about their drastic career choice.

'You never saw anything in your life like a Colombian club's dressing room immediately after a match,' Higgins commented in his despatch to the *Liverpool Echo*. 'It is worse than a Barnum and Bailey Circus. I first experienced it after the match in which Neil Franklin and George Mountford made their debut for Santa Fe. Naturally, I wanted to go along with them as soon as the game was over.'

Once Higgins got near the dressing rooms, as the latest British professional footballer thinking he was about to pick up his golden bounty on Colombian soil, he was in for a shock. 'I stood transfixed with amazement,' Higgins revealed. 'It was crowded from door to door with urchins, who were chattering away fifty to the dozen, swarming round the players, climbing on their knees and shoulders, and generally turning the place into pandemonium. Franklin and Mountford looked the picture of misery, although they were endeavouring to put a good face on it.'

Although none of the English contingent was a shrinking violet, they were also taken aback by the level of violence, an early taste coming in the game against Medellin. Higgins described the mayhem breaking out during Franklin and Mountford's debut. 'There were three periods of something like five minutes each when the game was completely held up,' he recalled. 'During one of these, every single player except the two Englishmen was engaged in actual fights or conducting heated arguments with opponents. Even the two goalkeepers ran to the centre circle and had a go! They were not going to be left out.' Higgins concluded it was 'anything but a happy introduction to Colombian football'.

Happily ensconced in Bogotá or not, the Stoke City players were now in breach of the rules and regulations of their domestic governing body back in England. Their act of rebellion was complete. Sanctions awaited them, if and when they returned home to Britain.

Sir Stanley Rous noted that despite his earlier appeals to the Colombians not to field Franklin, thereby jeopardising his international career, 'no compromise proved possible'. Therefore, 'Franklin was suspended on the grounds that he gave untrue reasons to the FA for not wishing to be considered for international matches; deceived his club and broke his contract and made statements to the Press and allowed articles to appear in his name likely to bring the game into disrepute.' More of those disagreeable articles in their opinion were to come. Hence Rous and the FA did not deviate from the original form of words on Franklin's charge sheet, once eventually and inevitably he appeared before them.

Neil Franklin and his Stoke City mate George Mountford were of course not alone among rebellious British footballers in turning out for Santa Fe on that fateful day. Everton's Billy Higgins had watched them make their debuts for Santa Fe from the stands. He remained in Colombia to take up a contract with Millonarios despite his reservations. Other British players were to follow.

'I know I have burned my boats,' Franklin admitted in the build-up to his Santa Fe debut. Defiantly, he added, 'Becoming the central figure in the biggest hullabaloo in the history of international football is not a role I particularly like.' But Franklin was adamant. He had done the right thing by flying off to Bogotá to take up his lucrative contract. Far from being a villain, he was determined, as proposed by his supportive Players' Union, to cast himself in the role of a footballing hero. It was to prove a difficult, if not impossible, task.

# BOGOTÁ BAD BOYS

NEIL Franklin did more than burn his boats or bridges with club and country as he began his Colombian adventure. He blew them out of the water. 'Why I left the Soccer Slave Market' splashed across the front page of the *Sunday Empire News* ensured the wrath of his former employers. Franklin insisted he did not care. His act of rebellion was for the good of the English game. He branded it corrupt.

'Though I have had 10 years of professional soccer slavery, I still have a conscience and I cannot reconcile it with some of the back-stage goings on in English League football,' ranted Franklin. 'The plain truth there is something rotten in the state of football today. It is no secret to those inside, but no player with his living to consider talks openly about it.'

Talk of 'slavery', even using the contradictory term 'professional slavery', was of course ridiculous. English players wanted more money but they were still paid. They may have been tied to club contracts with efforts to move elsewhere blocked but they were not marched back and forth from training in shackles. But, the hyperbolic and strident tone of Franklin's musings in the tabloid press did neatly serve to illustrate the extent of his anger.

After turning his back on Stoke City and England, Franklin felt he had the freedom to articulate his discontent, describing 'twelve months of misery in the Potteries'. He bemoaned the refusal of his club to grant him a transfer, complaining he had suffered deep 'unpleasantness' from those running his club. 'George Mountford and I agree that our only pang on leaving Stoke City was over the lads for whom we have respect and affection. Otherwise we have no regrets,' Franklin commented with the one diplomatic offer to his team-mates.

Franklin's central allegation was of the extent of illegal payments or 'backhanders' prevalent in the English league game, a practice, for all his other complaints about the club, he was anxious to excuse Stoke City of ever carrying out. For all his complaints, his boyhood club's directors and staff were honourable and honest in their financial dealings. 'Stoke have never paid a penny over the odds, but there are others who are not as particular. And, say it is downright dishonest,' Franklin insisted.

His main gripe centred on loyalty payments, namely the lack of them, and the signing-on fee given to players in the post-war years while being transferred from club to club. It was a flat £10 regardless of the size of the transfer fee. Franklin alleged, without naming any club, certain ones paid players considerably more behind the backs of Football League officials and more pertinently the tax man.

Franklin argued, 'Isn't there something radically wrong with a system in which soccer stars, pulling in record gate receipts, have to rely on odds and ends in the way of "perks" to augment their inadequate wage of £12 a week in the playing season and £10 during the summer months?'

As a result of the iniquitous system outlined by Franklin, he confidently predicted a raft of players were about to follow him and George Mountford out to Colombia to make their fortune, albeit in a league deemed illegal by football's world governing body FIFA. Stoke City's Frank Mountford, no relation of George, was among eight players named by the *Sunday Empire News* receiving 'approaches' from the Colombian moneymen.

In the event, Stoke City's future League Cup-winning trainer opted to stay at home. But a handful did travel. Everton's Billy Higgins, of course, was already there. Manchester United's Charlie Mitten was about to follow suit. Hearts' Bobby Flavell was set to provoke the ire of his club, the Scottish League, and the Scottish Football Association. Indeed, the FA at Lancaster Gate in London feared a rebellion on a much greater scale.

Franklin's acerbic comments in the Sunday newspapers made for uncomfortable reading for the men in FA blazers. They must have also felt his words insisting on his pride in wearing the England shirt were hollow. Meeting him years later with his England shirt and a cap pinned on the wall behind him I took them to be genuine. Back in the summer of 1950 with England's best player absent from a World Cup it mattered little to his critics.

Franklin wrote in attempting to justify his actions, 'Let me make it quite clear that I did not pull up my roots without a great deal of heart-searching. All the money in football cannot buy the pride that comes from playing for England. It is not without qualms that George Mountford and I cut adrift from Stoke City and our team-mates. Neither did we decide to take our wives to these far-off places without weighing up the situation carefully.'

On the weekend Franklin made his debut for Santa Fe in Bogotá, the England team-mates he had deserted were in action with a World Cup warm-up game against Portugal in Lisbon. They won 5-3 but failed to impress the English fans with typewriters sat in the press box, filing their copy for the national newspapers. All agreed Franklin was missed.

Commenting on his replacement, Bill Jones of Liverpool, Roy Peskett of the *Daily Mail* wrote, 'Though Bill Jones, playing his first game against a continental side, was not fully to blame, the absence of Neil Franklin upset the whole defensive plan and showed the paucity in England of centre-halves.'

But Franklin's merits as a footballer were, of course, not the exclusive focus of the international weekend for those following England. His act of rebellion, 'blow for freedom', in the opinion of the Players' Union inevitably drew further comment. It did so partly thanks to the fallout from a 'B' international against Italy in Milan, England losing 5-0.

It emerged that some of those players had been offered contracts by Italian clubs with a one-off payment of £4,000, and the promise of £50 a week in wages. At first journalists covering the match thought it was a joke. Once news filtered through of Franklin's flight to Bogotá they stopped laughing.

As Desmond Hackett of the *Daily Express* wrote, 'For official football, the Franklin story could not have come at a worse time. In Italy, British players attached to Italian clubs talked of the money that is picked up by star soccer players. The English team heard that the Juventus club have given their players an extra present of a holiday anywhere in the world for winning the Italian championship. Another team were given cars.'

Hackett revealed that while covering the 'B' international, the Italian club Napoli had approached him asking for help to hire three forwards, at any price they cared to mention, and even a coach. He wryly commented that the Napoli club officials did so, 'even after they had seen the shattering advertisement of our 5-0 defeat'.

Franklin's flight to Bogotá proved, at first, an irritating distraction for the rulers of English football as they looked forward to the national team competing for the first time in a World Cup. Franklin's rebellion, with other British players turning up in Bogotá to take up contracts in Colombia's 'pirate' DiMayor league, now threatened to turn into a full-blown crisis for the sport in England and Scotland.

'We may have appeared to stick the chin out when we said a week or so ago that the Neil Franklin departure for the fleshpots of Bogotá was a freak affair, not to be mistaken for the harbinger of a mass movement,' commented John MacAdam of *The Express*. 'Formidable? Maybe, but none of the football hierarchy is suffering from alarm and despondency on that account.' That was an optimistic view of the FA's position. There was clear disquiet.

As MacAdam himself put it, 'The general feeling is that the minor exodus is a good thing on account of the fact that it puts into focus the position in which British footballers find themselves. Maybe the blind men of football will begin to stir in their undergrowth and realise that a fair wage for a fair performance, to say nothing of the value of real training and coaching, is the professional footballers' view.'

And he noted, 'There is nothing new in the traffic except that this time it happens to have extended to Britain, the home of the game. The Latin Americans have been doing it to each other for years, unlicensed clubs poaching players from licensed ones and then throwing them aside when their turn had been served.'

Perish the thought that England's top-class footballers might be of interest on the international market, clubs licensed by FIFA and those unauthorised such as the members of Colombia's DiMayor league. On the eve of England's debacle at the 1950 World Cup in Brazil *The Express* correspondent confidently asserted, 'The thing is symptomatic of what is bound to happen when the great British game spreads. Pupils will filch away masters.'

The master Franklin and company had taken a grave risk. Predicting their fate, John MacAdam of *The Express* feared they may be quickly dumped by the fickle Colombian club owners. It was unlikely they'd be welcomed back into the English or Scottish leagues.

Naturally, the British Communist Party-supporting newspaper, the *Daily Worker*, struck a more optimistic note. It was predictably strident in its defence of the British rebel players, commenting in an editorial, 'Some will say that these players [Neil Franklin and George Mountford] have let the side down – Franklin in particular was England's automatic number one centre-half. Others, including members of the Players' Union will argue that the player has a right to do as he wishes during the close season. They will suggest, again quite rightly, that the footballer who delights the crowds for the main part of the year has a right to insist that the summer months should be his to do as he likes.'

The football establishment had easily resisted calls for reform of British players' terms of pay and conditions from the Players' Union and their supporters. Everyone in the English professional game knew Franklin's dissatisfaction at being tied to his club. His wages being capped despite being one of the finest players in the land was at the heart of his decision to desert the Potteries, even turn his back on the England national team.

One of his international team-mates, speaking on the basis of anonymity, commented, 'It is all very well talking about keeping wages to a limit but there is no limit when it comes to transfer fees. And once we've finished being big shots, we are through. We are just thrown out and invited to earn our living some other way. We cannot all keep pubs. There wouldn't be enough to go around.'

From the coach of the England 'B' team, Harold Shentall, there came a warning for his FA bosses and the Football League clubs. 'This [Franklin's flight to Bogotá and the approach of Italian clubs] is the worst thing that could happen to football,' he said. 'It is going to be very difficult to satisfy players that the present wage limit system is the best.'

Shentall was doing his best to argue for the status quo. Others felt differently, not least Jimmy Guthrie of the Players'

Union. He floated the idea of Franklin being at the heart of a test case, legal action against the FA and the Football League, if and when the FA suspended, then punished Franklin and his fellow rebels. He demanded players were paid their 'box office value' rather than a fixed maximum wage.

It would be well over a decade before such a scenario unfolded. Yet in the summer of 1950 thanks to the Colombian exploits of Franklin and company it seemed a realistic possibility. In the meantime, the FA stubbornly ignored a growing media frenzy, any calls for reform, and instead simply drew up its charge sheet for the British football rebels.

It did so at the beginning of June. The selection and disciplinary committees of the FA were convened to consider the cases of Franklin and Mountford. The international selectors, prior to sending an England squad out to the World Cup in Brazil, wanted to be seen to punish Franklin, furious he had made himself unavailable for Rio. They wanted him not just banned from playing in England but globally. The only flaw in their plan was Stoke City's reluctance, for the time being, to formally notify the FA that he was, in their view, in breach of contract.

Instead, Stoke City FC simply embarked on the more mundane task of repossessing the Franklin family home in Newcastle-under-Lyme. Club officials did so as the Franklins and Mountfords set about house-hunting in Bogotá. Mr and Mrs Franklin did so, unaware they had no home to go to on any return to North Staffordshire.

Even in the earliest stages of their time in Colombia, a flight back to England for Franklin seemed a distinct possibility. Once again, the restless player felt unsettled at a football club. Things at Stoke City were bad enough for him. But he did not anticipate some of the problems he would encounter in Colombia, not just a different national culture but different football culture.

There are contrasting contemporary accounts of Franklin's time in Bogotá – column inches full of optimism and joy from Franklin's de facto publicist, Capel Kirby in the *Sunday Empire News*. A far soberer assessment was delivered by Evelyn Webber of the *Daily Express*.

Webber travelled from her New York base for *The Express* to befriend the Stoke City players' wives in Bogotá. Her account of their attempts to settle into a new life ended up being splashed on the paper's front page the day after their husbands had made their unauthorised Santa Fe debuts. She described their mood as 'dispirited'. House-hunting, among other things, was not going well.

'It's nothing like we dreamed it would be,' groaned Mrs Franklin. 'The kitchens are primitive, great dirty looking iron coal cookers with a tank on top, old fashioned sinks, even a stone to scrub the washing on.' Unaware her husband's club had sent the bailiffs into their home on the outskirts of the Potteries, she commented her semi-detached was better than anything on offer in the Colombian capital.

Mrs Franklin also commented on her struggles with the language barrier, revealing it was even difficult to communicate to Colombians with a command of English because they failed to understand her Potteries accent. 'Today, we asked [the hotel staff] for thick soup like they make back home in Stoke. They brought us porridge,' she laughed.

Despite being described by Webber as 'dispirited', there was still a degree of optimism, a steely determination to enjoy her stay in Bogotá, one made all the better for her husband earning decent money for the first time in his career. 'We are looking for a house with servants' quarters. We'll be rich enough to afford that,' she told *The Express* journalist. 'And perhaps someone will come from home to look after the babies. Many a Stoke fan would jump at the chance. Our husbands are still popular there.' She further joked, 'Some of the [Stoke] team who knew we were coming said they'd even come to be our footmen.'

For the benefit of *Express* readers, Webber asked Vera Franklin and Phyliss Mountford what they thought of Bogotá's shops. 'They're full of things we've wanted for years,' they said. 'American nylons and toasters. Toys for the children. We want one of those marvellous streamlined American cars we see jamming the streets. But we haven't stopped to look at the price of anything yet.' Webber ruefully commented, once they did, they'd be in for a shock.

Additionally, of course, there was the backdrop of civil unrest. All their fame meant nothing to the Bogotá police. Neil Franklin and George Mountford, within days of arrival, were arrested for going out without their ID cards. Franklin noted, 'The political situation in Colombia is charged with dynamite. Never a day passed without some form of political demonstration, and when the Colombians demonstrate, they really demonstrate.

'We in Britain are so accustomed to having our political arguments made in a friendly and non-violent manner that we cannot visualise what happens when those hot-blooded characters beg to differ on politics. To me, it appears that the argument is never resolved until someone has his head cracked wide open.' Naturally he made those comments, hardly meant to endear him to his hosts, once safely back in England.

Despite initial problems, for the Stoke City players and their families generally, life in Bogotá seemed to be good. Franklin and Mountford were looking forward to a fruitful and lucrative stay. 'We've never seen so many people and they look as though they'd stepped out of a colour film,' Vera Franklin observed. 'They know us well now and whenever our husbands go out, they are mobbed for autographs while people shout in Spanish, "Good old England".'

Popularity with the fans was a given. Popularity with the other Santa Fe players: here Franklin, for one, struggled. 'Most of our players came from Argentina, and they rather resented the intrusion of George Mountford and myself,' Franklin noted. 'Before we arrived, the Argentinians had held the monopoly, but when they realised that English, Scottish, Irish and Welsh stars were likely to invade Bogotá, they became insanely jealous, because they realised the British players would train and train hard.'

Dismissively, he asserted the 'training was not quite the strong point' of Argentinians. He recognised they were 'very good ball players' and 'very good exhibitionists' but found them to be 'incredibly lazy' in training sessions. He observed, 'George and I naturally trained hard, just as any British player does, and when the Argentinians saw us throwing ourselves wholeheartedly into the training sessions, they took a dim view of it.'

Intriguingly, as much as he doubted the commitment of South American footballers to training, Franklin approved of the training regime. The one drawback was just getting to the training ground. A bus would pick the players up. Franklin and Mountford would turn up at the appointed time. The driver was nearly always two hours late, not a problem for their casual team-mates but a major irritant for the two lads from Stoke-on-Trent.

Once they arrived, Franklin and Mountford approved of what they encountered. 'The training was very different than the training we had been used to at home,' Franklin commented. 'It was much more varied and included much more ball practice, both of which are good points. Training in Britain is usually much too stereotyped, and there is nothing like enough ball practice.'

Franklin noted in his autobiography, 'Not only were the South American fanatics about practising with a football, they also included a lot of other ball games, such as basketball. But whatever ball games they chose, they made sure they were games played at speed, so that you had to keep agile, your eye had to be good and your stamina had to be good. I think we in Britain can learn a lot from this system.'

Decades before the advent of the Premier League, the arrival of foreign players and crucially foreign coaches advocating sports science and improved medical care, Franklin advocated the adoption of his South American club's more enlightened training regime. He was dismissive of the habits of British players of the fifties, sixties and seventies, himself included.

'We place too much reliance on golf, which is a good enough game and a pleasant enough relaxation, but it is useless for sharpening up the senses of a footballer,' Franklin observed. 'Footballers need to play games of quick movement so that they develop their ball sense and develop it at speed.' He rather bitterly concluded, 'So, one good thing about Bogotá was the training programme. The only pity was that everyone was too lackadaisical about timing and too many of the players did not buckle down to the programme seriously enough.'

Franklin may have had his problems winning over his South American team-mates but he did warm to the supporters. They also warmed to him as he tried to embrace the madcap world of Colombian football. 'The atmosphere is so electric that every ground has netting to keep the spectators off the playing pitch, but in my six games with Santa Fe I never knew that netting to succeed in its purpose,' Franklin recalled.

He also described the chaotic scenes prior to a match. 'The spectators even got into the dressing room at the start of the game,' he revealed. 'In Britain, dressing rooms are private. No one is allowed to enter them before a match except the players, the manager, trainer and directors (and few directors come in), but in Bogotá, the dressing rooms before a match were the scene of the gathering of the clans. Scores of people would jostle about, gibbering away excitedly in all sorts of languages, and it was a miracle that we players ever got on the field at all.' He went on, 'Almost anything could happen in football matches there and invariably everything did. For instance, everything in Colombia is highly commercialised and advertising appears to be just about the most competitive trade there is.'

He cited the example of a plane regularly flying over the ground, trailing an advertising banner, something not seen on a dreary winter's afternoon at the Victoria Ground in Stoke. 'Not content with that, they also engaged a man who parachuted out of the aircraft, landing on the playing pitch and then trotted around the track with a snappy advertisement pinned on his uniform,' Franklin remembered.

'The crowd loved that sort of thing, and they loved it even more one day when things went wrong. The wind carried the parachutist away from the stadium and he landed in some trees. He was badly cut and bruised, but he gallantly stuck to his job, ran to the stadium and although bloody and bruised, he trotted round his lap of honour.'

The level of violence Franklin found less amusing, from fans and players alike. 'Their tempers are always at exploding point, and it only needs a tiny spark to turn a football game into a brawl,' he moaned. 'I remember one occasion when 20 players got into grips in a terrible scrap. The only players who were aloof were George Mountford and myself. On another occasion one of our opponents was penalised for a foul, and the goalkeeper raced past me on the way to join in the scuffle, about which he could have known nothing. But a fight to a South American is a fight, and he must be in it.'

These observations were shared by Bill Higgins, but he denied the Colombian game of football was 'dirty'. Alright, he admitted fights did frequently occur but as he put it, 'really vicious fouls are rare'. Instead, he insisted, 'There is a lot of pushing and elbowing and obstruction galore, none of which is ever penalised.' As far as the British players were concerned Colombian referees seemed reluctant to send anybody off, no matter how grave the offence.

'There are two reasons for that,' Higgins explained. 'In the first place they fear reprisals from the crowd and the offending players' colleagues. Secondly, if they sent players off for fighting, very few games would ever be completed. There wouldn't be enough players left on the field.'

Along with the five British players in 1950, there were five English referees officiating in Colombia's DiMayor league. They quickly learned to adopt a lenient approach, doing so as a matter of survival as much as anything else. 'One English referee, who decided he would stand no nonsense and would interpret the rules according to the English manner, had the pluck to give a penalty in his first match,' recalled Higgins in a match involving Millonarios. 'You never heard such an uproar in all your life. The game was stopped for fully ten minutes.

'Spectators swarmed over the wire fence, players argued the toss in bunches all over the field, and a big bloke dashed into the middle and seized the referee by the scruff of the neck. The position looked decidedly ominous for a time, though eventually order was restored without anybody being hurt. The irony of it all was that the penalty was missed.'

Remarkably, the fan assaulting the ref escaped arrest. The police did nothing. Instead, as the hapless ref made his way to the dressing rooms after the game, his assailant waved at him and yelled an apology. For the Colombians and Argentinians this was all normal. For the British players it came as a complete culture shock.

The flight to Bogotá of English and Scottish football rebels can be summed up as a brave but foolish step for a group of British professional players of the fifties. Franklin boarded the plane along with his family insisting he did so with his 'eyes wide open'. Yet the man from the English Potteries struggled to adapt, found it difficult to fit in with his Latin American colleagues. For him, stories in the Colombian newspapers of more of what they called 'los maestros Inglese', 'the English masters' made matters worse. Higgins, Flavell and Mitten had joined Franklin and Mountford. Others seemed, at the time, certain to follow.

They did not do so because of the problems being encountered by Franklin and his fellow rebels. Gradually, word filtered back to England of the resentment felt by homegrown South American footballers of the British invasion. There were not just problems for Franklin and Mountford at Santa Fe but also their counterparts from England and Scotland at its fierce rival, Millonarios.

Everton's Bill Higgins made his debut for 'Ballet Azul' in an away match to Cali on Sunday, 21 May 1950. It did not go well for him. Millonarios lost 6-1 and he was substituted, an unfamiliar experience for an English player of the day. 'After playing for 75 minutes, during which time I was consistently cold shouldered and starved – I got one pass the whole time, and that a bad one – I was taken off by the Argentinian skipper and a substitute was brought on,' Higgins told the *Liverpool Echo*.

Despite not speaking a word of Spanish and only a couple of the Millonarios entourage being conversant in English, the man from Merseyside quickly picked up that the game may have been fixed. Months later he confided in the *Liverpool Echo*, 'There were all sorts of rumours that the game had been "sold". I am not in a position to express any opinion on that. My ignorance of Spanish meant that I could not follow the many and heated arguments which went on, but there certainly seemed a right royal "to do" about it all.'

Allegations of match fixing were the least of his problems. It was obvious to him his presence in the side was being resented, primarily by the Argentinian contingent. 'An Englishman on business in Bogotá told me that he had heard on good authority that the Argentinians had decided, no matter how long I remained with Millonarios, that they would refuse to cooperate with me,' Higgins explained. 'They feared my arrival might be the start of the invasion by English players which would eventually take their jobs away from them. Maybe one cannot blame them, but it certainly put me in a tough spot.'

Higgins took the snub from Millonarios' Argentinian players, noting they appeared to behave more favourably in the company of Scottish player, Bobby Flavell, once he arrived from Edinburgh at the club. He also felt Santa Fe's South American players were less antagonistic in their dealings with Franklin, Mountford and also Manchester United's Charlie Mitten once he eventually arrived in Bogotá.

Those players begged to differ. Higgins was not the only one struggling to make friends among his new colleagues. But, the biggest problems for British players seeking their fortune in football's El Dorado did appear to be at Millonarios with Di Stefano its star player.

*Reuters New Agency* revealed some four weeks after Neil Franklin and George Mountford's triumphant arrival in Bogotá, 'Resistance to the British football players who have been signed up to play for the Colombian Millonarios club has created a "grave crisis" in the club's management.' Speculation the club was unable to afford the wages of the British players hardly helped matters. There were signs of the great football rebellion fizzling out. Reality, even at an early stage, hit the British players. For them football's El Dorado was, of course, a myth.

Indeed, the most prominent rebel or mercenary depending on your point of view almost instantaneously appeared to have harboured doubts over his move to Bogotá. Neil Franklin began to advise other players against doing the same. 'Roy

Paul and Jack Hedley actually came out and we entertained them,' he recalled. 'We also told them a few home truths, and the pair of them were soon on their way back home.'

Both Paul and Hedley took fright at the prospect of heavy punishment for the Bogotá Bad Boys, returning home and hoping to resume their careers in the Football League. They stayed in Colombia enjoying what Paul later described as a 'land of sweeter song, headier wine and amorous women' than he even dared hope for. That was not enough to keep him there. Paul and Hedley declined to sign for their suitors in the form of cash rich Colombian football clubs, a £4,000 signing-on fee apparently on offer. Instead, they boarded a plane home.

Once Paul and Hedley arrived in New York on their way back home they were collared by journalists anxious to question them on their reasons for turning their back on the Millonarios club. Roy Paul commented, 'I will certainly warn all other British players against going out there. The Millonarios is run by a bunch of businessmen who don't know one end of a football from another.'

He went on, 'They made quite attractive offers by cable, but when we got down to business, they wanted first of all to put us on a 45-day probation period. They put us in a dreadful hovel with everything very primitive. They then started bullying us. They would not listen to what we had to say, or even consider our terms.'

According to Paul, the club's president, Alfonso Senior, gave him and Hedley a minute to make up their minds on whether or not to sign, tapping his stopwatch at the same time. The players turned turtle and left for home, Paul apparently to face the wrath of his wife. He had flown out to Colombia without even telling her of his plans. 'I'll be on the doorstep with a few words to say to "Roy the Wanderer" when he turns up,' Beryl Paul commented from her home in the Rhondda mining village of Gelli. 'Maybe if he knew what was waiting for him, he would stay in Bogotá!'

Asked how her husband might make his way home, Mrs Paul suggested, 'At the worst he could work his passage on a cargo ship. He's big and strong and it will do him good.' Just to add to the sense of comedy and farce, Paul's mother-in-law, Lena Stuckey, joined in. 'I hope they make him scrub the deck from end to end. That will teach him to fly off to the other side of the world without telling anybody!' Mrs Paul had yet to hear of her husband's admiration for 'amorous' Colombian women. That revelation came later. Still, she forgave him.

His club chairman, Abe Freedman, had been a little more relaxed about the promising Welsh international's jaunt to Colombia, at least in his missives for the benefit of the press. Swansea Town's boss told the *Daily Telegraph*, 'Paul is still on our books. If he wants to take a little trip to South America in the close season we can't stop him. We'll be glad to see him back.' Once Paul walked through the door of Swansea's manager, Billy McCandless, there was no sign of the warm welcome offered by the club chairman. A valuable asset, he was immediately transfer-listed, back on his travels, happily snapped up by First Division Manchester City.

Given neither Paul nor Hedley had technically broken their British club contracts, even the president of the Football League, Arthur Drewry, appeared sympathetic, happy to accept that most of the British players out in Colombia were there merely 'on vacation'. His generous interpretation certainly did not extend to Franklin, *persona non grata* for club and country.

Both the returning pair revealed they had been in touch with the Stoke player and his mate George Mountford, making no mention of their dissatisfaction with arrangements in Colombia. Indeed, they claimed the men were quite happy. 'Neil Franklin and George Mountford aren't too badly off,'

Paul told the press. 'They're with the other club, Santa Fe, and they have been well treated. And, they got the money in the bank before they left.' As Paul and Hedley were left penniless in Bogotá, Franklin even lent them money to help pay for the passage home.

Not only was he helping out some of his British colleagues eventually, it appeared as though he was still at the heart of recruitment for the Colombian businessmen intent on seeing out their football revolution. The *Daily Telegraph* revealed on 24 June 1950 that Manchester United's Charlie Mitten was on his way to Bogotá to play for Santa Fe after being given an invitation 'in the form of a phone call from his friend Neil Franklin'.

At the time, Manchester United were in New York after a successful tour of North America staying at a hotel on Times Square ahead of catching their flight home. For the Santa Fe boss, Robledo, it was an opportune moment for further recruitment. Mitten later recalled what happened when his hotel room phone rang. 'It was Neil Franklin. With him, he said, was the Santa Fe president Luis Robledo – the man who'd signed Neil and Mountford – would I have a word with him? Robledo said he was looking for the best left winger in the world and Franklin had given him my name. I said, "That's very flattering, Mr Robledo. What have you got to tell me?" Robledo said, "The offer is the same as the others – would you like to come down and have a look at us?" I said, "How do I get there?" He said, "We'll arrange it – an air ticket will be waiting downstairs in the foyer for you tomorrow morning. Just make your way down here, and we'll pick you up at the airport in Bogotá."'

Unlike Franklin and Mountford, Mitten, perhaps wisely, decided not to fly out to Colombia under the cloak of secrecy. Instead, on putting the phone down to Franklin and his Santa Fe boss, the Manchester United player took a deep breath and marched down the hotel corridor to knock on Matt Busby's door. Needless to say, the legendary Manchester United manager was not happy.

'He was very angry and upset,' recalled Mitten. Busby told him, 'You can't do that! You're not allowed to!' Mitten countered, 'I can. My contract has expired.' Busby still argued, assuring Mitten that the club was about to offer him a contract. 'Listen, I'm 29, not at the end of my career. Most of our team are 28 or 29, at the peak of our careers, and it's about time we started getting something out of life now. So, he [Busby] quietened down. When I told him the salary, he said, "Do they want a manager?" We had a good chat.'

Mitten went to Bogotá thinking, at the time, he did so with Busby's blessing. 'OK, you'd better go, or you'll die wondering' was Mitten's recollection of his final conversation with the Manchester United boss in their New York hotel. In reality, Busby was furious, losing one of his best players and a man daring to challenge his authority. Mitten was soon to be disabused of any notion of returning to Old Trafford.

Before taking his flight to Colombia from New York, Mitten tried to recruit other United players, including his room-mate, Henry Cockburn. All refused. However lucrative the offers from Robledo, they were not about to follow Mitten and challenge Busby. Mitten travelled alone to be met after the long flight at Bogotá Airport by Franklin, Mountford, their wives and children, and Luis Robledo.

Despite Franklin making the approach to Mitten, it was notably George Mountford who offered the Manchester United player reassurances, paying testimony to the Santa Fe owner. 'I had a chat with Robledo and took to liking him straight away,' remembered Mitten. 'George had told me he was a topper, one of the best. And I did find he was a perfect gentleman. I trained with the club, took a medical and signed a contract. Air fares for me and my family were paid in full.'

After signing his contract, Mitten briefly returned to Manchester to discuss the move with his wife and bring his family out to Colombia. In keeping with promises made to Busby in New York, Mitten went along to Old Trafford to inform the legendary manager of his decision to sign with Santa Fe. He made no attempt to stop him; nor did the FA.

Fatefully, Mitten firmly believed by going out to join Franklin and the other Bogotá Bandits as the *Manchester Evening News* referred to them, he was helping to foment a revolution. Surely, he reasoned it must lead to drastic changes in British footballers' pay and conditions. 'Any player in the land would have gone if offered such an opportunity,' reasoned Mitten. 'Even Stanley Matthews was interested in playing out there. He wasn't too old, always kept himself very fit. He would have filled the place. He would have done it; he was playing so well. I thought this was the start of players' freedom of contract.' This proved not to be the case, at least not in the short term. Indeed, as will be explained later, Mitten as a manager would be among those resisting radical changes to players' terms and conditions.

Franklin's role in recruiting Mitten came as a reassurance to Robledo, the businessman increasingly aware his prize asset was finding it difficult to adapt to life in Bogotá, both on and off the football pitch. There were no such concerns in the case of George Mountford. But rumours abounded back in England of Franklin's unhappiness, and speculation, for all his bombastic defence of his drastic actions, that the former international centre-half was about to return home.

Franklin anxiously tried to quash those rumours. Only a fortnight ahead of Franklin eventually heading home, he defiantly wrote with the help of his mate Capel Kirby from the *Sunday Empire News*, 'Forget any stories you may have heard or read to the effect that our little Potteries colony in Bogotá is divided in loyalty and regrets setting out on this goal-prospecting expedition to Colombia. Nothing could be farther from the truth. Such reports have been spread only by ill-wishers who would like to see our venture end in failure. If they are hoping to see us come crawling home with our tails between our legs, then believe me, they are doomed to disappointment.'

For good measure, the man regularly by then referred to in the tabloid press as the 'Bogotá Bad Boy' lobbed in more provocative comments. 'In England footballers are not so much club members as serfs,' he angrily commented. 'Here in Colombia it is all so different. The people are so hospitable. We are treated as friends and social equals of the club directors who are all men of education and substance.'

Yet for all these protestations Franklin and his family were far from being entirely happy with life in Bogotá. After arriving there to much ceremony, amid much controversy, just a few weeks earlier, they were soon to follow Paul and Hedley on their own way back to Britain. Franklin was about to come 'crawling home' with his tail between his legs.

At first this latest split with a football club was amicable. Officials at Independiente Santa Fe agreed to him accompanying his pregnant wife and their young son on the first leg of the journey back to England to have her baby. Once Franklin sprang another shock by turning up back in Stoke-on-Trent, his Colombian boss, Luis Robledo, was horrified. Effectively his audacious attempt to shake up world football had failed; his prize English asset lost from his grasp.

In a sense, Franklin felt his own decision to return home contributed to his union's failure to secure any meaningful reform of the terms of employment for English footballers. Now, he never quite saw himself as some sort of mid-20th century revolutionary, a man his union at first cautiously saw as one striking a blow for freedom. But he did recognise by dropping his bombshell and taking his flight to Bogotá he had focused the frazzled minds of those running the British national game on the treatment of professional players. Those minds were put at rest once Franklin returned home. Surprisingly, as will be outlined later, there was to be no immediate reform of footballers' pay and conditions.

While in Bogotá, he had received 'countless letters' from players interested in plying their trade in Colombia. 'If only 10 per cent of those players had made the trip, I doubt whether English and Scottish football would have recovered from the shock for years,' Franklin concluded. Then he rather bitterly added, 'That 10 per cent might well have taken the big step but for what George and I were able to tell them from our experience.'

Mountford stayed in Bogotá, and would do so for another year. Franklin though had had enough of playing on mud baths of pitches, the antipathy towards him and the jealousy from other Santa Fe players, the general frenzied atmosphere of Latin American football. In all he played just six matches, winning three, losing two and drawing the other. He was then off back to Blighty facing personal humiliation and professional ruin. He faced the ire of Stoke City, the Football Association and, to compound matters, the furious boss of Independiente Santa Fe, Luis Robledo.

# THE GREAT ESCAPE

AS far as the Football Association, the Football League and the directors of Stoke City Football Club were concerned, one man easily filled any Hollywood role of a stereotypical Latin American villain. That man was Colombian businessman and diplomat, Luis Robledo – the boss of Bogotá football club, Independiente Santa Fe. Quite remarkably Robledo and English bosses also ended up finding something in common. They were united in complete contempt for the behaviour of one of England's finest-ever footballers, Neil Franklin, the de facto leader of British football's 'Bogotá Bad Boys'.

First, Franklin flew out of the UK in relative secrecy with at best disingenuous pleas of innocence when it came to the matter of whether he had secured the agreement of his club. Stoke denied this was the case. So, at best he was being economical with the truth. At worst, he was telling an outright lie. It depends on who the reader might want to believe. Then just a few weeks later he flew out of Colombia, flying into London, and once again claiming he had the permission of his new club, albeit one without the authority from FIFA to sign him in the first place. Santa Fe denied giving him any such permission to return to England.

For the flight home, Franklin insisted it was unplanned. Indeed, this did appear to be the case. He was becoming increasingly anxious over the health and welfare of his wife and their unborn child. She needed to go home to England. The Franklins also learned earlier promises of their child automatically being entitled to British citizenship, even if born abroad in Colombia, were not true. It was a further reason for Vera Franklin to return home to her family in the Potteries.

'It was obvious that Vera could not stay in Bogotá to have her baby,' Franklin recalled in his autobiography. 'She was not keen on the climate, on the living conditions, or on the question of nationality. We both insisted that the new baby should be a British subject without any ifs and buts, and we had been assured that there would be no difficulty on that score. But, as on many other points, we had found that we had not been advised correctly.'

He added, 'Furthermore, like every other woman, Vera wanted to be near her own folk at such a time. She had never been 100 per cent fit in Bogotá and it was obvious she would be healthier and happier going home to have the baby.'

As a result, he approached the Santa Fe club for help. Its directors, much to the 'considerable relief' of Franklin and his wife, agreed she ought to go home to England to give birth. Consequently, the Franklins began to organise the trip home with the help of Santa Fe officials. Additionally, the club agreed for Franklin to fly with his wife, and their son, for the initial stages of their journey to New York, a gesture he described as 'most generous'. Quite naively Robledo and his colleagues felt confident they'd retain their prize English asset.

As his family set off early in July 1950, Franklin assured his club that he would return from New York to Bogotá. He failed to do so. His 'Great Escape' from an El Dorado rapidly turning into a personal hell was underway. Despite this he insisted in his autobiography it was not his original intention to return home to England. 'Let me say here and now that I had every intention of going back to Bogotá. I had my airline tickets which allowed me to land in New York, see Vera and

Gary off to London at four o'clock, and then fly back to Bogotá myself at midnight,' he wrote.

He also pointed out he took no luggage with him to New York, having only the clothes on his back. 'All my other clothes, personal possessions and equipment were back in my house in Bogotá. No man who was running away would run away without his clothes and possessions,' he argued. Among those possessions was a brand-new American car. His friend George Mountford, happily staying in Bogotá for the time being, agreed to help to pack up his clothes and football kit and send them back to the Potteries. The car was a different matter.

On arrival in New York, a city gripped in the middle of a July heatwave, a travel itinerary organised by Santa Fe football club once again began to unravel. 'Naturally, the heat upset Vera and she was even more upset when she discovered that despite all the assurances we had been given in Bogotá, no reservation had been made for her and Gary on the flight from New York to London,' Franklin groaned. 'So here we were, once again, stranded in New York because of a total lack of arrangements.'

The aircraft to London was full. There were no tickets in the names of Vera and Gary Franklin. They pleaded with airline officials to be allowed on to the plane to London but to no avail. Nobody was going to give up their seat. They were stranded in New York. It was off to find a hotel, Luis Robledo's favourite Manhattan bolthole of the St Regis Hotel, not to book a room but to phone him and rant at him.

'I was very annoyed and told him straight that I wasn't going back at midnight and that I was staying in New York until I saw my wife and son fixed up with a passage home,' Franklin explained. 'He pleaded with me to go back, telling me that his reputation depended on my playing on the following weekend. I told him flatly that I didn't care two hoots about his reputation. All I cared about was seeing Vera and Gary safely on their way home and that I was staying in New York with them until that had been arranged.'

Robledo gave up pleading with him and put down the phone, partially reassured that Franklin would be returning to Bogotá, once his wife and child were safely on a flight back to England. As Franklin ended his conversation with Robledo, he heard a familiar voice behind him. It was Evelyn Webber of the *Daily Express*. She was about to file her latest scoop: the Franklins in New York City.

The footballer even described the journalist as a 'friend'. Webber had certainly managed to build up a strong rapport with him and his family. She even offered to put them up in her New York apartment while they tried to arrange a flight to England, this time without the help of the hapless Santa Fe officials.

As the Franklins waited in New York, Vera Franklin, according to her husband, became more what he described as 'depressed and ill'. She was struggling in the heat, though grateful for the air conditioning in Webber's flat, worried about whether or not she would be able to board a plane home, and also fretting about her family from Stoke. They had travelled to London Airport to meet her off a plane she was unable to board. There was no way of contacting them to explain there had been a breakdown in arrangements.

As a result, Franklin took another dramatic decision. He explained, 'Now I ask you, what would be the reactions of any normal man to all that? I was so annoyed at the way I had been let down over Vera's trip home, and I was so worried about her health that I made up my mind on the spur of the moment. I would fly with her to London. Our luck was in. There was a spare seat on the aircraft, so instead of going back to Bogotá, I flew to London.'

Even then, Franklin insisted he had 'every intention' of flying back to Bogotá, once he was happy his wife had settled back into life in the Potteries. She would have to stay with her family given the decision of Stoke City FC to repossess the Franklins' family home in Newcastle-under-Lyme. Her parents' famous son-in-law would be a temporary lodger, one attracting more than casual interest from the neighbours.

He pleaded in mitigation once furious Independiente Santa Fe officials discovered in the newspapers their star English player was back in England. 'All I had done was fly through to London, instead of leaving half-way in New York, and if all the promised arrangements had been made there would have been no question of me doing that. Back home once more, I decided that I would wait and see how things turned out with Vera before flying back to Bogotá, because no matter what has appeared elsewhere, I was still determined to honour my contract.'

Naturally enough the first newspaper to reveal Franklin was on his way back home to Britain just happened to be the *Daily Express*, courtesy of their woman in New York, Evelyn Webber. 'Franklin on Way Home, "I quit Bogotá football" decision at airport' ran the headline to her piece. She insisted, as Franklin boarded his plane on 6 July 1950, he had packed in football in Colombia there and then, contrary to his later claims in the coming days, indeed also in his autobiography published some years later.

'I have quit. My wife did not like Bogotá,' Franklin is quoted as saying by Webber. She made no mention of helping out the Franklin family. Instead, she gushed, 'In New York, they stayed at a film star hotel, recommended by Luis Robledo, Santa Fe official and First Secretary of the Colombian Embassy in London, who arranged for them to go to Bogotá.'

Webber reflected, 'When I last spoke to him soon after he reached Bogotá he said happily over a plateful of steak, "This is the life. I think I might even sign for another year at another £2,500 signing on fee." Tonight, he said over a supper of milk and a sandwich, "The money doesn't mean so much now."'

Bizarrely, Franklin complained no one in Bogotá spoke anything but Spanish. His wife didn't like the living conditions. He added, 'Robledo gave me permission to go to New York and I'm supposed to be back to play on Saturday. I'm sorry to do this [fly on to London] but family comes first.'

After describing the botched travel plans, Franklin, who described himself as feeling 'homesick', then turned to the imminent row with Robledo and his colleagues at Independiente Santa Fe. Facing the wrath of Stoke City and the FA for signing for Santa Fe in the first place could wait.

'I will write to Robledo when I get back,' Franklin commented. 'Will I refund the £2,500 signing-on fee, deposited in my bank at Stoke? I am hoping Santa Fe will not ask me to.' As a precedent, he cited the behaviour of Argentinian players at Santa Fe. According to Franklin, 13 of them had broken their contracts a year earlier without a word being said by Robledo and other board members of Independiente Santa Fe.

'I am not too happy about football conditions there. A lot of Argentinians are in the team and some are difficult to play with,' he added for good measure. 'They withhold the ball from you and make things difficult.' Once this interview was published, Franklin had managed to burn his metaphorical bridges with Stoke City, the English FA, and Luis Robledo of Santa Fe.

Robledo would take a less relaxed view of Franklin's defection than the disappearance of his club's Argentinian contingent. As explained earlier, there were plenty more decent Argentinian players eagerly willing to replace them. For top-class English players, it proved to be a different matter. Robledo all along craved for one of the greats of the English game. He needed to hang on to Neil Franklin. Santa Fe's boss angrily demanded the player return to Bogotá forthwith or refund his signing-on fee. It was to no avail.

Once back in England Franklin quickly discovered any thoughts of resuming his career with Stoke City and England were just a little delusional. He was *persona non grata*. To be fair, he realised this was the case as he boarded his flight from New York to London. 'If England asks me to play again, I wouldn't say no,' Franklin told Webber. 'If I can't play there [at Stoke City], I'll open some kind of business with the money I got for going to Bogotá. But I won't leave Stoke in a hurry. Nor will my wife.'

Intriguingly there was a footnote to Webber's story splashed on the front page of the *Daily Express* alongside the latest accounts of the Korean War. It read simply, 'The England team at Rio leave for home today. It is reported, but not confirmed, that two of the players have signed for Santa Fe.' No names were mentioned.

As the England team, minus their centre-half, were returning home in disgrace after being knocked out of the 1950 World Cup by the amateurs of the USA, it was perhaps best the couple of players tempted to take up contract offers in Colombia kept quiet. It was the first time England competed at a World Cup. It was also the first of England's inglorious failures at a World Cup. Even so and quite remarkably, Neil Franklin's own ignominious return home garnered just as much publicity.

Within 24 hours of arriving back in Britain, Franklin had again changed his story, hoping presumably to appease his paymasters at Santa Fe. Yet again he was front-page news, his story vying for space alongside the war in Korea and the Labour government of Clement Attlee's struggles with his supporters in the trade union movement.

For Franklin, his own terms of employment, for that matter of other English footballers, were of more concern than any other workers. He pledged to go back to Colombia to play for Santa Fe. 'I feel I owe an apology to that grand fellow,

Senor Luis Robledo,' Franklin told reporters. 'I owe an apology to all the people of Bogotá, and I hope they will realise my explanation that Frankleen, that's what they call me, did not deliberately let them down. There's no question of my being a quitter.'

He further explained, 'I did what any decent-minded man would do, stood by my wife because it was desperately important I should. Vera was determined our baby should be born in England. Like every girl in those circumstances she wanted to be with her mother. And Bogotá didn't suit her because of her condition. We expect the baby early in August. Owing to Vera's health I can't go back earlier.'

She was happy to chat to the *Daily Express* and make diplomatic overtures to her Colombian hosts. 'Bogotá was lovely,' Mrs Franklin told the newspaper. 'Everybody was kind. But you can't help it if your heart turns to your own country. I remember sitting in our hotel one day and saying to myself, "You are mutt [fifties slang for fool]. You didn't like the idea of moving from Stoke to Hull when Neil talked of getting a transfer there. And here you are, thousands of miles from both places." I knew then that I would go back to England.'

As for her husband's decision to return with her to London she revealed, 'Neil had arranged to fly back to Colombia five hours after Gary and I left New York. He said he could not think of leaving us overnight. So, he let his plane go and he stayed on. As we drove away from the airport the feeling came over me that this was an omen. Neil and I were not meant to be separated. In the night, he had the same thought. And when we went to the airport the next day it seemed another omen that there was a spare seat on the London plane.'

From her famous husband came this parting shot to *The Express* journalist, 'My hope is that Senor Robledo will understand and also the people of Bogotá.' Warming to his theme, he boasted, 'There's a great future for me in Bogotá.

They hero-worship me. They are counting on me. They hope to build a team around me. I shall be bitterly sorry if anything I've done makes the plans Senor Robledo was building around me go adrift.'

Unfortunately, an angry Robledo was less than understanding. Nor were his Santa Fe team-mates. The people of Bogotá, the volatile Santa Fe fans, those Franklin assumed hero-worshipped him, were unquestionably unsympathetic. Franklin had raised hopes of glory for Independiente Santa Fe, a club founded by Robledo and his friends only a decade or so earlier. Franklin had just dashed those hopes.

Naturally enough Robledo was on the phone from Bogotá to Evelyn Webber of *The Express* in New York with a coruscating description of her new-found friend from Stoke-on-Trent. First off, he revealed he had quit as president of Santa Fe. 'I'm through,' he shouted to her down the line. 'Franklin's last words to me were, "I'll be back. An Englishman's word is his bond." The directors did not want to let him go to New York to see his wife off, but I persuaded them.'

He had initially pleaded with Franklin to return. His mates at Santa Fe didn't want him back. 'He says he can come back to play for us?' Robledo ranted. 'No club here will bear him now and I hope they don't take him back again to play in England. His contract is valid. He signed it in England and I can sue under British law. But that will now be a matter for the [Santa Fe] directors. I feel responsible for bringing Franklin out so I have offered to pay the club whatever they have lost.' He then bitterly complained, 'I got the Franklins a house. They stayed a few days and Mrs Franklin did not like it. I got them another. They stayed one day. Now people in Bogotá will laugh at England.'

Given the expressions of bitterness and resentment expressed by Robledo on behalf of the good people of the Colombian capital, Webber thought it wise to check on the

Mountford family. 'I feel terrible,' George Mountford told her. 'Are Neil and I still friends? Well I suppose so. I'll be embarrassed when I go on the field tomorrow. But I won't go home. We are happy here.'

Years later Franklin gave his sanitised account, mentioning he had been in touch with George Mountford. Their relations remained friendly. 'A lot of sensational stories came out of Colombia, and it appeared that my journey to London had created quite a furore,' Franklin reflected. 'But of course, if their organisation had been as good as their promises, there would have been no flight to London. It would have been Bogotá–New York–Bogotá.'

Charlie Mitten revealed that the British Consul also decided to check up on Mitten and the Mountfords, concerned for their welfare rather than, in the case of the *Daily Express* correspondent, trying to grab a story. 'Santa Fe officials were furious when news reached Bogotá that Franklin had returned to England,' remembered Mitten. 'There were some hard things said to George Mountford and myself about Englishmen breaking their word.'

It turned sinister for the two remaining English players at Santa Fe, thanks to the surprise defection of their friend Franklin. 'For weeks afterwards, private detectives followed us around everywhere, obviously checking up that we were not going to leave town,' Mitten explained. 'Even the British Consul was concerned and asked whether we were happy in Bogotá and asked whether we intended to honour our contracts. He said British prestige was at stake.'

Back in Stoke-on-Trent, Franklin composed an explanatory letter to Robledo after reading the Colombian diplomat's bad-tempered interview with Evelyn Webber of the *Daily Express*. 'In this letter, I told him of our experience in New York, of how Vera was very ill, and of how disappointed I was of the breakdown in the arrangements I had been assured were made by the Club,' he said. 'I also told him that I would soon return to play for Santa Fe and that no one need worry. No one seemed to believe that attitude.'

Regretfully, he recognised he had not just angered Santa Fe fans. Back home in the Potteries the gravity of his bombshell decision to turn his back on his hometown club and, to compound matters, his country on the eve of a World Cup, began to sink in. A section of Stoke City fans and England fans failed to recognise him as a football revolutionary, a 'champion of freedom' for professional players across the land. To them, albeit a minority, he was a greedy mercenary, nothing less, nothing more.

'They [the Colombian fans] seemed to think that I had ducked out of Bogotá and that I had no intention of returning,' Franklin lamented. 'Even some of my own countryfolk thought that. Many of them wrote long and abusive, and of course anonymous, letters to Vera and me, and I can only hope that they did not represent the majority of opinion in Britain.'

For the time being, he ignored the brickbats, verbal or written, being directed at him by irate fans across the transatlantic divide from Stoke-on-Trent to Bogotá. Many others were prepared to give him a sympathetic hearing, not least his fellow pros. Franklin went along with Stoke goalkeeper Dennis Herod to Burslem Cricket Club, ostensibly to play as 'ringers' for a Port Vale side in a charity match. The throng of supporters gathered for the game sat in shock once they recognised the man walking out on first wicket down for the Vale cricketers. It was Neil Franklin. He was out for a three-ball duck, disconsolately walking back to the pavilion before being mobbed by autograph hunters.

'I was much happier to meet my former Stoke City colleagues the day after returning from Bogotá,' Franklin remembered. 'I played with them in a cricket match for a combined Stoke City and Port Vale team. I got a duck!' He then posed the question, 'If I was so sure I was going back to Bogotá, what made me decide to stay in England? The simple fact that the Santa Fe officials announced that I was not returning, said I had broken my contract and let them down.'

Robledo and his Santa Fe directors did not want to listen to what they deemed lame excuses, especially from a man less than open with his true motives for turning down an England international call-up for a World Cup, a scenario they themselves had engineered. Given the Colombians had lost their prize asset there also came the dawning realisation their raid on British football talent was coming to an ignominious end. Their mood turned to bitterness and anger.

As Franklin simply put it, 'They just would not understand my point of view, so I decided I would be foolish to go back. They would have made misery for me. I would have been let down on the field by my Argentinian colleagues, and they would have seen to it that the crowd turned against me. And when a Colombian crowd turns against you it is time to duck.'

Instead, he chose to face the wrath of his home club and country. Quite reasonably a footballer, unbelievably managing to generate more headlines than his former England team-mates being sent packing from a World Cup, decided he would in his words, 'rather be an unpopular figure here in Britain than an unpopular character in Bogotá. It is safer.'

Even the man acting as Franklin's unofficial public relations agent in Bogotá offered little comfort. 'Franklin's actions in coming home instead of bidding his wife goodbye in New York and turning back looks like a double cross,' Capel Kirby almost mournfully wrote in the *Sunday Empire News*. 'Unfortunately, that seems to be the general impression, especially in the north [of England] and in the Potteries where he was once a hero.' The last comment must have hurt.

For the time being Franklin settled back to life in the Potteries, playing cricket rather than football, going out fishing in the Staffordshire Moorlands. His Stoke City club chairman, Harold Booth, commented, 'Franklin's return is a surprise. The club has decided nothing yet. The FA's international committee will meet soon to discuss the Bogotá signings and Stoke's attitude will be governed by its findings.' Franklin, a glittering football career seemingly in tatters, awaited his fate, as did the other rebels as they planned their return home to Britain.

# FRANKLIN'S PUNISHMENT

JUST a few months earlier Neil Franklin revelled in the role of one of the 'crown princes' of mid-20th century English football, universally acknowledged as the finest defender in the land. As he sat in his wife's parents' home at close of summer in 1950, he must have felt more the 'clown prince' instead. He flew to Bogotá full of optimism, relishing a new venture, free of the shackles imposed on him and his fellow professionals by the rulers of English football. A golden future beckoned for, in his naïve and rather patronising view, an English footballing missionary landing on the shores of Latin America in search of football's El Dorado.

Sadly, for Franklin and his family, those dreams began to turn into a nightmare even as he made his flight to Bogotá. Travel plans began to unravel, accommodation failed to live up to expectations. Playing frenzied, violent football proved a joyless experience. Furthermore, from being an English football hero, he turned overnight into a sporting pariah. For some he was a hero blazing a trail in the campaign to give those offering up their 'working man's ballet' to millions their just rewards. To most, Neil Franklin had turned into a mercenary villain.

Quite bizarrely there was almost as much focus on Franklin and his fellow rebels following their Colombian adventures as on the hapless England footballers' humiliation in Brazil. Franklin's escapade in Colombia may have turned out to be a joyless experience. His former England international team-mates experienced worse. They lost two of their three group games at the 1950 World Cup in Brazil, including that infamous 1-0 defeat to a United States team largely made up of amateurs. Yet, as much newsprint, if not at times more, was devoted to Franklin and his band of mates in Colombia as the humiliation of the hapless English football team in Brazil.

It was for two reasons. Firstly, the World Cup was not taken too seriously by British sports writers of the day, harbouring a rather insular attitude to global football. It would only be truly shattered once Hungary thrashed England 6-3 at Wembley in 1953.

A young Ron Atkinson – later to become Manchester United manager – played against Franklin in the twilight of his career. Atkinson summed up the mood. He told me, 'I am not sure at the time the World Cup mattered. As far as we were concerned, international football was the home countries [England, Scotland, Wales and Northern Ireland]. It wasn't until Hungary came to Wembley and turned us over that we thought that there was anything outside. It wasn't until the World Cup in 1954 [won by West Germany] and the European Cup began a couple of years later that people really started to take notice of another world out there.'

The second reason, along with their curious indifference to the World Cup, was that the English footballing establishment felt genuine alarm at the Bogotá players' rebellion, fearing it had reignited the spluttering campaign for footballers to be paid according to their box office value.

In his travails with Stoke City's board, Stanley Matthews regularly insisted top footballers were worth as much as film stars of his day. To him it was no surprise that regular England internationals, other than Franklin, had been approached by Colombian representatives of the DiMayor league. Aside from Manchester United's Charlie Mitten, his clubmates, John Aston and Henry Cockburn, received offers but rejected them. Both went to Brazil with the England World Cup squad.

Matthews denied he took any offer to play club football abroad 'seriously' and in the late eighties told David Miller, 'Not many players in the league were too impressed with the [Colombian] offers. We knew we were tied by a contract; and although that contract was unfair, nobody thought about the alternatives too much. What's more, those that went to Bogotá soon got homesick.'

By way of a stark example of the unhappiness over pay and conditions, Matthews pointed to the experiences of Willie Watson, a dual international footballer and cricketer, and member of England's 1950 World Cup squad in Brazil. On travelling down from Yorkshire to London for a training session ahead of the trip to Rio, Watson upgraded his train fare from third class to first class. He reasoned that the train was full and didn't think it was right to stand up all the way before working out with his fellow international players. To his annoyance, the FA rejected Watson's expenses claim for the upgrade.

In his autobiography *Double International* Watson revealed, 'On my return from Rio, I received a cheque for £60 being my fee for the trip [now roughly £2,000 allowing for inflation]. I didn't play in any of the three matches and included in my letter was a note saying that I overcharged on expenses. I must say this annoyed me. I received sixty pounds for going to Rio and not kicking a ball, and at the same time I lost something like three hundred pounds by not playing cricket for Yorkshire. Yet, here was the FA quibbling about expenses. I don't think I've been so hopping mad.'

Such was the discontent over pay, international players briefly considered breaking their Football League contracts, even as Franklin skulked back home from Colombia. It was not to go off to an unauthorised league. Instead, a more novel plot was hatched – set up a touring party to play exhibition matches, football's version of basketball's Harlem Globetrotters. Franklin, Mitten and the other Bogotá Bandits no doubt would have been welcome to join.

None other than Franklin's old mate, Sir Stanley Matthews, revealed this bizarre plan to be the brainchild of former Scottish international defender, Andy Beattie. 'Of course, there was resentment over the size of our wages,' Matthews recalled. 'Andy Beattie had said some of us should get together and go touring all over the world, that twenty players should break away from the Football League and get paid what we were really worth.'

Matthews revealed that Beattie put the idea to him along with many other players. He did not name them. The plan was considered unworkable. 'We all wondered where we would be able to play such matches? Normal stadiums would be unavailable because of FIFA regulations,' Matthews told David Miller for his authorised biography. 'Anyway, nobody had the nerve. Andy always thought that his idea was the future but most of us just accepted the situation.'

Previous hollow threats of strike action to boost footballers' wages had been easily seen off. Losing players to foreign predators was another matter. Given, aside from Colombia with its unauthorised DiMayor league, the international market for players was beginning to open up, there appeared to be a serious threat to football's established order. Instead of recognising the need for at least cautious reform, the FA and the Football League hardened their stance. Franklin and company did possess the nerve to rebel. They needed to be punished severely. How the FA responded to the exodus to Colombia would be a matter of intense scrutiny.

Just like Franklin, the media in late summer 1950 was in limbo, waiting for the FA to act. Just to fill up some column inches, there was even febrile speculation on the eve of a new football season over the whereabouts of Franklin. Had he gone back to Bogotá after all? News agencies quoted an anonymous official at Stoke City, not only confirming the player had not been in contact with the club, but also bizarrely claiming it was not clear whether he was still in the city of Stoke-on-Trent.

Given his wife was about to give birth and her stated wish to be with her mother while doing so, it was a fair bet he was in the vicinity of the North Staffordshire Royal Infirmary. Franklin sat at his in-laws' home in the Shelton district of the city, the area in which he grew up, weighing up his options or rather lack of them. Going back to Colombia was certainly not one.

The Stoke official being quoted by regional newspapers summed up the club's position in selecting a team for Stoke's opening match of the 1950/51 season against Newcastle United. There would be no room for Franklin or for that matter George Mountford, who was still in Colombia. 'In any case the FA have yet to come to a decision on the entire situation,' he commented. 'Bob McGrory has selected a team in which no space has been left for Franklin.'

Stoke's vice-chairman, Arthur Preece, weighed in with some additional pithy comments. 'We have not seen the player since he left for Santa Fe with George Mountford,' Preece told the press. 'It was the player's duty to get in touch with us. The club has made no effort to speak to him and is not likely to.' Franklin knew he was *persona non grata* with Stoke City. For the time being he had no intention of contacting his old employers at the Victoria Ground. He waited, instead, for contact from the FA.

On 24 August 1950, Vera Franklin gave birth to a daughter at the Haven nursing home in North Staffordshire, a cause for celebration following weeks of turmoil and, at times, misery. On the same day, Sir Stanley Rous, the FA secretary, popped a letter in the post to Neil Franklin. It was not to congratulate him on the new arrival.

'When I made the decision to remain in Britain, I knew that the Football Association would have to move in my case. I didn't know what to do. I made no move to approach Stoke City, and when the season opened, I spent the day fishing,' Franklin later explained. 'On August 25th 1950, I received a letter signed by Sir Stanley Rous, the Secretary of the Football Association. It told me quite bluntly that I was suspended, and any move to lift the suspension must come from me.'

This 'blunt' letter from Sir Stanley Rous stated, 'I am writing to inform you that for leaving their clubs while under contract and for playing in unaffiliated football in Bogotá in contravention of the Football Association, the Football League and club rules and regulations, the following players are suspended forthwith: N Franklin (Stoke City), W C Higgins (Everton), C Mitten (Manchester United), G F Mountford (Stoke City). The suspensions must remain effective until the players apply to this Association for, and are granted, reinstatement.'

In some respects, confirmation of a suspension from playing professional football and the summons to appear at a disciplinary hearing, if he wanted it to be lifted, came as a relief to Franklin. In his autobiography he commented, 'So that was that. If I wanted to get back into English football, I would have to appeal to the Football Association and take what punishment they cared to mete out to me. If, of course, I made no move towards reinstatement, then I would have to suffer some punishment in return for any reinstatement that might be granted.'

At first, Franklin put his application on hold. As he put it, he had too much on his mind given the birth of his daughter. He wanted to spend as much time as possible with his wife and their newborn baby before focusing on his application for reinstatement. If and when he was allowed to return there was also the additional problem of finding a new club. As far as Stoke City were concerned, he was out the door.

His manager did agree to allowing him to train at the Victoria Ground but on his own, in the afternoons and evenings. From some of the players he received a warm welcome as he turned up at lunchtimes but not from all. There was outright hostility from those believing, far from being a rebel striking a blow for professional footballers, he was a greedy mercenary, one turning his back on his hometown club and country.

Once the FA formally suspended him the facility was withdrawn. McGrory informed him the directors thought it was 'better for all concerned' if he stayed away until the FA ruled on his case. Instead, it was back to the Stoke Police sports ground for solo training sessions. It was then that the new Stoke captain Jock Kirton revealed the level of hostility towards Franklin from some Potters players.

Kirton commented, 'When Franklin visited the ground for training before the Stoke directors had considered this decision [by the manager McGrory], several first team players took exception to the matter. As captain I was deputed to raise the matter with Mr McGrory, who in turn reported this minority attitude to the directors.'

Just to further stress most players were quite comfortable with their former captain returning to the Victoria Ground, Kirton insisted, 'The training ban was purely a decision of the directors. Since then a number of the players have made it known that they are not opposed to Franklin training at Stoke and do not identify themselves with the present position. They have nothing personal at all against Franklin.'

A few short years earlier Franklin, as Stoke captain, offered words of comfort to Stanley Matthews as he fell out with the club. Franklin's reassurances to Matthews of there being no animosity towards him were met with relief. The overtures from Kirton to Franklin were of limited comfort. Looking back in hindsight, he was quite sanguine about the matter.

'It was a change from what I had been used to but I had no grumbles,' he mused. 'I had gone to Bogotá of my own free will. I had come back of my own free will, and I had asked for reinstatement of my own free will. So, I had to be prepared to be an outcast until the powers-that-be decided what to do with me. And, of course, I had to take anything that was coming my way.'

Franklin was informed he would need to go before a joint committee of officials from the FA and the Football League at a hearing at the Adelphi Hotel in Liverpool on 2 October 1950. Of course, he was not allowed representation from the Players' Union. But, much to his eventual relief, a director of his club agreed to go along with him to provide a character reference.

It followed revelations the Stoke City directors had fallen out among themselves over just how to deal with Neil Franklin. One or two were surprisingly sympathetic, mostly though for their own commercial reasons as much as any warmth for Franklin as a human being and as a Potteries lad, one of their own. Another group wanted him cast to the football wilderness, something within their power. If they had their way, he would never play professionally again.

Those taking the latter view won the argument. Above all, they recognised a prodigiously talented homegrown player might generate some lucrative income for a cash-strapped club. As Clifford Webb of the *Daily Herald* newspaper put it, 'However badly Franklin may have behaved, he is still a most valuable asset. A good many clubs would be glad to buy him for a record fee.'

It wasn't just Stoke City officials angry at Franklin letting them down – Santa Fe directors simultaneously demanded revenge for him walking out on them. It threatened to sue him for the return of his initial lump sum payment of £1,000 [roughly £35,000 in today's money] plus damages for alleged breach of contract. Both of Franklin's clubs seemed determined to make his life a misery. It was all becoming a little farcical.

Commenting on Santa Fe's angry overtures, Franklin casually told the English press, 'Until I receive official notification of the matter from the solicitor acting for the Santa Fe club, I'm not going to unduly worry. My chief concern now is to have my reinstatement application considered by the FA and to get back into English soccer. If I can do that, the Santa Fe business takes second place. If any litigation does take place, there could be quite a showdown on the issue.'

In the meantime, Stoke's directors settled their differences and decided to support Neil Franklin's application to the Football Association to be reinstated as a professional footballer. Much to their disgust, the FA seemed reluctant to set a date, leaving the player and club in a state of limbo.

This reluctance followed legal advice. At the time, several directors of English football clubs were suspended from all football activities for a variety of misdemeanours, mostly financial. If the suspension of Franklin was lifted, along with the other football rebels, then the case for lifting all suspensions became inarguable. It meant effectively an amnesty for all football miscreants.

Franklin took the short trip from the Potteries to Liverpool along with Stoke City's vice-chairman, Arthur Preece and the club's manager, Bob McGrory. On arrival in Merseyside, there were some well-wishers to greet the man vilified by many in the English game, but hailed as a 'hero' by the Players' Union. It was the weekend of the professional footballers' annual golf tournament. Many of his old mates were staying at the Adelphi, and as much as he had split opinion over walking out on club and country, most were more than happy to wish him well.

It was a joint hearing of the FA and the Football League. From the FA the chairman, Amos Brook-Hirst, fellow FA council members Albert Ansell and Sir Leslie Bowker were present along with the secretary, Sir Stanley Rous. The Football League was represented by its president Arthur Drewry, who had also served since the Second World War as an England international team selector. As the man who had allegedly overruled the England manager, Walter Winterbottom, in his team selection for the game against the USA, he might have been quietly relieved by the fuss made over Franklin's antics. Drewry was joined by the Liverpool FC chairman, Will Harrop, the League's chairman, Joe Richards, and its secretary, Fred Howarth.

Before hearing what Franklin had to say for himself, they listened in silence to a character reference delivered by Preece, the Stoke director. 'It was gratifying to learn that the vice-chairman, Arthur Preece, described me as the nicest player Stoke ever signed,' Franklin mused in his autobiography years later. 'That must, I am sure, have helped me, because if my club had attacked me and shown me in a bad light, the punishment might well have been more severe than it was.'

It was then Franklin's turn to take a deep breath and begin to make his case to a group of men viewing him, to put it politely, with immense disdain. 'I realised that it would be silly to hide anything, so I told the Commission everything,' Franklin recalled. 'Not a single incident was left out. The story I told was pretty well the same story as I have related in the previous chapters, the story of the offers, the prospects, and the fulfilment, which did not quite measure up to the promises. I admitted frankly that I made a mistake, but at the time I thought I was doing the right thing, not only for myself but for my wife and family.'

He also, for all the antagonism from the FA and the Football League, gratefully noted, 'There was no bitterness on either side at the inquiry. It was just an honest effort by everyone to get the whole matter settled and as far as I was concerned, the sooner it was settled the better.'

It had been a workmanlike session, settled before lunch. The joint Commission quickly came to a conclusion. Neil Franklin's suspension would be lifted on 31 January 1951. It was a relief to Franklin. In the circumstances, he thought he got off lightly. 'Not too bad' was his own verdict.

Sir Stanley Rous went out to address the waiting media at the Adelphi Hotel, reading out the following statement:

> A report of a joint Commission appointed to hear an appeal by N Franklin, a professional player of Stoke City FC against a suspension imposed on him for leaving his club whilst under contract and for playing in unaffiliated football in Bogotá in contravention of the Football Association, the Football League and Club Rules and Regulations. The Commission having questioned Franklin on all the aspects of his case, decided that his suspension will be removed as from the 31st January 1951. In the meantime, Franklin remains a retained player of the Stoke City FC, but may not receive wages or payment of any kind from his club in respect of the period of his suspension.
>
> The Commission also decided that no payment should be made by the Stoke City Football Club to Franklin in respect of the unexpired period of his contract from the date of his leaving this country. In communicating the foregoing decision to Franklin, the Chairman informed him that the Commission deprecated his actions for:

1) *Giving untrue reasons to the Football Association for not wishing to be considered for international matches.*
2) *Deceiving his club and breaking his contract.*
3) *For making statements to the press and allowing articles to appear under his name likely to bring the game into disrepute.*

A copy of the verdict was duly sent to Franklin's temporary home in the Potteries, a further copy sent to Stoke City FC at its Victoria Ground. Vice-chairman Preece, and manager Bob McGrory formally informed him at the meeting in Liverpool that he was no longer welcome at their football club, the one he supported as a boy, played for with distinction since a teenager but fell out with on not just one or two but three occasions. Franklin had in quite bizarre and dramatic circumstances finally got his way. He was on Stoke City's transfer list.

'One thing was certain. Stoke City and I had come to the parting of the ways,' Franklin ruefully reflected. 'The club announced officially that it would "be better if we parted company" so I was left with a lot of time to ponder on the tragedy of the situation. Here was I, a player, who had wanted to get away from Stoke City because of the niggling attacks on my style of play. Now I was being given that release, but only after the long-drawn-out business of going all the way to Bogotá and being plastered all over the front pages of the newspapers.'

The editorial in his local newspaper, the *Evening Sentinel*, not surprisingly made for uncomfortable reading. 'In North Staffordshire, opinion upon "the Franklin case" has been sharply divided,' it noted. 'Some would have "welcomed the prodigal", others consider that his actions might have debarred him from resuming what has been a very distinguished career in the great national game. Now the decision of the joint Commission of the Football Association and the Football League should everywhere be accepted in the same way that the judicial findings of the court are accepted. Obviously, there is no harshness here because authority was flouted.'

It concluded, 'Neither Stoke City, whose interests have been adversely affected, nor the player himself view the decision in any light other than fair and just. All followers of the game, realising that we all make mistakes and have to pay for them, should now recognise the fact that, when the period of suspension expires, Neil Franklin will have paid fully for his transgressions in infringing the laws and the rules of the game. Indications are that he will not again play for Stoke City. If that be so, it may be not the least part of the punishment suffered by one of the most accomplished players ever produced by this North Staffordshire district, so rich in football tradition.'

Following Franklin's disciplinary hearing, the player seen as the ringleader for an act of rebellion to shock the British sporting nation, 'punishment' was meted out one by one to the others daring to ply their footballing trade in a foreign land without permission from the English and Scottish football authorities. Just like Franklin, one by one they also brought home tales of woe, sob stories unlikely to wash with the patrician rulers of the FA.

# QUASHING A FOOTBALL MUTINY

ALL too briefly for the Colombian dreamers running their outlawed DiMayor league, they threatened to undermine and shatter the world order of the sport of association football. Ultimately, they were doomed to failure. FIFA, with the English arch-schemer Sir Stanley Rous to the fore, managed to reassert their authority.

Domestically, Rous recognised it was vital to do the same at home, fearing those growing opportunities for players going abroad. Perhaps grudgingly, he later recognised Franklin and his mates as more than just rebels but perhaps even pioneers.

In his 1978 autobiography *Football Worlds: A Lifetime in Sport*, Sir Stanley wrote, 'From my own and the FA point of view there was no bar to movement within clubs affiliated to national football associations, although the League was naturally resistant to depredations from Europe as well as South America.' Above all, Rous was troubled by the overtures from Italian clubs noting, 'The FA made no objections to the trickle of players abroad to clubs within FIFA's orbit. John Charles, Denis Law, Gerry Hitchens, Eddie Firmani and Jimmy Greaves were free to make a name and money in Italian football after Franklin pointed the way.'

Franklin, of course, never went to Italy to play club football. It was the plain audacity in going abroad which appeared to leave Rous troubled. Going to an unauthorised league served almost as a convenient technicality to punish Franklin. Jimmy Greaves returning homesick from Italy as Rous believed Franklin did from Colombia was of odd comfort to the former FIFA boss. In fairness, he did profess to admire them for their ability as footballers.

Back in 1950, Franklin was considered by Rous as no pioneer, nor his mates in Bogotá. Along with the rest of the English football establishment, the then FA boss set about quashing a mutiny. They were deaf to calls for reform. Failure at a World Cup, the flight of top stars to Bogotá, the temptation of others to do the same, mattered little.

Meantime, as foreign stars, especially the British, began to return home from Colombia or, in the case of the Argentinian stars, depart for alternative destinations, the Colombian FA, Adefutbol, reapplied to FIFA for recognition. FIFA agreed at a special conference held in the Peruvian capital Lima but only on the condition that the remaining foreign players packed their bags and left Colombia. A deadline was set for 31 December 1953. The dream of a football El Dorado was over.

Against the backdrop of spiralling political violence, to the point of a de facto civil war and inevitable economic turmoil as a consequence, DiMayor, at least the model pursued by Luis Robledo and company, became unsustainable. Franklin and his fellow British rebels no doubt suspected as much.

George Mountford and Charlie Mitten stayed at Santa Fe to see out their contracts, only returning to England once FIFA bosses met with the godfathers of Colombian football at their fateful meeting in Peru. There was no golden future. Yet again El Dorado turned out to be a myth. Independiente Santa Fe suffered financial collapse with Robledo resigning, even garnering sympathy and support from Mitten. 'He'd put in a lot of money. He deserved better than that,' reasoned the former Manchester United player.

Everton's Billy Higgins returned from Bogotá just as Neil Franklin was learning his fate at the Adelphi Hotel in Liverpool. The Evertonian immediately applied for reinstatement with the FA setting a date for a hearing in London of 7 November 1950. On the eve of his disciplinary hearing the contrite Higgins declared, 'Naturally, I am a bit anxious to know what action the FA and the Football League are likely to take in my case. I am hoping that the governing body will temper justice with mercy as they have invariably done with offenders against football laws in the past.' He added, 'I can only await the verdict. The sooner it is over the better. My own personal problems, however, are of a minor consideration. I shall have to face the music and I am ready to do so.'

Just as Franklin was unimpressed with his club Santa Fe, Higgins felt the same of Millonarios. 'Take it from me, Bogotá is no football paradise, even for a player on top salary and drawing big bonuses. The money sounds tremendous, whether you say it quickly or slowly, but the high cost of living skims the cream off it,' he informed readers of the *Liverpool Echo*. As almost an act of contrition he noted, 'I realised more than ever the English players even though they don't get as much [money] as they feel they should be in a paradise compared with Colombia.'

Higgins faced the same group of men as those who sat in judgement on Neil Franklin. This time the joint FA and Football League Commission delayed its deliberations. Higgins was forced to wait for some of them to decide on another matter, the England team to face Wales. Not surprisingly they had a problem position. Who to play centre-half, the position vacated by Neil Franklin? In the event they opted to create some football history by calling up Arsenal defender and Middlesex cricketer, Leslie Compton, brother of Test cricketer Denis. Thanks to Franklin's antics, Leslie

Compton became the oldest England player, at the age of 38, to make his full international debut, though admittedly he had played wartime internationals before being usurped by Franklin.

Once the committee men eventually finished sitting down in judgement on the Everton centre-forward, Bill Higgins, they delivered what many observers considered a light verdict. His suspension would be lifted almost immediately on 30 November 1950, a contrast to the prolonged suspension imposed on Franklin. Afterwards, Higgins commented, 'I am happy that it is all over. I feel that the committee were sympathetic, and realised that I had learned my lesson.'

As he left FA headquarters as a relatively relieved man, Hearts winger, Bobby Flavell, was writing from Bogotá to the SFA asking for his case to be considered. Unlike his British colleagues Flavell had adapted more enthusiastically to Colombian football, too enthusiastically. He managed the nigh on impossible feat of being sent off, earning a seven-day suspension from the Colombian FA. By Christmas 1950 he was back home in Scotland for good, hoping to overturn the SFA's suspension for going out to Colombia in the first place.

Flavell landed at Prestwick Airport on Friday, 15 December 1950 along with his wife Pearl and their one-year-old daughter Linda. Somehow, he had managed to persuade the Millonarios club to pay for their flight home with the promise of returning to Bogotá. He had no intention of doing so. 'They think we are just home for a holiday or I don't think they'd have let us go,' Mrs Flavell helpfully informed reporters waiting at the airport.

On 24 January 1951, the SFA executive committee ruled on Flavell's case. Fearing more Scottish players might be tempted to fly out to South America, it decided to make an example of the Hearts player. It fined him £150 and set a date for the lifting of his suspension for the end of the 1950/51 season. 'When the suspension is up [1 May 1951], the season is over. This sentence is going to cost me nearly £500,' Flavell commented.

Asked if he would consider going back to Bogotá, Flavell responded, 'No. I think it's washed up over there.' Shunned by his club Hearts in the same manner as Stoke treated Franklin, Flavell even feared his football career was over. 'I suppose I'll need to take my medicine, pay up and hope for the best,' he mournfully commented. 'I'll have to find a job or something and it won't be easy. I sold my hairdressing business some time ago. I've no trade, but I did some office work before I turned full-time footballer.'

So, just two English remained in Colombian football: Manchester United's flamboyant forward, Charlie Mitten, and Franklin's Stoke City mate, George Mountford. Neither appeared to do so with a great deal of enthusiasm. Mitten's wife, Betty, returned home to Liverpool for Christmas 1950 along with her three children, John, Charles and Susan. 'Bogotá just needs getting used to,' she ruefully told the *Daily Mirror*. She was not going back, though hinted her husband might try to extend his contract. Mitten instead decided to return home to his wife.

'My contract expires in June and I shall be returning home,' he wrote in his letter to his wife. 'I must return to Manchester United, but whether they decide to transfer me or keep me is something I shall have to talk over with the directors.' Once she revealed the contents of the letter, British football writers concluded, 'the Bogotá bubble has burst'. To compound matters, they noted FIFA had settled its differences with the Colombians. The British football rebels were coming home whether they liked it or not.

On his arrival back in England in the summer of 1951, Mitten admitted to feeling more than a tad embarrassed given the fuss over his homecoming. Throughout his time in Bogotá, Mitten like Franklin milked the British press, sounding off to anyone caring to listen about the injustices suffered by professional footballers.

At Heathrow Airport, a throng of journalists gathered, hungry for more juicy quotes from Manchester United's rebellious star player. The pilot even went on the plane's tannoy asking Mitten's fellow passengers to let him off first to face the crush of reporters waiting in the arrivals lounge. 'Adulation never meant a thing to me. It always embarrassed me,' Mitten later commented. 'I liked to let my football do the talking. But it really hit me that publicity was part of the game that day sitting in the aeroplane coming into Heathrow on the way back from Colombia. Until that moment, I was not really aware how much the press and football feed off each other.'

His disciplinary hearing was set for 18 July 1951. As he walked into the hearing at a London hotel, the Football League secretary, Fred Howarth, apparently greeted him with the comment, 'Hello Mitten. I see you've caused us some trouble.' Mitten recalled cheekily replying, 'The Lord helps those who help themselves.'

As far as Mitten was concerned, he was up before a 'kangaroo court' with men on the bench displaying little interest in football despite running the English national game. 'Every question at the tribunal concerned finance,' lamented Mitten. 'How much had I made? What was my contract? What were the bonuses? I told them nothing. What business was it of theirs? The whole tone of the tribunal was that here was a thieving little boy who had to be taught a lesson.'

To his angst, there was little support from the Players' Union, despite its earlier support for the Bogotá rebels. Nor of course did he receive the backing of his club, quite the opposite. Manchester United manager, Matt Busby, and its secretary, Walter Crickmer, sat alongside him at the tribunal. Yet it was left to the Football League and FA's committee men to tell him that his club had decided to put him on the transfer market. They even implied that Manchester United felt 'forced' to sell him given his recalcitrant activities.

Mitten's punishment turned out to be the harshest – fined £250 and ordered to carry on serving his suspension until 31 December 1951. Even Franklin got off more lightly. The main reason was the contention that Mitten had broken not just one but two contracts with his club, something he denied.

His club claimed he had broken his 1949/50 season contract once he turned up in Bogotá in June 1950. But he had also re-signed for Manchester United to play in the 1950/51 season and was therefore in breach of another contract. 'This tribunal of nine tradesmen wanted to discipline me somehow. They were determined to make an example of me,' lamented Mitten. 'Those nine people sitting around the table on that committee were so stupid; they refused to see that it was all going to change.'

Charlie Mitten never played for Manchester United again. It was not just the men he dismissed as 'tradesmen' wanting to make an example of him. To Mitten's shock and horror Matt Busby felt the same. As many more players were to learn, you didn't cross Matt Busby. Foolishly, Mitten thought he might be welcomed back at Old Trafford, even as he claimed turning down a chance to join Di Stefano at Real Madrid. The Spanish club's boss, Santiago Bernabéu, apparently offered him a contract while he was still in Bogotá. Instead, Charlie Mitten ended up at Fulham.

As for George Mountford, the man flying out to Bogotá with the most high-profile rebel Neil Franklin, he also decided to honour his one-year contract with Santa Fe. It is clear he did so reluctantly. At one point, Mountford wrote to his parents informing them he was bringing his young family back home to England, booking a flight to New York, planning to board a cruise liner due to arrive in Southampton on 5 November 1950.

Mountford's bosses at Santa Fe scuppered the homecoming plans, refusing to release him from his contract but mindful, given the imminent and inevitable collapse of their unauthorised enterprise, they were not going to be able to field him for much longer. His dad, George Mountford senior, told the Stoke *Sentinel*, 'We are disappointed George is not coming yet glad in a way that the whole thing will soon be finished.'

Even former diplomatic colleagues of Santa Fe's Luis Robledo at the Colombian Embassy in London saw fit to comment, no doubt after being briefed by him. One official told British journalists, 'I have received reports from Bogotá that none of the British players in Colombia will be playing there next season. All will seek to end their contracts before the end of the season.'

The anonymous diplomat pointedly added, 'I believe that the lenient view taken by the Football Association over the Franklin case has made the other players feel that it is easy to get back into British football. That and homesickness, which some of them are feeling, is the reason.' Final confirmation for British observers of what some viewed as Colombian football's act of 'piracy' was over.

Mountford finally returned to England in May 1951. On arrival in the Potteries, he received a significantly much warmer welcome from Stoke City than the reception the club gave to its former England centre-half. There would be no debate over whether or not to banish George Mountford to the football wilderness. Stoke's manager, McGrory, wanted this Bogotá rebel back in his club's red and white stripes, leading the attack.

Mountford dutifully put in his appeal to the FA for reinstatement. His hearing was scheduled for 19 June in Manchester with McGrory and Stoke's vice-chairman, Arthur Preece, going along as they had done with Franklin, some nine months earlier. For Mountford, the joint FA and Football

League Commission fined him £250 and agreed to lift his suspension from 3 September 1951, meaning he would miss the first fortnight of the forthcoming season.

Afterwards, the FA's Sir Stanley Rous dryly commented, 'Mountford remains a retained player of the Stoke club, and although he can receive no wages until September, he will be allowed to train on the club's ground.' Intriguingly, he also offered, for the first time, a degree of sympathy for the players who had taken flight to Colombia observing Mountford, 'indicated to the commission that the promises made by the [Colombian] negotiators to players in this country were not kept with regard to housing etc.' Even the patrician boss of the FA appeared touched by some of the contrite players' tales of woe.

As by accompanying Franklin, he helped to lead the mini exodus of leading British footballers to Colombia, he got off relatively lightly. George Mountford accepted his punishment. His club, quite oddly, appealed, complaining it was too harsh. McGrory wanted him available for the start of the season. But the FA refused to answer his entreaties. His player went off to train with his old friends at non-league Kidderminster Harriers.

He went back to his hometown club because there was nowhere for him to live in the Potteries, given Stoke City had repossessed the house the club had given him. He returned in September, the keys to his house returned and a place in Stoke City's starting line-up guaranteed. George Mountford was welcomed back to the Potteries as a prodigal son, yet the hometown poster boy Franklin was treated by the embittered Potters board as a pariah.

Yes, Manchester United's Mitten was handed out the harshest punishment but only on a technicality. At the time, Franklin was the poster boy of English football, the 'crown prince' reduced to the status of 'clown prince'. His union feted him as a 'hero'. Yet the Bogotá affair had set back its campaign for better wages and conditions for British professional footballers. The FA, the Football League and the clubs had reasserted their authority. They were even able to make light of a forthcoming government inquiry into the treatment of professional footballers, one in part arguably prompted by Franklin's flight to Bogotá.

In the meantime, Franklin had a few months off to mull over how to perhaps rebuild a once glittering career. The omens were not good, cast out by his hometown club, temporarily banned by the men selecting the England international. Franklin could have been forgiven for packing the game of football in altogether. He chose not to. 'Perhaps, football is a drug,' Franklin commented. 'Once you have tasted it you cannot leave it alone.'

*England's Neil Franklin dispossesses Scotland's Jimmy Delaney after the forward had beaten goalkeeper Frank Swift to a through ball, Wembley, 12 April 1947 (PA Images)*

*Franklin pictured at Stoke City's Victoria Ground after being made captain of his hometown club, August 1946 (Getty Images)*

*England line up for the anthems ahead of playing world champions Italy at the Stadio Comunale in Turin on 16 May 1948. The team was Frank Swift, Laurie Scott, Don Howe, Billy Wright, Neil Franklin, Henry Cockburn, Stanley Matthews, Stan Mortensen, Tommy Lawton, Wilf Mannion and Tom Finney (Popperfoto/Getty Images)*

*Neil Franklin holds off Italian centre-forward Guglielmo Gabetto as England captain and goalkeeper Frank Swift makes a save at the Stadio Comunale, Turin, 16 May 1948. England won the match 4-0. ( Keystone/Hulton Archive/Getty Images)*

*Stoke City centre-half Neil Franklin enjoys a cup of tea before leaving for the ground on match day, 19 February 1949 (Haywood Magee/Picture Post/Getty Images)*

*After England training, Franklin signs a football watched by his team-mates Stan Mortensen, Jimmy Dickinson, Jackie Milburn and Tom Finney along with an excited group of autograph collectors, Cardiff, 14 October 1949. (Bob Thomas/Popperfoto/Getty Images)*

*England team group versus Wales, Ninian Park, Cardiff, `16 October 1949 (top l-r) John Aston, Bert Mozley, Neil Franklin, Bert Williams, Jimmy Dickinson and Johnny Hancocks. (front l-r) Tom Finney, Jackie Milburn. Billy Wright, Stan Mortensen and Len Shackleton. (PA Images)*

*Neil Franklin's last game for England, playing against Scotland at Hampden Park, Glasgow on 18 April 1950, goalkeeper Bert Williams making a save. A 1-0 victory assured World Cup qualification for the finals in Brazil just a couple of months later. Franklin failed to turn up. (Popperfoto/Getty Images)*

*Ready for Take Off, Neil Franklin poses for photographers at the Victoria Ground Stoke, 13 April 1949 (S&G/S&G and Barratts/EMPICS Sport)*

*England footballer and ex-Stoke City centre-half Neil Franklin returning from Bogotá, Colombia after walking out on his club to play for the South Americans' Santa Fe, 8 July 1950 (Davis/ Express/Getty Images)*

*George Mountford, Neil Franklin's Stoke City and Santa Fe team-mate, pictured at Southampton docks wih his wife Phyliss and their children, Jill and Kay, after returning from Colombia, 15 May 1951 (Express/Getty Images)*

*Back in a Stoke City shirt, Neil Franklin pictured with England international winger Mark Chamberlain at the Victoria Ground Stoke, 15 August 1983 (PA Images)*

# FALLEN IDOL

SAT at home, cast as he put it into the 'football wilderness', the rebel leader Franklin refused to dwell for too long on a disastrous career decision. Most of the Bogotá Bad Boys managed, albeit with a degree of difficulty, to pick up the pieces of their careers – some even thrived. For the 'poster boy' Franklin it was a different story.

His punishment, he accepted without complaint. 'I couldn't grumble,' Franklin noted in his autobiography. 'I had broken the laws, which have been laid down by the Football Association, the Football League and the clubs, so it was inevitable that they should hand out punishment. But to those who like to throw bricks, let me say and underline the fact that I returned to the country of my own free-will (greatly encouraged, though, by the action and inaction of the Santa Fe club) and it was of my own free-will that I applied to the FA to inquire into my case [for reinstatement as an English professional footballer].'

In conclusion he commented, 'I knew when I wrote to Sir Stanley Rous that my action could only result in punishment. It was worth the punishment, though, to get back into English football. Football, you see, is my life. I chose the profession myself, and I loved every minute I spent in the game.' Presumably out of support for the other rebels being punished as mercenaries, he also insisted he had never met a player who didn't love the game.

There was just one snag for Franklin. He needed to find a football club to embrace him in his love of the game. There were plenty of prospective suitors, but crucially the biggest top-flight clubs appeared wary. Normally, they would bombard the likes of Stoke City with record bids for the transfer of a player once regarded, until his act of rebellion, as an automatic choice for England.

Premature retirement was not an option. As much as he loved the game, he wanted to play, not watch on from the stands, especially not at the Victoria Ground as he wanted to be out on the pitch in the red and white stripes of Stoke City rather than be back stood on the terraces with his old mates.

'Sitting in the stands or standing on the terraces watching your pals go through the motions is not enough,' he explained. 'You find yourself playing the game with them and for them. Your neighbouring spectators look at you with queer looks on their faces as you mutter to yourself, "Take it this way, boy. No, not that way." And so, you go on. You even move your legs and your body as your imagination transports you from your seat or position on the terraces right out there on to the field.'

As Stoke City's board considered whatever offers came in, the Victoria Ground switchboard hardly lighting up with calls from other clubs, Franklin prepared for his return, training yet again alone at the Stoke Police sports ground. 'Yes, football is a drug. Once it has you in its clutches it never lets you go, but there cannot be a pleasanter drug, or indeed a more beneficial one,' he enthusiastically proclaimed. 'So, throughout my suspension I counted the days until I would be back in the fighting line.'

Fearing any comeback might backfire on him as he came under inevitable close scrutiny, Franklin added, 'I religiously prepared myself for my comeback for I knew that all eyes would be upon me, and I also knew that many people were already throwing me on the scrap heap as a has-been. I knew that my past reputation would not help me one little bit for the average sporting follower, or rather sport follower, has an incredibly short memory.'

Thanks to his infamy, Franklin understandably reasoned that any criticism might be inevitably harsh. Sympathy for a player, who had turned his back on club and country, was notable in most quarters from football fans for its absence. 'I knew then that I would come back as "Neil Franklin, the man who went off to Bogotá",' he acknowledged. 'I knew that people would watch me critically, be only too glad to find faults with my speed or with my play, and be quite unconcerned about writing me off as finished.'

Franklin boasted he 'trained hard' despite enduring the fate of the loneliness of the long-distance runner rather than enjoy the camaraderie of team training. Intriguingly, despite admitting at the time he was a poor spectator, Franklin did return to the terraces, as part of his preparation for a comeback. 'I watched all the football I possibly could, trying to spot faults, and pick up tips,' Franklin revealed.

'One great thing I did learn was that you can see more from the stands and terraces than you can from the field of play itself,' he confided. 'Your field of vision is much wider. You can see the pattern of the game. You can see how moves are built up, how they can be counteracted.' In describing football as tactically akin to a game of chess he used the curious phrase, 'there can be an antidote to every antidote'. Despite this observation, he still insisted professional players and coaches knew far more about the game than the average fan just popping along to a game on a Saturday afternoon.

As he left his disciplinary hearing at the Adelphi Hotel in Liverpool, speculation raged over where he might go to resume his career. Franklin made protestations to the contrary in his autobiography. Yet despite not kicking a ball in anger for months on end, his name was rarely out of the newspapers.

'Once you are out of the game you are out of the limelight, and overnight you can be forgotten,' Franklin reasoned.

This might generally be the case, for not just footballers but any sport stars, but such was Franklin's notoriety in the mid-fifties there was an insatiable appetite for stories of the man considered to be the leader of the 'Bogotá Rebels'. Citing interest in the Stoke player from Derby County and Wolverhampton Wanderers, Clifford Webb of the *Daily Herald* wrote, 'Only 26 years old and with more than 20 consecutive appearances for England, Franklin is certain to command a fee pretty close to the existing record.'

From the *Daily Telegraph*, its football correspondent Frank Coles commented, 'There will be keen competition to bid for his [Franklin's] services if he is put on the transfer list.' There was no 'if' because both the club and the player made it clear their parting of the ways was mutual. He was on his way. But much to both their surprise, the offers trickled rather than flooded in to the offices of Stoke's Victoria Ground.

Along with Leicester, Derby and Wolves, West Ham United expressed interest in signing Franklin. Also, Arsenal were thought to be interested in securing Franklin's services. The Gunners' manager, Tom Whittaker, denied any interest, preferring instead to stick with 38-year-old Leslie Compton, the player FA selectors chose as Franklin's replacement in the England international team.

Franklin's friends in the game monitored events with increasing bafflement, not least his England mate, Tom Finney. He described the failure of England's top clubs to show any interest in signing Franklin as 'criminal'. At one point, he even went to see his Preston manager, Cliff Britton, urging him to make a bid. 'I understand Neil Franklin is heading back [from Colombia] and looking for a club,' Finney recalled telling Britton. "What an excellent signing he would be for us," I said. The manager shrugged his shoulders in a gesture of "thanks but no thanks" and I couldn't believe it.'

Franklin was forced to consider dropping down a division in order to rebuild his shattered career. During the course of his perennial requests for a transfer from Stoke City, Franklin's name was constantly linked with ambitious Second Division club Hull City. It appeared more likely Humberside was his destination of choice, once he began to turn up at the club's ground, Boothferry Park, to cast an eye over potential team-mates and opponents.

On the evening of 21 October 1950, Neil Franklin held talks with Hull City's board of directors after watching the club's Second Division game against Coventry City. He had gone there after again being approached by the Hull manager, his old friend and England colleague Raich Carter. 'Franklin came over at our invitation so that he could have a look at Hull, see our club, meet our directors and officials, and form general impressions as to whether he would like to come here or not,' commented Hull's chairman, Harold Needler. 'He did not commit himself but is going to give us a definite reply later.'

Five days later, Hull City formally put in its bid for Neil Franklin, offering the sum of £20,000. Members of the Stoke City board were individually contacted by the club's manager Bob McGrory to garner their opinion. Each one rejected the bid. 'Surely, we can attract more money from a First Division club,' they reasoned.

As a result, an asking price was cited. Any bid above a then British transfer record of £25,000 would be accepted. Vice-chairman Arthur Preece told the press, 'It is not our wish to make a long drawn out affair of Franklin's transfer. If we receive a bid above £25,000, we shall act without delay.'

From the *Yorkshire Post* came a ringing endorsement of Franklin, despite him being pilloried as 'the Bogotá bad boy' among many journals of the day. Richard Ulyatt wrote,

'Franklin remains the outstanding English centre-half of the post-war period. His successor in the England team has not yet been found; his record of having played in every major post-war representative game for England until the end of last season is likely to stand for many years.'

Citing the views of football fans on Humberside in regards to Franklin's controversial reputation, he commented, 'I do not know what the public demand is in the dock area of London or in Derby, or in Leicester, but I can testify in the tremendous public interest there is in Hull in Franklin's future. On my last visit supporters were discussing him; one of them casually mentioned that he would subscribe to a fund for him if the club opened one to secure Franklin's transfer.' Ulyatt, though, further ventured Hull City, wherever it found funds from, would not be able to afford Stoke's asking price.

Ignoring setbacks and doubts over the club's ability to come to a deal, Hull City persevered, even rumoured at one stage to be offering one of their rising young prospects of the day in a part cash and part player exchange – a young man by the name of Don Revie. 'I am quite happy with Hull City,' responded the future Manchester City cup winner and Leeds United manager. 'I have never wanted a move, nor do I intend to ask for one. Moreover, I have never heard any suggestion in official quarters that the Franklin negotiations would involve me in any shape or form.'

As Revie made it clear he had no intention of moving to Stoke, his ambitious board at Hull managed to find the cash to raise their bid. The Stoke board met to consider the latest offer on the evening of 9 November 1950. This time, they agreed, the fee reportedly £22,500, £750,000 in today's prices despite being a near record bid back then.

A statement was put out on Franklin's behalf by his manager, Bob McGrory. It read, 'I [Franklin] am very pleased that it has been settled. It has been a worrying time but now that I know I am going to Hull City; I can get down to preparing for the day when I shall be able to play again. The sooner I am settled in Hull and training for the big kick-off the better. That is my main aim now. It has been a bad business but I shall be all right when I am playing again.'

On more than one occasion Franklin fell out with McGrory. He was not the only high-profile Stoke City player to do so, Stanley Matthews chief among them. Nevertheless, McGrory, for all their differences over playing styles and tactics, admired the local lad he guided through the ranks at Stoke City to England stardom. Franklin left with his old manager's best wishes.

From his new manager at Hull came enthusiastic backing. 'Neil Franklin is the best centre-half in the game and I am pleased he is coming to join my club. I have played with him in many international games and I know his worth,' proclaimed Raich Carter. Feelings of admiration were mutual, Franklin declaring Carter as a 'great student of the game'.

Hull City's delighted club president, Kenneth Percival, declared, 'As soon as I received the news from Stoke, I had a word with Neil Franklin. He was delighted that the whole matter had been cleared up, and he is looking forward with enthusiasm to the day when he can settle down at Boothferry Park and do his stuff.' As an opening practical measure, Percival revealed he would ask the FA for a ruling on whether Franklin could train at Hull while remaining under suspension. The FA, in a first act of conciliation towards the recalcitrant player, agreed.

Because he was still under suspension, Franklin was unable to formally sign for Hull once terms were agreed with Stoke. Effectively, the transfer was a gentlemen's agreement between directors of the two clubs and the player. Meantime, Franklin went to Humberside to hunt for a house his new club had agreed, much to the annoyance of Football League bosses, to buy for him. He was not allowed to put pen to paper until 1 February 1951.

'I felt like a schoolboy on the first day of the holidays when I had signed for Hull,' remembered Franklin. 'I threw myself into training with more vigour and enthusiasm than I had ever done before, and when Raich Carter asked me if I felt up to playing for the first team on the Saturday I felt like replying, "Just try and keep me out."'

His comeback was greeted with enthusiasm, not just by Hull fans, but the wider football public, not least those concerned by the state of the England national team, just months after their humiliation at the Brazil World Cup of 1950. For them, Franklin, for all his hot-headed faults, remained the best centre-half in the land. On the day Franklin made his comeback England's international selectors were due to meet to pick the side to play Scotland, doing so after a less than convincing victory over Ireland in Belfast. Surely, it was argued, the FA must swallow its pride and restore him to the England line-up.

Among those advocates of an England recall for Franklin was the legendary sports editor of the *Daily Express*, later tragically to become one of the victims of the Munich air disaster. On the morning of the defender's return to competitive football on 3 February 1951 against Blackburn Rovers, Henry Rose commented, 'I have been asked a dozen times whether Franklin will be chosen by England if he shows no decline in form after a seven month lay-off. My reply was a definite "yes". I am on the side of the selectors and Franklin.'

He further explained, 'The player committed no crime when he went to Bogotá to earn more money. He committed one when he broke his contract and came back. For that, like anyone else culpable, he has paid the penalty – a four-month suspension and loss of wages. Having paid the penalty, he should not be victimised. I do know the FA were deeply impressed by the manner in which Franklin made a clean breast of all the details of his runaway trip and return.'

There were doubts in some quarters as to whether or not Franklin ought to be recalled, summed up by John Thompson of the *Daily Mirror*. Thompson wrote, 'Many football lovers must be wondering whether technical skill will be considered all-important by the selectors when they name England's centre-half. Even if Franklin regains his old greatness should he usurp Laurie Hughes of Liverpool [England's centre-half in the last match against Ireland]?'

He concluded, 'Some will say that Franklin has already been sufficiently punished for his Bogotá blunder. Others might claim that it would be wrong to reward him with an international cap, the symbol of success which every boy who plays football dreams of gaining.'

Sadly for Franklin, the latter view prevailed. Henry Rose of *The Express* and other leading English sports writers sympathetic to Franklin were too generous in their opinion of the FA's powers of forgiveness. As far as Sir Stanley Rous and company were concerned hell would freeze over before Neil Franklin donned an England jersey again.

'That was my great ambition and I tried everything I knew to produce the form worthy of a restoration to the England side,' he lamented. 'The Press rooted for me. Many fans rooted for me, and frankly I often thought my chances of selection were good, especially when the England selectors were struggling to solve the centre-half problem. But the selection never came and I was bitterly disappointed.'

As he took to a football field in a competitive match for the first time since his infamous Colombian adventures, Franklin still harboured hopes of an England recall. More than 39,000 fans turned out to greet him in a city keener on rugby league than association football. The club had boasted prior to the match it expected Franklin's debut would guarantee a crowd of 50,000.

Unsurprisingly with his lack of match practice he struggled but still took many plaudits. The *Daily Herald*'s David Williams wryly noted, 'His playmates got only a £1 bonus instead of two because of his first-half slip-up that gave Blackburn's Paul Todd the first of two goals. Neil's positional genius was there, however, and judging by the way he waved his colleagues into clearances, Hull look like having two tactical directors, Raich Carter [Hull's manager] looking after things in front.'

Alan Holby of the *Sunday Express* wrote, 'Franklin certainly lacked match practice. But all the old touches and moves were there. The skilful placing, the lovely heading and that perfect positional sense. In my opinion, Franklin will regain his place as England's centre half.'

The Press Association's correspondent described his performance as 'satisfactory', arguing his 'surety of touch' and 'accuracy of timing' would come with match practice. Contrary to the views of the FA selectors he further argued, 'England will need the man who came back from Bogotá.' The advice of those advocating an England recall for Franklin was of course ignored.

In his autobiography, Franklin commented, 'I would love to have gone through my first game for my new club without making a serious error, but football doesn't allow luxuries like that.' At the time he took comfort from the plaudits pouring forth from the press box, not least the thoughts of Henry Rose. Writing in the *Daily Express*, this doyen of football writers noted, 'Franklin played as well as ever, in my judgement.'

As for Franklin's howler, Rose commented, 'He had always taken risks in the goal-mouth, and the fact that he failed to trap a ball almost on his own goal-line and presented Paul Todd with a scoring chance is to me sufficient evidence that he has not been affected by his long rest. Only a player confident of his own ability would have dared to stop the cross. The ordinary man would have belted it away first time.'

Franklin declared his Hull debut himself as 'satisfactory'. Yet he was destined never to relive past glories, left in the cold by England's selectors, partly down to the obduracy of those running the English game but mainly because for the first time in his career he was about to be bedevilled by, in comparison with his antics out in Colombia, the relatively mundane matter of injuries.

'I had read about players who received injuries from which they never recovered, but I never thought that I should be the subject of one of these hard-luck stories,' Franklin ruefully recalled. 'Hitherto in my career I had been lucky. True, I had been injured but nothing serious had ever gone wrong.' In December 1951, the injury curse struck Franklin, with what he described as a 'gammy knee'. It put him out of action for the rest of the season.

A surgeon in Newcastle-upon-Tyne operated on his knee, hoping to save a career now in jeopardy less than a year after Franklin returned to action after his Bogotá ban. 'Nursing my way back to fitness was a long and laborious job,' Franklin commented. 'At times it was heart-breaking but, as every footballer knows, the important thing when you are fighting an injury is not to give up the struggle.'

Briefly, he was able to make another comeback. Restored to full health and appointed as the Hull City captain, Franklin lined up for the beginning of the 1952/53 season for his club's opener in the Second Division away to Everton. Hull won 2-0, drawing rave reviews, not least of the performance of the club's centre-half. Henry Jones in the *Sunday Express* wrote, 'One-time England centre-half Neil Franklin was the kingpin in a great Hull City victory.' The *Sunday People*'s Ray Raymond described him as 'the focal point of this triumph', while Franklin's old friend Henry Rose hailed his performance as up to a 'display of his best England vintage'.

Sadly for Franklin, his latest comeback lasted just a few short weeks, forced off the field in excruciating pain during a testimonial match against Lincoln City. 'I always thought the period of suspension was bad,' Franklin bitterly recalled. 'I then thought that nothing could be worse than my first period on the injured list, but this second dose was worse than anything I have ever experienced.'

Already his thoughts turned to retirement, a premature end to a great but turbulent career. Almost inevitably for a professional footballer of the day, life as a publican beckoned. At first Hull City thwarted his plans, the club's directors still hoping their star turn would return to his playing best. He vainly hoped much the same. His request to return to the Potteries to run a pub and commute to Humberside was, at first, turned down flat.

Hull City, a club only a year or so earlier harbouring grand ambition, was, as Franklin put it, in the 'doldrums'. From promotion hopefuls, dreaming of a first taste of top-flight English League football, a relegation battle loomed. Hull's directors were desperate for him to return. 'I was continually asked whether I was anywhere near playing fitness. Every time I was asked, I had to shake my head sadly,' Franklin admitted. 'I knew that if I went into a game without being 100 per cent fit, I might break down again and this time there would be no return. I would end the season as an incurable cripple as far as soccer was concerned.'

Hull City survived relegation. The injured Franklin's relationship with his club and manager did not survive. Once again, he was at odds with his bosses at a football club. This particular set on Humberside reluctantly agreed in July 1953 to him taking a pub in the Hanley district of Stoke-on-Trent, the Blue Bell Hotel where he would live and work while still playing from time to time for Hull City. They even went as far as asking Stoke City to allow him to train with his old mates.

Not surprisingly, the Potters refused. A similar request was sent to Port Vale, then based in Hanley, only once again to be met with a refusal. Franklin was back training at the Stoke Police sports ground.

From then on, his first team appearances for Hull City were few and far between; one of the greats of the game was reduced to playing regular reserve-team football. Inevitably, Franklin went on the transfer list but there were no firm offers for his services. Hull City priced him at £5,000, too much of a risk for football clubs of the day, especially for an injury-ravaged and temperamental player.

There was one last hurrah. Port Vale relented, giving him permission to train with its players. Then, at the start to the 1954/55 season for Hull City, his manager Bob Jackson took him by surprise by not only restoring him back to the first team centre-half berth but also giving him the club captaincy, 'a wonderful gesture' acknowledged Franklin. It meant, for his latest comeback, being reunited with his old boss Raich Carter, by then manager of Leeds United, Hull's opponents on the opening day of the season.

Franklin described marking one of Leeds United's all-time legendary players John Charles as an 'ordeal'. Hull lost 2-0, Charles scoring both goals. An even greater ordeal, in his mind, was to come, playing against Stoke City at the Victoria Ground. 'I had not played on the old ground since my flight to Bogotá and I wondered how the crowd would receive me,' Franklin explained. 'As soon as I trotted on the field the fans gave me a great welcome and that put my mind at rest.' It was a form of redemption.

The 10,000 Stoke fans who turned up to watch the match and give Franklin his 'great welcome' probably wished they had never bothered. It was a goalless draw between the two clubs; Stoke, with whom Franklin nearly won a league title less than a decade earlier, arguably in the greater decline.

Still, there were plaudits for the former England centre-half. Bill Fryer of the *Daily Dispatch* wrote, 'Neil Franklin may or may not be England's centre-half but at least I have not seen a better one this season. How pleasant it was to see a centre-half with his thoughts constantly on attack, even from his own penalty area, how pleasant to see such calmness under stress.'

Remarkably, talk of an England recall lingered, despite the player struggling with injuries and labouring with a Second Division football club. This was partly down to the inability of the England selectors to find a player capable of making the England number 5 shirt his own. Once Sir Stanley Rous and England selector, Joe Mears, turned up for a game between West Ham United and Hull City the press speculated they may just swallow their pride and welcome Neil Franklin back as the prodigal son of English football. They were mistaken.

Sadly, Franklin put in what was described as an 'average' performance in a 1-1 draw. Frank McGhee of the *Daily Mirror* observed, 'He [Franklin] has shivered under the chill of the cold shoulder from them ever since he went to South America in 1950. Since then thirteen men have been tried for the problem position but never did they consider Neil, the Bogotá Badboy. This was his big moment. He said, "I've been playing and feeling as well as ever." Then he trotted out to give an ordinary, solid Division Two club performance.'

Lingering hopes of a return to international football were dashed. In truth, he was struggling to remain as an effective player in domestic football. 'Happy though I was in Hull's first team, there was one dark cloud,' lamented Franklin. 'Despite the letters, the newspaper articles, and general public opinion, I remained on the outside looking in at the England team. Everybody but the selectors were shouting, "Franklin for England" and Franklin himself was desperately keen to get back into the famous white jersey.'

Franklin's career petered out, dogged by persistent injury and, as a result, unable to hold down a place in an extremely average Second Division team. From his pub in the city centre of Stoke-on-Trent, the former England star indicated he wanted a move. Such was his desperation, Franklin opted to drop down yet another division, moving to a club neighbouring the Potteries, Crewe Alexandra. He did so despite the club consistently finishing rock bottom of the old Third Division North.

Going to the Railwaymen of Crewe metaphorically signalled his playing career, once a glittering one, had hit the buffers. They even struggled to raise the money for his transfer. Hull City demanded £2,000 but eventually settled for £1,250 with £500 of the sum being raised by Crewe's supporters' club. Despite being a fading star, Franklin's capture in February 1956 guaranteed a boost in attendances at the club's Gresty Road ground even if only for a short while.

'I have always played for a struggling club and liked it,' Franklin commented, forgetting he had captained a Stoke City side vying for the league title less than a decade earlier. Reassuring his fans, he went on, 'I am as fit as a fiddle and hope to go on playing for some time.' He brought a touch of class to the Alex defence but it made no difference to the results.

There was little change in fortune for club or player. His low point occurred in a game at home to Cheshire rivals, Stockport County. Throughout Franklin's domestic and international career, including his stint in Colombia, he only managed to score one goal. Against Stockport he was given the opportunity to double his tally from the penalty spot. He missed, skying his kick over the bar.

Crewe's perennial applications for re-election to the League failed to end despite fielding a man once considered the best footballer in England. Franklin once again felt the need for a move, ironically enough ending up at Stockport County in October 1957, almost exactly a year after his infamous penalty miss against them. Taking up the role of player-coach, he didn't last long there either.

A once glittering career petered out in failure. Franklin's demise was best summed up by a despairing Tom Finney. 'With all due respect to Hull, Crewe and Stockport,' wrote Finney, 'they were hardly clubs at which you would have expected to find a footballing star such as Neil Franklin. He was for the bigger stage but one ill-advised decision cost him his career.'

Franklin's final hurrah as an English professional footballer came with the Southern League part-timers of Wellington Town, once again as a player-coach. There had been wild rumours of him teaming up with the Tottenham Hotspur manager, Bill Nicholson, as a member of the coaching staff at White Hart Lane. Those rumours proved unfounded. It was off to seeing out a playing career and carving out a coaching career in non-league football. In any event, his career as a Staffordshire publican, running the Blue Bell Hotel in Hanley, appeared at the time to be more of a priority.

As Franklin saw out his playing career in non-league football, a future Manchester United manager was beginning to make his way in the game. Ron Atkinson recalled with fondness coming up against the former England centre-half while playing for Oxford United in a game against Wellington Town. He told me how he was proud to have played against him, share a pitch with a legendary footballer.

But how was he going to get the better of him? Atkinson's manager at Oxford, then known as Headington United, just happened to be Stoke City's centre-half in the 1930s and helped to mentor the young Franklin. Arthur Turner warned Atkinson of one of Franklin's favourite tricks. 'Franklin had many,' Atkinson told me.

'Before the game Arthur Turner took me to one side and described to me this little trick of Franklin. He liked to feint to pass back to the goalkeeper, and then turn past his opponent, and dribble out of the penalty area. He did it once to me but I remember Arthur Turner's advice and put in a tackle. I robbed Franklin of the ball.' Ron described the moment to me with a chuckle as if it was one of his proudest in football.

After a playing career in the lower divisions of English football, Ron Atkinson went on to become one of the country's finest club managers with not just Manchester United but, among others, West Bromwich Albion and Aston Villa. Put simply, great players enjoying international stardom rarely make great coaches or managers, Franklin being a prime example.

Franklin had joined non-league Wellington Town from Stockport County in June 1959 as a player-coach. He lasted just 12 months there, moving across the Shropshire town to the Cheshire League side Wellington Sankey, a former works team run by the GKN engineering company. Franklin didn't last long there either, despite being promoted to manager. His business commitments, running a pub, took priority. Just turning out as a player with the old works team suited him better.

Still, a man in love with football refused to give up on the prospect of a career as a coach. As a former international footballing centre-half, deemed ahead of his time, he held strong views on how the game ought to be played. It originally brought him into conflict with Stoke City's manager, Bob McGrory, as a prelude to his infamous decision to take up a contract in Colombia. As a player, he wanted to be remembered as a pioneer of the beautiful game rather than a mercenary rebel. In playing retirement, he desperately wanted the chance to share his vision of the game with young professionals, moulding them as a coach at a Football League club.

To showcase his coaching credentials, Franklin, once seen as one of England's finest only to be cast into the football wilderness in an act of seeming madness, decided to go back on his travels. There was another call offering the chance of an adventure on foreign shores. He packed his bag in the summer of 1963 after being offered the job of coaching APOEL Nicosia, runners-up in the Cypriot league and cup winners the season before he took up his post. For the club's new head coach, it meant his first and only taste of European club football.

For Cypriot football in general it was an opening foray into European football. It began well for Franklin and his players. Up against the Norwegian side SK Gjøvik-Lyn in their first tie, the Cypriots won the first leg at home emphatically, 6-0. They completed the job in the away leg with a 1-0 win for a 7-0 victory on aggregate. This European football lark seemed easy. As soon as the draw came through for the next round, Franklin realised his players were going to be in for a rude shock.

APOEL Nicosia drew Sporting Clube de Portugal, otherwise known to English fans as Sporting Lisbon. If Franklin took his players to the Portuguese capital with a sense of trepidation, it was justified. They were thumped 16-1. 'You have to remember that this was the first time APOEL had played under lights, the first time they had ever played on grass, and it was also the first time they ever tried to play in the rain,' Franklin told the *Daily Mirror*'s Frank McGhee.

He then sorely commented, 'It bucketed down, the pitch was a swamp, my lads, all of them amateurs, were pathetic. None of them wanted to play and they did not realise it was possible to play in those conditions. They didn't know how to tackle the job and just stood there and took it.'

The second leg was less embarrassing, losing just 2-0 for an 18-1 defeat on aggregate, still a European club record. It was of scant consolation to APOEL that Sporting Lisbon went on to win the competition, knocking out Manchester United on the way.

Life in the Mediterranean sunshine was brief for the perennially restless Franklin, just a few short but eventful months. This time there were no quibbles with a decision to leave one club for another. In Colombia, Franklin and his Bogotá rebels were largely isolated from the civil disturbances raging there. It was not the case for him in Nicosia. As Christmas approached in 1963, Cyprus was riven by its own bitter sectarian and nationalist conflict between the Greek and Turkish communities. APOEL Nicosia bosses reluctantly advised their English manager to return home to England for his own safety. Fortunately, he did so with the offer of gainful employment.

Finally, a Football League club was prepared to give one of England's finest-ever players a chance in management. Colchester United, a Third Division club, ignored his chequered rebel past, offering him the manager's post. It was a lower division club but, once Franklin took up the Colchester manager's job in December 1963, the former rebel was now a member of the football establishment given a 'free hand' to put his views into practice. No doubt his board heard with relief his promise not to do anything 'drastic'.

Franklin's tenure as manager of Colchester United was, to put it mildly, fitful. Eighteen months after being appointed manager his club was relegated to the Fourth Division. These days it would almost certainly guarantee the sack. But the Colchester board of directors decided to back Franklin.

Armed with his own coaching checklist, emphasising dedication to honing ball skills, supreme levels of fitness but curiously a liberal dietary regime, Franklin set about restoring his club's fortunes after suffering the indignity of relegation. Perhaps in hindsight, his players had eaten too many pies during their relegation season. More ball practice and fitness sessions were needed. His loyal Colchester directors were rewarded with immediate promotion the season after relegation, albeit by the tightest of margins.

On the last day of the 1965/66 season, Colchester United lost 2-1 at Newport County, leaving Franklin and his players anxiously awaiting news of other results. For five minutes after the final whistle, Franklin sat in the press box alongside *The People* newspaper correspondent and ITV Sport commentator Hugh Johns. 'I would never have dreamed I could experience this sort of nervousness,' he gasped to Johns. Finally, he heard that Luton Town, Colchester United's nearest rivals, had only managed a 1-1 draw at Chester.

It meant that under the odd system of goal average used at the time, Franklin's club had secured promotion back to the Third Division. For the record, Colchester's average was 1.48, Luton's 1.28. 'Colchester go up – by a decimal' ran the headline to Hugh Johns's piece in *The People*. 'We'll need strengthening next season,' reflected Franklin in a statement of the obvious. But within two years, he once again suffered relegation. This time he also suffered the sack. His brief foray into coaching and football management was at an end. Franklin packed in the professional game, once and for all.

It was an ill-starred flirtation with coaching and management, never capturing the heights Franklin rose to as a player. Sadly for Franklin, any hopes of a glorious end to that playing career, perhaps even a belated England call-up, given the selectors' persistent failure to find an English international class centre-half, were dashed.

At the twilight of his playing career, not once did Franklin reflect that he had only himself to blame for being an England international outcast. Instead of being feted as an all-time great of the English game, Neil Franklin was cast as the Bogotá Bad Boy, the rebel mercenary. For the patrician rulers of England's national game of football, players needed to know their place, tugging their forelocks and just being grateful to be paid whatever was on offer to play the game they loved.

Franklin insisted he had no regrets but he paid a heavy price for his own act of rebellion and trying to secure a better financial future as a professional footballer, arguably heavier than any of his fellow Bogotá rebels. It meant to serve as a deterrent to any high-profile player daring to challenge the rulers of the English game. If so, it failed. Franklin's treatment at the hands of the FA, the Football League and his club Stoke City did not end the campaign for better terms and conditions for professional footballers – far from it.

# EL DORADO'S AFTERMATH: THE CAMPAIGN FOR REFORM

ALRIGHT, even Neil Franklin's greatest fans might dismiss his flight to Bogotá, along with the other British rebels, as nothing more than a brave but futile effort in the campaign for improving professional footballers' wages. As much as his supporters argued otherwise, it was an abject failure. He was no revolutionary 'hero' as his own Players' Union tried to make out in the spring of 1950. Quite the contrary. Franklin just went to Colombia intent on securing his own future, the same for George Mountford, Charlie Mitten, Billy Higgins and Bobby Flavell. Nevertheless, their actions did begin, albeit over the course of a decade and more, to pave the way for reform of UK footballers' pay and conditions.

Of course, as the rebels headed for Colombia, they wanted the best in the long term for all their fellow professionals, hoping their gripes about being treated badly by English and Scottish clubs might be heard. Yet above all, Franklin, for one, maintained he was quite understandably focused on the interests of himself and his young family. So was Mountford, so were all the other British players going to Colombia, the Bogotá Bad Boys or 'Bandits' as they were termed in the national press.

Why would they not be acting for their own best personal interests? Their actions, led by Franklin, made absolute sense to many football fans of the day. Forget turning your back on club and country as the chance of becoming world champions beckoned. At the time, the World Cup did not matter. Well, it didn't until England were humiliated at the 1950 tournament with Franklin absent from the side.

Yet this mini rebellion, actually in fairness a massive shock to the English football establishment with Franklin refusing to go to a World Cup, cut more than just a raw nerve. It was a kick in the men in blazers' metaphorical body parts. Indeed, shock waves reverberated through the national media of the time, reflecting interest in the country at large. As eventually borne out by the holding of an official inquiry into professional footballers' terms and conditions, reform seemed inevitable.

It turned out not to be the immediate case. Reform took another decade or so. There's no doubt those flights to Bogotá by British players turned out to be a failure for campaigners hoping it might immediately provoke a change of heart among the British establishment. Thanks, in part, to the then weakness of the Players' Union, there were to be no fairer terms and conditions of work for British footballers of the early fifties. It was clearly not the end.

There was a chance to regroup, perhaps, with respect to Franklin and his 'mates', for some more level-headed people to press for reform in the late fifties and early sixties. A new regime at the Association Football Players' and Trainers' Union rebranded the Professional Footballers' Association [PFA] under the guidance of its new visionary leader, the Fulham player Jimmy Hill, certainly thought so.

As Franklin and company began to pack their bags for Bogotá in the early fifties their hapless trade union leaders were making their latest futile efforts to come to an agreement with the Football League and Football Association over their terms and conditions of work. It had been doing so since its foundation in 1907. It made next to no progress. On 1 May 1950, the various parties met, ostensibly to come to some form of accommodation. The meeting was pointless. Franklin and his mates would have told their union bosses so. A week later, Franklin and Mountford were making their flight to Bogotá.

By the time the succession of disciplinary hearings of the Bogotá rebels ended a year or so later, minds were refocused. Yet again the threat of strike action by players loomed. Yet again, the club bosses, the Football League and FA refused to budge. Indeed, they were becoming even more belligerent, even denying players the basic human right of legal representation in any dispute. A lawyer, for example, had not been present at any of the disciplinary hearings of the Bogotá rebels, a state of affairs they stoically accepted.

Yet, as much as the authorities and even the union denied it to be the case, Franklin and his chums' drastic act of rebellion only intensified the calls for reform, the need at the very least for some form of compromise. With the 1951/52 season imminent the Players' Union threatened strike action. Talks to avert the walkout became deadlocked so in desperation union bosses appealed for government intervention.

Aware of public disquiet, awoken to the power of football as part of the fabric of national life, Clement Attlee's outgoing Labour government agreed to try to broker an agreement among the warring parties. At least it agreed to be seen to be doing so. It wanted an end to a period of hostilities between professional footballers and their bosses, which had slowly intensified since Franklin's 'bandits' turned up in Colombia.

Prior to, throughout the Bogotá saga and beyond, the Players' Union only managed to eke out the tiniest of concessions. Club bosses openly mocked some of its demands. Not only did union officials want to secure the freedom to change club contracts and better pay from gate money but were also eyeing up the new market of broadcast rights. In an almost visionary move, they recognised, long before the clubs themselves, that radio and fledgling TV broadcasts of football matches can be exploited for lucrative income.

Broadcasts, even radio broadcasts, were controversial enough at the time, vigorously opposed by smaller Second and Third Division clubs on the basis commentaries on the big First Division matches affected gates. There was even the remarkable prospect at the beginning of the 1950/51 season of radio commentaries being banned.

If they were to go ahead the Players' Union wanted a share of the cash. Jimmy Guthrie, its chairman, proclaimed, 'The players are the stars of any football broadcast. Their talents are used without cash recognition by the BBC. The union believes that professional football and radio can go side by side. But not in the present set-up. The BBC pays for all professional entertainers except footballers. Even boxers are part of the fee.'

As the season kicked off, the BBC carried second-half commentary of Burnley v Arsenal, the union's gripes on pay, from whatever source, and contracts left unresolved. A man without any pay packet, Neil Franklin, as mentioned earlier, opted to go fishing rather than watching his old Stoke City mates lose 2-1 at home to Newcastle United.

His union's campaign was hampered not only by the obduracy of clubs, the FA and Football League, but also a lack of unity in the trade union of professional footballers. Just as the 1950/51 season began without the Bogotá rebels, Arsenal's players resigned en masse from the union. West Bromwich Albion players followed their example. They cared not one jot for the plight of Franklin and his friends, nor the inability of their union to defend them.

Just out of seeming jealousy, the pay on offer to a football union boss was of more concern than apparently any other issue. In the early fifties, that man was Jimmy Guthrie. Rather than focus on the battles to reform their terms and conditions of employment, union delegates held an extraordinary meeting in Manchester on 16 October 1950 to discuss Guthrie's pay.

The plight of the Bogotá rebels, outcasts from the game, may have been informally discussed. It was not formally on the table. There was a distinct lack of support for Franklin and his mates. There was not much love from some quarters for Guthrie either. His critics turned out to be a vocal minority.

West Brom's delegate, Billy Elliot, explained his team-mates' grievances with their boss. 'We do not agree with the amount that Jimmy Guthrie is getting,' Elliot bluntly commented. 'The majority of footballers get £12 and we do not think a man associated with us should get more.' Most delegates disagreed. A pay increase for Guthrie was approved, the recalcitrant Arsenal and West Brom caving in, agreeing to resume paying their subs.

After dealing with his own pay – £16 a week rather than the players' maximum wage of £12 a week plus a yearly bonus of £150 for the union boss – Guthrie then turned to his members' wages. He boasted that the negotiations for new contracts to be on offer from Football League clubs were making 'satisfactory' progress. It was anything but 'satisfactory'.

Guthrie and his team failed to make any progress. Instead, they turned to the government, specifically the Ministry of Labour, to act as intermediaries in the dispute. Along with the perennial complaint with the maximum wage, talks centred on the ability of players, or more pertinently lack of ability, to leave from one club to another. They were not automatically allowed to another club even while out of contract. Franklin, George Mountford and company had spectacularly circumvented this rule by going to Colombia to play in a league not recognised by the world-governing body, FIFA.

A fruitless series of meetings ended with civil servants advising the football authorities and the unions, the Scottish

Players' Union also locked in dispute with their members' employers, to go away and settle any differences on their own. There was nothing they were able to do for them. But, as the cricket season took over from the football season in the summer of 1951, government ministers, alarmed by the prospect of the paralysis of the national sport, invited the warring parties back.

All along, the FA, the Football League, the clubs and the unions acted as though the rebellion had never happened. If anything, the humiliating return of Franklin and his fellow rebels helped to further entrench the football establishment in its opposition to improving players' terms and conditions. They were able to exert the commercial muscle at the expense of a chronically weak Players' Union.

Such was the level of hubris, the Football League unilaterally changed the start and end date times of contracts, taking them from July to July rather than August to August. It also imposed a pay rise of £2 a week, less than demanded by the Players' Union. In addition, it upset fans by putting up admission charges.

As a result, the unions threatened strike action for the 1951/52 season. 'If we don't get some form of settlement of our differences, next season will not start,' union chairman Guthrie ranted. 'We are referring the latest development to the Ministry of Labour, and will repeat the previous advice to our members, not to re-sign for the clubs until this matter has been settled. It is now entirely up to the ministry and the clubs.'

Yet again they backed down with the outgoing Labour government of the day now agreeing to a formal inquiry. After Ministry of Labour officials met the FA, Football League and Players' Union on Friday, 28 July 1951, it issued the following statement: 'It was recognised by all parties that the proposals for a new form of contract put forward by the Players' Union raised issues of a far-reaching character. The Minister has therefore, in agreement with each of the parties, decided to appoint a committee to investigate the questions raised regarding the terms and conditions of employment of players, including their form of contract.'

More than 12 months after Neil Franklin, George Mountford, Charlie Mitten, Bobby Flavell and Bill Higgins took flight to Bogotá in their own desperate, some might claim greedy, escapade in the hope of securing a better future as professional footballers, a government minister finally recognised there were 'far reaching' issues in the state of English football, professional players, their bosses and the paying fans. Even then, it was difficult to get them around the table.

Correspondence from the UK National Archives reveals the depth of enmity and contempt among all the individuals involved in the running of the English national game of association football. For the FA's Sir Stanley Rous, dealing with Whitehall civil servants from the Ministry of Labour and union leaders clearly served as something of a chore. His nonchalant, almost ambivalent attitude clearly wound up the players' leaders, chief among them the combative secretary, James Fay.

On being contacted by the Ministry of Labour in August 1951, setting out the parameters for the inquiry hearings to be held on 15 October and 16 October 1951, Fay politely suggested they were held in public. Sir Stanley rather oddly claimed this would not be possible because the Albert Hall would need to be hired to accommodate all the reporters. And, the FA boss further argued their presence might harm 'freedom of expression'. Once Fay got word that the Football League secretary, Fred Howarth, also demanded they be held in private, albeit at the suggestion of the Ministry of Labour, he responded angrily.

Fay wrote back to the ministry insisting, 'Although I stated in my letter of August 26th that the union had no objection to the sessions being held in public, I now have to inform you the union definitely request they be held in public. What are the objections? The union have nothing to hide. Let the British Press have the opportunity of placing the full details before the public, to which they are entitled. This is not an industrial dispute; it is one of National interest and concerns the livelihoods of the men who entertain millions of the community.'

Fay's pleas, to the annoyance of the British press, were ignored. On the eve of the hearings the union made its case again, James Guthrie telling the *Daily Mirror*, 'Football is our biggest national sport and the people should have the right to hear all the evidence given. The union want the public admitted, the FA doesn't mind one way or the other but the League prefers secrecy. It is obvious that the League's desire for a meeting behind closed doors is born out of the fear that the public will support the Players' Union demands for professional footballers to be freed from conditions which go back to the feudal system.'

On Monday, 15 October 1951, the hearings went ahead in private, journalists banned along with the general public. On the panel hearing the professional footballers' case were the former England and Yorkshire cricketer Herbert Sutcliffe, Max Woosnam, a director of the chemical firm ICI and a former England amateur football international, the general secretary of the rail union, the Transport Salaried Staffs' Association, George Thorneycroft and a board member of the Rover car company, George Savage. They were chaired by Sir John Forster, the aristocratic president of the UK's industrial arbitration service, the Labour Court.

Counsel for the Players' Union, Christopher Shawcross, King's Counsel, outlined his case to them at almost painful length. It centred on three demands: the right for players to work for whoever they liked, the removal of the maximum wage, and finally the right to be legally represented, something that had been denied to the 'Bogotá Bad Boys'. Oddly, perhaps out of diplomacy, he never mentioned the escapade of Franklin and his gang of footballing bandits.

Remarkably, sports writers of the day treated the Players' Union case with a strong degree of scepticism. It appeared few lessons had been learned from the desperate measures employed by those going off in search of football's equivalent of El Dorado. Their cries of being reduced to serfdom by their British clubs and the authorities were treated scornfully.

A leading football correspondent for the next few decades, Brian Glanville, wrote in a syndicated piece: 'The Players' Union, taking their case to government arbitration, talk loudly though not very convincingly about "slavery" in football.' He further argued, 'It may seem that the unfortunate footballer is at the mercy of his club, who can exploit him to the full; but for my part, I think it is a ludicrous exaggeration. Clubs, after all, have rights, as well as players. There is a most irresponsible spirit among British footballers in general, a craving for rights without duties.'

Glanville, along with others, did recognise the need to reform, perhaps following the example of European continental football, especially in France and Italy with transfers only allowed in the close season, and the end of rolling year-on-year contracts. None of this the FA, the League or the clubs were prepared to countenance.

Against this backdrop, Christopher Shawcross KC took to his feet to address the Ministry of Labour inquiry, a formal hearing where bizarrely no one was prepared even to whisper the words Bogotá, Colombia or Franklin. Instead, Shawcross chose to deliver a history lesson. He did so in grandly informing the inquiry, 'The grievances of the Union and its members, if it is a grievance genuine or imaginary, is of very long standing.'

To assist him in delivering his lecture on the development of English football history, the KC cited a damning report into the state of the football industry published just a few months earlier by a forerunner to the modern-day Policy Studies Institute. It had painfully charted the development of association football throughout the previous decades in order to make its assessment. Rather cheekily Shawcross also chose, as a primary source to back his arguments, the Football League's own official history, published to mark its 50th anniversary in 1938. Embarrassing his adversaries into submission appeared to be the tactic.

Crucially he questioned the notion of Football League clubs being clubs in a conventional sense of the word, a group of people banded together either to play sport or support and assist those going out on to the field of play. As much as many professional football clubs were at the heart of their communities they did not exist for the benefit of players, coaching staff and supporters. It was a painful truth many in football will dispute to this day.

Two key factors brought about this development, he argued. First was the Football Association's decision to found the FA Cup in 1871/72, leading to other competitions, making the transformation of a recreational sport into a professional one inevitable. The next key development was, of course, the formation of the Football League in 1888.

There was the chance to make money, lots of it. For the best part of a century, this did not include players, the major bone of contention for Franklin and his mates. That was despite, as Shawcross put it, a game entertaining millions of people served to provide 'a profession rather than a recreation' for those who play the sport at the highest level.

To be a bit more precise about the popularity of the national game, gate figures in England showed that the 92 Football League clubs in the early fifties were attracting 40 million spectators a season. Before the outbreak of the Second World War, the figure was considerably lower, at 31.4 million a season. Yearly rises in prices at the turnstile meant that within a decade or so profits for First Division clubs doubled. Money was pouring into the game; players wanted their fair share.

Why was this not the case? The Policy Studies Institute had noted claims fans might be jealous. It found this an unconvincing argument. Mind, if the writers stepped into a time machine and landed in the early 21st century they may well have found many echoing the following comment, 'There may be a vague argument, resentment against anyone getting very large sums of money for what is, after all, a sport to them, even if it is a profession to a few.'

Back in 1951, Shawcross and his clients, the Players' Union, found this view highly arguable. Criticism of the Bogotá Bad Boys largely avoided condemning the size of the players' contracts. Cries of 'mercenaries' were largely mute. Most of the opprobrium heaped on Neil Franklin was for letting down his country and surreptitiously walking out on his hometown club.

Franklin and George Mountford had broken their contracts with Stoke City Football Club, the others the same with their clubs. If anything, Shawcross argued, the question of professionals' contracts, especially for restless players, was more important than the wages problem. Tying down players to simply rolling yearly contracts and still holding on to their registration as professionals with the FA, even if deemed surplus to requirements, smacked of gross unfairness. Yet, the FA and the Football League clubs were unyielding.

Shawcross then set about coruscating the system of 'disciplining' players in English professional football, whether their misdemeanours were real or imagined. Reflecting on the procedures of the game's governing body, he condemned FA hearings as being carried out on the lines of military court-martials. As for individual clubs' internal disciplinary hearings, counsel for the Players' Union reiterated demands for independent arbitration. In both cases, he deplored the refusal to allow players legal representation.

To back his case, he cited the findings of the Policy Studies Institute. It concurred with the Players' Union's view. As Shawcross explained, it argued, 'In disputes between the player and the club, the union suggests it be dealt with first, at the club concerned by discussion between club and union representatives. If the dispute is not settled there, the matter should be referred to the League Management Committee and the union for discussion. If no agreement is reached it could then be referred to arbitration in the same way as other industrial disputes.'

This was something the Football League management and club directors were not prepared to countenance. Shawcross accused them of being stuck in the 1890s, the decade the Players' Union was formed. It became defunct thanks to the Football League's refusal to give it any recognition before being revived in 1907.

The Football League's own account of its first half century of existence gave the Players' Union's fifties lawyer what he deemed a 'vital' insightful passage into the attitude of his clients' employers towards them. It concerned the fear of players being poached without a penny in compensation being paid, effectively what threatened to happen in the summer of 1950 with Franklin leading the exodus of players to Colombia.

'This history will have made clear that one of the main foundations of the Football League was the power to retain registered players, that clubs could not be permitted to approach other players surreptitiously, make them settled by improper overtures and then get their forced transfers for nothing,' intoned the authors of the Football League's tome.

Franklin maintained in his dispatches from Bogotá 'surreptitious' and 'improper overtures' were rife in the post-war years. This was flatly denied by the Football League and club bosses. They were either being naïve or far from honest. This became clear in fractious exchanges as King's Counsel for the Players' Union began to examine, as a witness to this government inquiry, the Football League's president, Arthur Drewry.

Before Drewry began to make the League's case, Shawcross reminded those present of Franklin's explosive accusations of players being treated by their employers as 'soccer slaves'. Admittedly he did so without quoting the former England centre-half's strident articles in the *Sunday Empire News*. Instead, he resorted once again to reading out passages from his out-of-print history book.

Such accusations were prevalent throughout the twenties and thirties. There was nothing original in Franklin's contentious comments. Similar arguments had been made by his predecessor at Stoke City – as a local hero, the biggest football star of the day in Sir Stanley Matthews. League bosses angrily rejected such claims.

For Christopher Shawcross KC, the following summed up the condescending and patronising attitude of the Football League: 'The vital principle which was forgotten in all the loose charges of "slavery" and "trafficking in human flesh" is that no player can be transferred without his consent, and in any case the clubs through the League, "are better armed than anyone else to judge of what is the fairest practice for the protection of, not merely themselves, but the player".'

Neil Franklin, his fellow Bogotá rebels, his old Stoke City mate Stanley Matthews, who was still at the height of his powers despite nearing 40 years of age, and the rest of their fellow professionals flatly rejected the view of the clubs and the Football League. To them it summed up the patronising, arrogant and ignorant approach of those running the English professional game of football.

As King's Counsel for the Players' Union began to outline the painful series of disputes with almost annual threats of footballers going on strike, tempers began to fray. Shawcross noted wages at the start of the 1946/47 season were the same as for 1938/39. 'The competition [the Football League] was in abeyance,' protested its president Arthur Drewry. 'Yes, there was a war, of course, as some of us remember,' Shawcross tersely responded.

To further raise hackles, he then accused the English football establishment of feudalism. Never mind living in the 1890s, they behaved as if they were living in the 1390s. It was an accusation to meet the approval of the likes of Neil Franklin, if he had been allowed in the room to hear it being made. Christopher Shawcross KC grandiosely took up the lingering complaints of serfdom.

Addressing the chairman of the inquiry, he began, 'You may think, Sir, that there is something of an analogy between the constitutional history of this country because you may think that whilst the Football Association is the original "King", these professional clubs, members of the League, and the League itself, is now almost stronger, or in many respects stronger than the "King".' Given the state of relations between the FA and Premier League clubs such a comment has a resonance for football fans today.

Shawcross went further, something unrecognisable today when it comes to the terms and conditions of professional footballers. He commented, 'Then, at the other end, the lowest end of the scale, come the "serfs"; that is the players, because it is the case, and one does not want to use exaggerated language, but it is not an exaggeration to say that this [players'] contract and the conditions under which these players are obliged to serve, rightly or wrongly, are such as to amount to a servitude as had been unknown since the Middle Ages; the sort of conditions of servitude, which we are told exist in Soviet

Russia and other countries but are quite unknown in any other form of industry, sport or anything else, and as I suggest have never been known in this country since the Middle Ages.'

As a tactic, an exercise in hyperbole perhaps, accusing Football League bosses and club owners of acting like medieval barons was bold. To add further stinging insult, comparing them to Stalin and his acolytes in the Kremlin, was bound to provoke anger. It was also a tactic doomed to failure. If the hearing was held in public, the resultant outcry from such a dramatic intervention with colourful language to the fore may have been guaranteed to focus hearts and minds of fans and the country at large on what footballers considered their 'ill-treatment'. Instead his flowery speech fell on the deaf ears of Whitehall civil servants, the men in blazers from the FA and Football League and crucially the 'independent' inquiry panel sitting in judgement.

Even as the hearing came to an end, much to their frustration, the realisation must have dawned on the Players' Union bosses that they were yet again wasting their time in even trying to rope in the assistance of government. Perhaps given the level of resistance to reform, including at government level, the drastic unilateral actions of Franklin and company appeared not so unreasonable after all.

Just one MP displayed any consistent interest in holding the government to account in the weeks following the hearing with an interminable time to come up with any conclusions. Naturally, it was Neil Franklin's old MP Ellis Smith, the Labour member for Stoke during the footballer's spell in Bogotá.

On 12 March 1952 the members of the committee of inquiry convened by the Ministry of Labour and National Service sent their findings to the Ministry of Labour. It was almost a fortnight later before the Minister of Labour, Sir Walter Monckton, released them. On being pressed by Ellis

Smith to do so he confessed to feeling a 'little embarrassed' because he had once appeared as a barrister on behalf of the Players' Union. Maybe his tardiness in releasing the committee's report was down to recognition that it would leave his former clients in despair.

The inquiry committee rejected calls for the abolition of the maximum wage and any meaningful changes to the retain and transfer system. 'Unusual as are the existing provisions relating to maximum wage and to which a professional footballer's contract is subject,' the inquiry concluded, it did not think the union's alternative proposals would be 'to the ultimate advantage of professional players as a whole'.

Instead, the Commission simply recommended a pay rise, a rise in the maximum wage of £14 a week without specifying by how much. It also proposed a transfer cap of £15,000. Just months earlier, Stoke City sold Neil Franklin to Hull City for substantially more. There was no chance of the clubs accepting such a salary cap. They were happy with the non-binding recommendations on pay but warned it would be passed on to the fans passing through the turnstiles.

As for players being given legal representation during disputes with clubs or the FA, the inquiry did conclude it constituted 'a denial of justice'. But the members of the Ministry of Labour Commission did not put forward any formal proposals to do anything about it. Instead they suggested the FA and the Football League might merely give the matter their 'consideration'.

Naturally, the rather lame findings, essentially a general recommendation to maintain the status quo in fifties football, left union bosses feeling frustrated, in some cases even incensed. James Fay, the secretary, wrote back to the Ministry of Labour politely and diplomatically noting that his committee was 'unable to agree with the report of the findings of the inquiry'.

Franklin's old MP, Ellis Smith, urged the minister to give an undertaking to 'get all parties together as soon as possible in order that their relationships can be placed upon a much better basis than they had been in the past'. No such undertaking was given. Worse, Ellis Smith was not helped by the flippant attitude of his own Labour front bench with a glib intervention from Clement Attlee's former Home Secretary, James Chuter Ede.

In recognising that Monckton once represented the Football Players' Union, Ede took to his feet to ask, 'Can the Right Honourable and learned Gentleman tell us what was the transfer in his case?' Sir Walter answered, 'It has been a very unsatisfactory financial undertaking.' Cue much hilarity in the House of Commons chamber. For the MP for Stoke-on-Trent South, his former constituent Neil Franklin, and all other footballers, it was no laughing matter.

The Association Football Players' and Trainers' Union needed a new approach. Members decided they needed a new leader. Jimmy Fay retired after a lifetime campaigning for his members. Chairman Guthrie was ousted in favour of a new visionary leader, Jimmy Hill. Crucially, Hill found a rebel player to prosecute a test case, one a tad wilier and appearing more reliable than Neil Franklin.

Quite bizarrely the last man Franklin persuaded to fly to Bogotá, Charlie Mitten, unwittingly played a crucial role. Prior to his Colombian venture, Stoke City's Franklin effectively went on strike after being refused a transfer by his manager, Bob McGrory. A decade later Newcastle United's George Eastham did the same. An England international, he was at loggerheads with his club manager, Charlie Mitten, one of Franklin's Bogotá Bad Boys. A decade on in the summer of 1960, Mitten, despite his protests to the contrary, had metamorphosed into a fully reformed and paid-up member of the football establishment.

Looking back on the row, Mitten appeared remarkably sanguine about his accidental role as a manager in the ultimate reform of English professional football. He recognised that it was in a 'state of unrest' thanks to the failure to reform in the immediate aftermath of the rebel move to Colombia. In Richard Adamson's biography of him, *Bogotá Bandit*, Mitten commented, 'I could understand the young lad's point that he was in the game only a set number of years to earn as much as he can get. "I'm one of the good players and I want my worth in the short time I've got." I'd felt exactly the same way before I went to Bogotá – now I was on the management side, so I understood both arguments. The League never understood this. They just saw the players as cattle to be discarded, disposed of, as the club pleased.'

Mitten rightly suspected more was at stake than just one player's desire to leave his club. 'The negotiations reached stagnation point, and in the summer, he went to the PFA. He just wanted to move, and the club came to the conclusion that what he really wanted was freedom of contract,' Mitten noted. 'The transfer market had rocketed, and the board seemed more concerned with the fee than defending the retain and transfer system, which they assumed would go on. My board wasn't interested in the contract dispute. I didn't want Eastham to go, but what could I do if he wouldn't play for me?

'All I could do was keep him out of football by not signing his transfer. I had nothing personal against the lad. He was principled and acted perfectly honourably. He played it straight – and he was a brilliant player for me, an automatic selection at Newcastle, and deservedly went on to be an international. But as regards to earning money, the only way open to him was what he did.'

Eastham, a player eventually to join Neil Franklin in the select pantheon of Stoke City greats, gave a blunt but straightforward account of his spat with Mitten, Newcastle

United and the football authorities. Yes, it was about money but, at first, more about his innovative plans to earn more moonlighting elsewhere being frustrated by Newcastle's directors.

'You see we didn't really train in the afternoons for the first team. You'd come in at ten and finish at twelve,' he told BBC Radio Stoke as he looked back on his career. 'So, I said can I get a job in the afternoon? I was at this time getting married and I'd like to supplement my wages.' At first Mitten and his board agreed but Eastham struggled to find a job until one of the directors offered him part-time work at his glass company. 'It was selling glasses to pubs,' Eastham explained. 'So, it meant I had to go around the pubs in the afternoon. And you know what happens there. They say "have a drink". It wasn't an ideal job so I said "no, that's not for me". That was it. There were no more attempts to find me a job or something to be going on with.'

It was then Eastham put in his transfer request. 'I said can I try and go somewhere else. Can I get a move to another club? And they said no, you can't go anywhere. You're committed to the club. You've signed a contract and that's it. We don't have to pay you. If you don't play for us, you don't play for anybody.' On that note Eastham headed down to London to take up a job as a sales representative for cork, earning £30 a week, £10 more than he was earning as a footballer at Newcastle United.

Naturally Eastham's prolonged absence from football, roughly eight months, provoked uproar in the footballing hotbed of the North East of England, if not the rest of the country. Eastham explained, 'The months went by and the papers used to give us a hard time. "Why's he not playing?" And eventually the League got fed up with all the publicity, which wasn't good.' The Football League's churlish decision to prevent Eastham playing for a showbiz 11 in charity matches and the ensuing bad publicity had brought matters to a head.

'They said [to Newcastle] you'll have to sell him,' recalled Eastham. 'So, that's when I went to Arsenal for £47,500. And they [Newcastle] couldn't even be bothered to give me the money they owed me.'

Supported by Jimmy Hill, leading his rebranded union the Professional Footballers' Association, Eastham sued. It was off to the courts. Eastham explained, 'The PFA, who'd been backing me all along, said "Look, we've got enough money to take this to court and will you be prepared to take it to court?" And, I said "Yes, why not? You've done enough for me and I will take it to court with you." So that's how it all came about with Jimmy Hill and Cliff Lloyd and the other union representatives. That's how it came about.'

Franklin and the future Newcastle manager Mitten's escapade in Bogotá gave the football establishment, club owners, the FA and the Football League a jolt, ultimately nothing more. It concentrated minds among fans and the public at large on the gripes of professional footballers, but that was all. Ultimately, a widespread rebellion was averted. Franklin came home humiliated. Hill and Eastham's strategy, acting within and using the law of the land, proved far more effective. It truly put the frighteners on the men running football.

Alarmed by Eastham's test case in challenging football's retain and transfer system and the latest threat of strike action, the Football League and club bosses caved in on the issue of the maximum wage. In January 1961, Eastham by then at Arsenal, the maximum wage was finally abolished. They refused to back down over the retain and transfer system. A showdown in the High Court became inevitable, Eastham's costs paid for by the PFA.

On 4 July 1961, US Independence Day, Eastham won what his supporters termed 'his fight for footballers' 'freedom'. Mr Justice Wilberforce, sitting in the High Court, ruled in his favour. The retain and transfer system, governing the employment of English professional footballers, was illegal. Remarkably, Eastham modestly reflected decades later, 'I wasn't particularly looking to force anybody to do anything.'

Yet again, during the course of Eastham's court case, Franklin's favourite theme of 'soccer slavery' had been raised. Gerald Gardiner QC, for the PFA, argued professional footballers were treated like cattle or, as he curiously put it, almost echoing Franklin's words from more than a decade earlier, 'paid slaves'. As with his predecessor, Christopher Shawcross KC, he condemned the transfer system as being akin to the feudal system of the Middle Ages.

It was an historic victory, one of course applauded by Neil Franklin. Even Mitten in hindsight applauded the decision. He did so despite his own intransigence as a manager sparking the case, reflecting, 'I advised Newcastle that the issues of freedom of contract, as being pursued by the PFA through the courts, would be accepted in law. In all these years of stagnation it was the Players' Union who had let the players down, and failed to challenge the issue in the courts. But it was also stupidity by the people at the top – the clubs who refused to accept that those who were doing the job should be given more consideration.'

More reforms were to follow as billions of pounds began to flood into the game courtesy of subscription television revenues, the balance of power shifting from clubs to players. Those reforms arguably came to a head thanks to an obscure Belgian footballer by the name of Jean-Marc Bosman in a dispute with his club Standard Liege. It ended up in the European Court of Justice (ECJ).

In 1995, the ECJ ruled in Bosman's favour, essentially deciding that football's transfer rules were in breach of European Law, which guaranteed free movement of labour between member states of the EU. Given the most powerful clubs and leagues on the planet all operated back then in European Union countries, radical reform to the retain and transfer system became inevitable. It led to England's Premier League and Football League revising their rules on the awarding of contracts to players. Their counterparts in Scotland and in the rest of Europe did the same.

There remained disputes. Newspapers across Europe reported several cases of players wanting to leave their clubs but being blocked from doing so. This was highlighted by the case of the French international, Nicolas Anelka's desire to leave Arsenal and join Real Madrid. Arsenal, not surprisingly, tried to block any such move.

Anelka did eventually go to Real Madrid but in the meantime the EU Commission formally opened up legal proceedings against FIFA. Thanks, partly, to political intervention from most notably the UK government under its Prime Minister, Tony Blair, and Germany's Chancellor Gerhard Schröder, a compromise was reached between FIFA and the EU Commission. The pair had argued in a joint statement that the fundamental reform of football's transfer system being demanded by the EU Commission jeopardised the survival of smaller clubs relying on transfer fees. Under pressure from the heads of government of two of the EU's most powerful member states – nations with major domestic leagues – the EU Commission had no choice but to back down.

FIFA implemented new measures to come into force worldwide in September 2001. Any disputes ultimately go to the Court of Arbitration for Sport based in Switzerland and therefore operate under Swiss law. FIFA's *'Regulations on the Status and Transfer of Players'* do not go as far as the original Bosman ruling. But, those revised regulations still meant as the sports historian John Harding observed in his history of the PFA that, 'professional footballers gained a measure of self-determination' unheard of since the foundation of the

Players' Union in 1904. Pound note signs were lighting up in the minds of not just the players but their agents. Unlike for Franklin and his peers, modern footballers' version of El Dorado was for real.

# FOOTBALLING PIONEER OR MERCENARY REBEL?

ALL along, Neil Franklin made his primary motive for turning his back on club and country clear. It was to make money, secure his family's future. His head was turned by the promise of golden riches in a footballing El Dorado. The same applied to his travelling companion and Stoke City team-mate, George Mountford. It was true of the other rebels taking up contracts in Colombia's DiMayor league.

There was clearly one other factor playing on Franklin's mind. It was in causing outrage that he was given by the media in Bogotá a platform to highlight what he and his friend Charlie Mitten argued was the urgent need for the reform of English and Scottish football. What followed in response from the rulers of British football was, of course, less than urgent.

Mountford, Higgins and Flavell were also far less strident in their comments on the state of the professional game of football. In assessing both aspects of what motivated them, whether it be the desire for immediate financial reward, or as unlikely rabble-rousing shop stewards, politically agitating from their South American lair, they failed.

Nevertheless, as already explored, the Bogotá rebels or bandits certainly gave the complacent and arrogant rulers of England's beautiful game a brief but, without question, an almighty fright. Yes, they resisted change but with the Bogotá episode firmly planted in the minds of all those involved in

English professional football of the fifties and sixties there was the slow, painful but inexorable march towards the reform demanded by Franklin – at least the changes he called for in his missives as an angry young man.

What is bizarre is just how much the older Franklin singularly failed to embrace the PFA's campaign to change the system of a maximum wage and retain and transfer contracts. If anything, he appeared to treat it with disdain. For all his protests of 'serfdom' while holding forth from a hotel in the Colombian capital, the de facto rebel leader appeared at best lukewarm as Jimmy Hill, George Eastham and company went through the courts, at worst almost hostile.

For this contradictory figure the reforms had gone too far. His mate Mitten, the hapless Newcastle United manager, might be taken for feeling much the same as he battled with the recalcitrant Eastham. But unlike Franklin he all along recognised that professional footballers in the English and Scottish leagues were being short-changed by their bosses. He just baulked at the overnight changes prompted by legal action from Jimmy Hill's PFA.

For Mitten the sensible thing for the clubs to do was phase in wage reform upon the return of the rebel players from Bogotá. That would have been all too sensible. It was never going to happen. Instead, the men in suits wanted to punish the recalcitrant players, quash any rebellion, keep the irritable but weak Players' Union at bay, and most of all make sure the most high-profile rebel, Neil Franklin, suffered.

In all this the chief prosecutor was the FA's secretary and future FIFA president, Sir Stanley Rous. On his retirement in the seventies, Rous looked back on the entire episode with a deep sense of sadness, even surprisingly a degree of sympathy for Franklin.

As noted earlier, Rous did view Franklin and the others as pioneers in terms of leading the way and plying their trade abroad. But in his autobiography and using the benefit of hindsight, Rous went further. First of all, while careful not to excuse England's embarrassment at the 1950 World Cup, he acknowledged that Franklin's absence from the side was a severe blow.

'The team for that 1950 World Cup was weakened by the loss of one of the best centre-halves to play for England, Neil Franklin,' Rous wrote. He went on to acknowledge, 'In those days of a maximum wage of £20 a week it was not surprising that lucrative overseas offers should be particularly attractive. And, Franklin had accepted just such an offer from Bogotá in Colombia after secret negotiations.' [In 1950, the maximum wage was £12 a week, not the sum quoted by Rous.] Unfortunately, as Rous did correctly point out, the Stoke player had broken his contract with his club and rejected an England call-up for a World Cup – there was no choice but to suspend him.

Despite calls for Franklin's reinstatement as an England player once he had served his suspension, Rous simply and dismissively referred to an 'international career in ruins'. There was never going to be a way back into the England team. Playing out his career at a Second Division club lucky to have him on his books mattered little. It was the act of turning his back on his hometown club and his country on the brink of making its World Cup finals debut.

But Rous in this memoir was in a sense contrite and full of admiration: 'It was particularly unfortunate that Neil Franklin should be at the centre of this tug of war, for he was the nicest of men and a fine player, vital to the England team of the time.'

Decades after the controversy, the pair met at a match between Arsenal and Stoke at Highbury. 'He was as pleasant as ever and with no rancour over the past,' recalled Rous. 'He recognised that in preserving a principle, England's loss had been as great as his own.' It was a lament for a great player.

Former Manchester United manager, Ron Atkinson, who played against Franklin in the England rebel's twilight years, agreed that he was a huge loss to the international game. 'It was a different world. They were on £12 a week back then, which was an ok wage,' Atkinson told me. 'First and foremost, they wanted to be footballers. It was an added bonus [going to Colombia]. There was no back way back for them, especially Franklin and Mitten as international players. It was an unknown thing. You'd never heard of a player going abroad. Going to South America was not something that was done. For English footballers it is not even done now.'

'Big careers ended,' lamented 'Big Ron' in assessing the Bogotá rebels. 'Franklin missed the 1950 World Cup. England missed him. At 28 for a centre-half, it was no great age. He would have gone on to play for England at the 1954 World Cup.' Franklin was irreplaceable in the position. Billy Wright played there as an emergency measure. 'I knew Billy Wright,' commented Atkinson. 'He was a big fan of Neil Franklin.'

In preserving the 'principle' of holding players to unpopular contracts with their clubs, English football's other power brokers won an initial skirmish in resisting calls for reform. In the long term, as football grew into a truly global sport, they were doomed to defeat.

Oddly then, once early reforms did come, the once disgruntled Stoke City and England centre-half bemoaned the state of a changing game. Even, for him, the putative reforms made it unrecognisable, not necessarily for good. Yet for all his curious reservations, he had few gripes. 'Good luck to them,' Franklin argued while reflecting on the relative riches enjoyed even by players of the sixties and seventies, some argue still a relative pittance compared with the rewards on offer for the superstars of the 21st century.

Assessing his own career, Neil Franklin made one simple understated observation, 'Not what you would call quiet and uneventful, was it?' Before he had boarded his fateful flight to Bogotá, Franklin had made 39 consecutive appearances for England in wartime, victory, and full internationals, captained his boyhood club Stoke City to within a whisker of capturing the Football League title and was widely recognised by even the sternest of football critics as one of the finest defenders ever to play the game. Crucially he will forever, as he recognised, be remembered as being at the centre of a football sensation which rocked the sporting world.

In doing so he became a rebel hero for some, not least his supporters in the Players' Union, those stoically campaigning for professional footballers to be treated with decency by their employers, those demanding players were allowed to earn their box office value.

To others, Franklin and the other Bogotá Bandits were nothing more than reckless hotheads acting in self-interest rather than acting in the wider interests of the professional game. He was no pioneer, just a mercenary rebel. Perhaps, as alluded to earlier, in truth he was neither. Deep down Franklin was a working-class kid wanting to do his best for his family. He also wanted tangible rewards for his mates, whether it be those lucky enough to wear an England shirt, his pals with First Division Stoke City, or professionals at any level of the beautiful game.

Most people mellow in later life. It appeared the same for Franklin. Quietly, he became a member of the footballing establishment he once railed against, not a significant figure – lower league manager and member of the football pools panel – but still one worthy of respect from his peers and fans alike. His career as a coach and manager was, to put it politely, fitful. His time as a friendly publican, welcoming wide-eyed football fans, myself included, to his hostelries, maybe proved far more fruitful.

His view of football was just of it being a simple game to play. Fortunately, for him, he had the God-given talents to make playing the game look simple. On the role of defenders, especially centre-halves, there's little doubt he was something of a revolutionary in an era when the man in the number 5 shirt was undervalued in the rigid tactical systems employed in English forties and fifties football.

Indeed, he was as scathing of coaches as his parsimonious tight-fingered directors in assessing their tactics. Long before the emergence of England's World Cup-winning captain, Bobby Moore, Neil Franklin advocated the role of a footballing centre-half. 'The theorists, the point grabbers, blame who you like, have killed the centre-half footballer and it is no coincidence that the death of the footballing centre-half and the drop in the general standard of play came at one and the same time,' Franklin moaned. No doubt he did so while reflecting on the 'strait jacket' imposed on him by his managerial nemesis at Stoke City, Bob McGrory.

He went on, 'To my mind the centre-half should be first and foremost a ball player. I was so definite in that view that I refused to be swayed by the early criticism of my play. People used to accuse me of loving to fiddle with the ball near my own goal, but I have always believed that it is better to be robbed in possession than to become just another kicker of a football. Anyone can kick and chase it, but football demands more than that.' In fairness there were instances of Franklin being caught in possession of the ball, making defensive errors, but these were rare. Few of his peers possessed his talent, unable to take the risks he did as a defender of consummate artistry.

Then again, he modestly challenged such assessments from pundits of his day as a player. To him, his talents were those expected of any top-class player. 'Maybe I am wrong, but I assume that any footballer worthy of hire, as a professional or as an amateur, is able to propel the ball, either by head or by foot, accurately and swiftly,' he mused. 'You might tell me that there are many people in football who cannot do that, in which case I shall reply that those people are not footballers. They may go through the motions but that is all.'

Just to hammer home the point, he concluded, 'Don't get obsessed with the "stopper mania". A centre-half is a member of a football team and he should therefore be as good a footballer as anyone else in the team. He should tackle hard. He should try to intercept, and he should use the ball when he has won possession. And by using the ball, I don't mean just kicking it.'

Curiously, once he put his playing and brief coaching career behind him, Franklin made the switch from poacher to gamekeeper with relative ease. For all his rebel antics in Colombia, this self-proclaimed football visionary expressed some odd reactionary views. Chief among them was his opposition to the abolition of the maximum wage. As the leading figure in an episode threatening to shake the football world to its foundations, an angry young man ranting to anyone who'd care to listen of the need for some intense navel-gazing into the terms of employment of professional footballers, his contrary opinions in later life seemed bizarre.

'I am against unlimited wages myself,' he wrote in his autobiography, *Soccer at Home and Abroad*, published just five years after playing unauthorised league football in Colombia. There, in the capital Bogotá, he railed against the English football establishment, citing accusations of 'serfdom'. Players needed to be paid their true worth as entertainers to millions of fans, especially the superstars of which Franklin back in his pomp as England's first-choice centre-half and Stoke City's captain was clearly one.

Yet a brief few years later he concluded, 'I feel that if the maximum wage was abolished you would get all sorts of undignified and underhanded auctions taking place, and that would be bad for the game.' Of course, Franklin unwittingly became a world-leading expert in 'underhanded auctions' of footballers as he took his infamous flight to Bogotá. There was perhaps just a small lack of self-awareness in those autobiographical comments.

Then again, he was also rightly wary of the spectre of corruption and illicit gambling in the English game, something he articulated in ghosted newspaper articles during his time in Colombia. Those underhand practices carried on during the fifties and into the early sixties as the PFA fought for reform. The PFA's job was made easier once these were exposed in the media.

Surprisingly though, Franklin trashed some of those comments, opinions he appeared to begin to regret in hindsight, intemperate over-the-top rants. Recognising many clubs, especially in the lower divisions were struggling then as they do now, he wrote, 'We must forget all our old quarrels, all the silly talk about slave markets, and realise that now players are well paid it is up to us to attract more spectators by improving the standard of play.' The Bogotá Bad Boy was no longer a rebel, let alone a mercenary rebel. Franklin by the mid-fifties and early sixties preferred, if possible, to be seen as a visionary of the game, an aspiring pioneer.

By the time he became a Football League manager with Colchester United, the maximum wage he belatedly supported had been abolished, and the detested retain and transfer system he himself vehemently opposed scrapped, thanks to George Eastham, Jimmy Hill and a sympathetic High Court judge. Sadly, he only had the briefest of time to put his ideas on how the game of association football ought to be played into practice.

Those ideas, part based on his brief experience of South American football, were, for the time, more than a tad unconventional. Much meets the approval of a modern-day Champions or Premier League coach. In other aspects, they would choke over their energy drinks on reading accounts of some of his methods.

Above all, unsurprisingly, he advocated there was no substitute for ball practice. 'No player becomes such a master that he has no need of further practice,' Franklin insisted. Of course, as a young player at Stoke City he enjoyed being mentored by the footballing genius, Sir Stanley Matthews. 'After all, the whole basis of a footballer's art is that he can master the ball, so surely he should spend hours and hours practising the various tricks and moves with the ball at his feet,' Franklin commented. 'Stanley Matthews does [comments made in the mid-fifties] and the supreme wizardry of my old colleague is good enough for me.'

To sum up his views, he offered the following coaching checklist:

1. *Train hard and make sure you are always fit.*
2. *Don't be bored with your training. Make it interesting.*
3. *Remember that the strenuous pre-season training is the important time during which you must get fit, whereas after that you just have to KEEP fit.*
4. *There is nothing better than match practice.*
5. *Ball practice is all-important.*
6. *Eat what you like.*
7. *Smoke and drink, if you want to, but always in moderation.*
8. *Training at home is usually better than special training at some health resort.*
9. *Never just THINK you are fit; always know you are.*

Emphasis on fitness and ball practice might meet the approval of his esteemed successors in an England shirt, especially those entering a career as a coach. His 'eat what you like' mantra might make a few modern-day coaches splutter. His approval of smoking and drinking, at least in moderation, might raise eyebrows but in fairness it remained in the English game up until the nineties.

His brief foray into coaching and football management ended abruptly, another great player failing to make it as even a half-decent manager. After being sacked by Colchester, Franklin packed in the professional game, once and for all. His only contact came as a member of the football pools panel, alongside, among others, his former England team-mate Raich Carter. A relatively quieter life in the North Staffordshire countryside running a popular country pub, the Dog and Doublet at Sandon beckoned.

Gone from the professional game, no longer working as a player or coach, but Neil Franklin, thanks to his exploits both on and off the field of play, could never be forgotten. Here was a player derided for turning his back on club and country yet eulogised for decades after his flight to Bogotá in search of a crock of gold as one of England's finest-ever players.

For all the qualms over his behaviour in the summer of 1950, Franklin's peers long recognised him as one of the greats of the game of football. They did so while perhaps baulking at some of his odd reactionary and contradictory views. His curious opposition to the abolition of the footballers' maximum wage while openly rebelling against the self-same suffocating financial restraints of English football served as just one example.

This surprisingly complex figure cast doubt on many innovations in fifties and sixties football, everything from midweek matches under floodlights to the use of substitutes. 'We must set our faces against substitution. Substitutes are undesirable,' Franklin insisted. Even then he reluctantly offered a caveat. Basically, he was against players only to be replaced in the event of an injury. It was a system open to abuse, with some disreputable teams faking injury, Franklin argued. Mass tactical substitution was something he was happy to countenance. He welcomed its eventual implementation, while at the same time describing it as a 'dreadful' Americanisation.

Yet thanks to his experience in South American football, the infamy he revelled in as his name was splashed across front and back pages of the nation's newspapers, he did welcome one aspect of professional sport from across the Atlantic. Franklin applauded any explosion in media interest in not just soccer but sport in general. Sadly, for him it came in the twilight of his life. 'We allow ourselves the luxury of a rosette and maybe a rattle or a bell, but on the continent and in South America the whole world stops for a big game,' Franklin observed of fifties football. 'The newspapers too give far more space to football abroad than they do in this country. An international or a big cup game will be the excuse for page after page of comment and page after page of report after the game.'

One arch manipulator in the British media of interest in football, for good or for bad, served as one of Franklin's greatest admirers as a player. Former England team-mate and future England manager Don Revie ignored his friend's spectacular fall from grace with his flight to Bogotá, brushed aside some of Franklin's more bizarre views in playing and coaching retirement. To Revie his old mate was one of the greatest to ever play the game of association football.

As Revie was about to lead his Leeds United team to FA Cup success in the competition's centenary year of 1972, he was asked to pick his all-time British team. There were, unsurprisingly from someone to more than easily rival Franklin as a divisive figure, one or two picks that raised eyebrows. Revie picked his old Manchester City team-mate Bert Trautmann in goal ahead of England's World Cup-winning goalkeeper, Gordon Banks. Whatever Trautmann's merits, it was lost on Revie that his old mate was German, not British. It was also lost on him that his central midfield pick, Johnny Giles, was Irish rather than British. Giles was one of four of Revie's late sixties and seventies Leeds players to make it into his 'Great Britain XI'.

But the standout pick for Revie was his centre-half. He ignored another of his Leeds players, Jack Charlton, England's World Cup winner in the number 5 shirt. He also ignored the captain, Bobby Moore. Instead, he went for the player who refused to go to England's first-ever World Cup, Neil Franklin. Revie admitted some of his picks might raise a few hackles but argued in Franklin's case, 'Few people will quibble with my choice of Neil Franklin at centre-half, for the former Stoke City and England defender stands out easily as the most skilful pivot Britain has produced.'

High praise for Franklin. More came a couple of decades later as the Football League celebrated its 100th season. A Football League committee selected 100 'league legends' in the summer of 1998, a list of the greats of the game going back to the opening 1888/89 season. Naturally, Franklin featured among them.

Fellow professionals remembered his exploits as a footballer fondly, paid tribute to his genius. 'Franklin was a very good footballing centre-half,' remembered Ron Atkinson. 'He would easily fit into the modern game.' Sadly for Franklin, he, more than any other of his fellow Bogotá rebels, including his Stoke City mate George Mountford, will be forever remembered for his ill-fated decision to grab the illusory Colombian riches.

Not surprisingly, Franklin's former Stoke and England team-mate, not least mentor, Sir Stanley Matthews was full of praise but lamented Franklin's fateful decision to go to Colombia instead of joining him at a World Cup. It perhaps mattered little the legend's own rebel streak as much as his genius as a footballer may well have rubbed off on the young Franklin. After all, it was Franklin who had to sort out one of Sir Stanley's many spats with the powers that be at Stoke City, doing so as the club challenged for the championship!

Even so, he admitted to feeling a degree of sympathy on hearing Franklin and George Mountford had landed in Bogotá. 'I didn't at the time think Neil was unwise to go, if he wanted to. It was big money,' Sir Stanley told David Miller for his 1989 authorised biography of the England winger. 'I realised afterwards what a mistake it was.'

There was no hesitation in assessing Neil Franklin's qualities as a player. Sir Stanley rated many of his fellow England internationals in their respective positions for David Miller. 'The best I've played with. He made it look so easy, a master,' Matthews enthused. 'The way he played, wanting the ball, always passing, you'd suppose he couldn't tackle but he could. He had all the time in the world. I don't know how he did it. Yet, I can see him now. If he was playing sweeper these days, he'd never need a bath, he'd never break sweat. He floated about the pitch, playing the ball with both feet, and would beat opponents on the edge of his own area. What a player!'

Franklin's old England colleague, Tom Finney, a lifelong friend, offered support but with key reservations. In his autobiography, he wrote, 'I cannot help feeling but a sense of despair when recalling Neil Franklin, the best defender I played against or with – yes, that good.' But in assessing the decision to play in Colombia, Finney commented, 'The move rocked the football world, coming as it did just a few weeks before the 1950 World Cup. It was an astonishing decision and I believe he regretted it until his dying day.'

So, as Finney suggested he might, did Franklin have any regrets? It seemed he most certainly did. Concluding his own autobiography, Franklin offered remorse but was careful not to seek any sympathy. 'Usually when people look back on their lives or careers, they say they wouldn't change it in any way. I am going to be different,' Franklin wrote. 'If I could have my time over again, knowing what I know now, I would not make the trip to Bogotá. That was probably the greatest mistake of my career, but it is little use crying over spilt milk. I went with my eyes open, but the only trouble was that I got them opened even wider when I arrived!'

As for the rest of his career, at time glittering, he offered no regrets, especially looking back fondly at his time with his home club, Stoke City. Admittedly, he had his difficulties at times with the club's irascible manager, Bob McGrory; this hardly made him unique. His mentors Stanley Matthews and Frank Soo suffered much the same. What Franklin most enjoyed at Stoke was the camaraderie of his fellow players, the majority local Potteries lads, the same as himself.

'We had all grown up together, all played together as juniors and we all graduated together into first-class football,' Franklin happily recalled. 'It was not unnatural, then, that we had a team spirit second to none. In fact, nowhere in my travels have I met team spirit to rival that which prevailed at the Victoria Ground.'

There were myriad reasons for Franklin failing to settle into life as a player for Independiente Santa Fe in Colombia, the biggest being the broken promises of the club's co-founder, Luis Robledo. All the British players found it difficult to settle, come to terms with the language barrier and to them an alien culture. For their Argentinian counterparts, not least the great Alfredo Di Stefano, immersing themselves in the culture of Colombia was less of a problem. They not only adapted to Colombian life relatively happily but made life for the British players as difficult as possible.

In retirement he was happy to pass on the benefit of his wisdom to aspiring players, young lads making their way in what he proudly called the world's 'greatest' game. 'Since I entered the game as a misty-eyed youth, I have had my ups and downs,' offered Franklin. 'I have tasted the glamour of big matches. I have sampled the honour of playing for

England. But I have also sampled the loneliness of exile and the worry of ever recurring injury. Yet all that is part and parcel of a professional footballer's life, a life of changing moods, changing scenes and changing fortunes. A life that has its thrills and its spills. A life that has its light and its shade, its joy and its sorrow. A life that has its honours and its heartbreak.'

It was a wistful summing up of a broken career, one to celebrate with so much more promise until it effectively ended, at least at top level, with the boarding of a flight to the Colombian capital Bogotá. Perhaps, in his regret, it informed his footballing philosophy for young players. 'Go into football determined to work, determined to learn. For the life of a professional footballer demands hard work, and it is a life which can never bring you to the end of the road of knowledge. Soccer is a game no one ever learns thoroughly,' he ventured in way of advice.

Franklin died on 9 February 1996 in the Staffordshire market town of Stone, just outside Stoke-on-Trent, taken from the football world as it soared in popularity. Vast riches he only dreamed of, by then were available to the best players; no need for them to resort to embarking on rebel tours.

During his lifetime, he reflected, 'The public remembers, idolises its footballers, but the public soon forgets them and idolises the new generation. For the public was never equipped with a lasting memory.' On this he was wrong. Great footballers are remembered but unlike other legends of Stoke City and England, namely Sir Stanley Matthews and Gordon Banks, Cornelius Franklin quietly slipped away.

Stoke City fans of a certain vintage remembered him for good and bad. By far the majority of them told fans such as myself watching Tony Waddington's trophy-winning side of the seventies that Franklin was one of the finest ever to wear an England shirt, let alone a Stoke City shirt. But unlike

Matthews and Banks his passing was not to lead national TV and radio news bulletins.

Forever he lived in the football memory as the leader of the Bogotá Bad Boys, viewed by critics as a player throwing his career away in an act of impetuosity. He had done so while genuinely seeking to guarantee his young family's future given the constraints on English players of his day.

Aside from his contemporaries, such as Sir Tom Finney, Don Revie, Raich Carter and indeed Sir Stanley Matthews, few remembered his greatness as a player, just the ill-fated trip to Colombia. As a defender, Franklin had no equal in the post-war years, arguably not even his friend Billy Wright. Indeed, Franklin treated other defenders with their thuggish tendencies in post-war domestic and international football with disdain.

Unlike them, Franklin read the game superbly, possessing great positional sense, able to tackle and intercept at will, a priceless distributor of the ball to his team-mates. As an England centre-half, he proved for more than a decade after being axed to be irreplaceable, Billy Wright only eventually persuaded to move from his favoured position and wear the number 5 jersey out of desperation.

Put simply in one tribute on Franklin's departure to an alternative footballing world, he was 'a delight to the eye'. In summing up his own career he concluded, 'All the same, if I had my time over again, I would go into football. Never was there a greater game, a more exciting or exhilarating game. Never was there a more worthwhile career. I have had my disappointments. I have had my downs. I have known moments that I never want to experience again. But looking back on the whole career, I can only say I have loved it, and good luck and good fortune to all those following in my footsteps and the footsteps of my contemporaries.'

Those now following in his distinguished footsteps do indeed earn a good fortune for their work both on and off the field. Do they owe this to Neil Franklin, a footballing pioneer or mercenary rebel? Given the football establishment regrouped after the initial bombshell dropped by Franklin and his mates, probably very little. Meeting him at his country pub in the early eighties along with other curious Stoke fans, I suspected it did not matter to him anyhow.

Yet in many respects his rebellion along with the other Bogotá Bandits did matter. The status quo in the professional game was never going to last, the shaken pillars of the British football establishment in the summer of 1950 about to come crumbling down. Quite what Franklin might now make of the modern billionaire game, the inadequacies of the FA in its governance and the largesse of FIFA, just one organisation he fell foul of, sadly we will never know. Good luck to the players he might say but no doubt while condemning greedy leaching agents and, of course his favourite target, the men in blazers.

Throughout the history of world football nobody challenged the rulers of the game as brazenly and outrageously as Franklin and his fellow band of rebels. No doubt he wanted to be remembered for his greatness as a player, one of the finest in an England shirt. Instead, Neil Franklin will be forever remembered for boarding his flight to Bogotá.

# SELECT BIBLIOGRAPHY

## BOOKS


*Behind the Glory, 100 Years of the PFA*, John Harding, Breedon Books Publishing Ltd (2007)

*Bogotá Bandit*, Richard Adamson, Mainstream Publishing (1996, 2005)

*Football Worlds: A Lifetime in Sport*, Stanley Rous, Faber & Faber (1978)

*League Football, and the men who made it*, Simon Inglis, Willow Books (1988)

*Potters at War*, Simon Lowe, Desert Island Books Ltd (2004, 2009)

*Stanley Matthews, The Authorised Biography*, David Miller, Pavilion Books Ltd (1989)

*Refereeing Round the World*, Arthur Ellis, The Sportsman Book Club (1955)

*Soccer At Home and Abroad*, Neil Franklin, Stanley Paul and Company Ltd (1956)

*Stanley Matthews, The Authorized Biography*, David Miller, Pavilion Books Ltd (1989)

*The Ball is Round, A Global History of Football*, David Goldblatt, Penguin Books (2006)

*The Football League*, Bryon Butler, MacDonald Queen Anne Press (1988)

*The Football Man*, Arthur Hopcraft, Aurum Press (1968, 2006)

*The Irish Soccer Split*, Cormac Moore, Cork University Press (2015)

## BIBLIOGRAPHY

*The Way It Was*, Stanley Matthews, Headline Book Publishing (2000)

*Tom Finney, My Autobiography,* Tom Finney, Headline Book Publishing (2003)

## NEWS SOURCES

Associated Press (AP)

BBC News

BBC Sport

BBC Radio Stoke

*Coventry Evening Telegraph*, Coventry

*Daily Express*, London

*Daily Herald*, London

*Daily Mail*, London

*Daily Mirror*, London

*Daily Telegraph*, London

*Daily Worker*, London

*Evening Post*, Leeds

*Evening Sentinel*, Stoke-on-Trent

*Evening Standard*, London

*Hull Daily Mail*, Hull

*Lancashire Telegraph*, Blackburn

*Liverpool Echo*, Liverpool

*News of the World*, London

*Reuters*

*Sunday Empire News*, London

*Sunday Express,* London

*Sunday People*, London

*Sunday Telegraph*, London

*The Guardian*, London

*The Newsletter,* Belfast

*The Observer*, London

*The Times*, London

*Western Mail*, Cardiff

## ARCHIVE & OFFICIAL SOURCES

British Library, London http://explore.bl.uk/

Hansard, Westminster https://hansard parliament.uk/Commons

European Law Journal: *Sporting Justifications under EU Free Movement and Competition Law: The Case of the Football Transfer System, Geoff Pearson (September 2014)*

FIFA, *'Regulations on the Status and Transfer of Players'* (2020), https://www.fifa.com/who-we-are/official-documents/ UK National Archives, Kew, London, https://www.nationalarchives.gov.uk/

*Committee of Investigation: Football Association and Football League Ltd and the Association Football Players and Trainers Union (October 15/16th 1951), Ministry of Labour and National Service; Association Football, Report of a Committee of Investigation into a Difference Regarding the Terms and Conditions of Association Football players (Published: March 14th 1952*)